PREFABS

STUDIES IN HISTORY, PLANNING AND THE ENVIRONMENT

Series editors   **Professor Gordon E. Cherry,** *University of Birmingham*
Professor Anthony Sutcliffe, *University of Leicester*

PREFABS
A History of
the UK Temporary
Housing Programme

BRENDA VALE

E & FN SPON
An Imprint of Chapman & Hall

London · Glasgow · Weinheim · New York · Tokyo · Melbourne · Madras

Published by E & FN Spon, an imprint of Chapman & Hall, 2–6 Boundary Row, London SE1 8HN, UK

Chapman & Hall, 2–6 Boundary Row, London SE1 8HN, UK

Blackie Academic & Professional, Wester Cleddens Road, Bishopbriggs, Glasgow G64 2NZ, UK

Chapman & Hall GmbH, Pappelallee 3, 69469 Weinheim, Germany

Chapman & Hall USA, 115 Fifth Avenue, New York, NY 10003, USA

Chapman & Hall Japan, ITP-Japan, Kyowa Building, 3F, 2-2-1 Hirakawacho, Chiyoda-ku, Tokyo 102, Japan

Chapman & Hall Australia, 102 Dodds Street, South Melbourne, Victoria 3205, Australia

Chapman & Hall India, R. Seshadri, 32 Second Main Road, CIT East, Madras 600 035, India

First edition 1995

© 1995 Brenda Vale

Typeset in 10/12½ pt Times by Cambrian Typesetters, Frimley, Surrey

Printed in Great Britain at the University Press, Cambridge

This book was commissioned and edited by Alexandrine Press, Oxford

ISBN 0 419 18800 2

A catalogue record for this book is available from the British Library

CONTENTS

PREFACE

After the Second World War a new type of state-subsidized house appeared in Britain. The two-bedroom temporary bungalow was produced ostensibly to provide much needed housing in the immediate post-war period and some 156,623 houses were supplied between 1945–1949 as part of the scheme. The bungalows differed from pre-war state-subsidized housing in a number of ways including their method of construction. For the first time in Britain one of the ideals of the Modern Movement was realized: a house was manufactured on a production line in a factory.

The hypothesis that underlies this particular investigation into the history of the prefab is that, as a housing form, it was in essence a public success. Certainly the bungalows have survived long beyond their design life of 10–15 years, even if their prefabricated skin has now sometimes been replaced with conventional materials such as bricks and tiles. This survival has also occurred in the face of adverse contemporary criticism from all sides when the provision of temporary accommodation after the war was first suggested. At the time there was also little consultation with the public over the type of temporary housing that might be required or whether the public even wished to live in such housing. The fact that the temporary bungalows represented a major innovation in public housing, as they were both prefabricated and factory produced, had also to gain public acceptance. The method by which this radically different housing was introduced to the public, assimilated by them and lived in by them must, therefore, form the focus of any investigation of its apparent success as a housing form.

The purpose of this particular history is not only to tell the story of the prefab and its people but also to attempt to understand why this technological advance in housing provision (in terms of both production and materials) received little acknowledgement in the architectural press either at the time or since. It may also be of value to try to discover why the temporary bungalows were popular with the public and why, also, this experiment in the mass-produced house from the factory has not been repeated in the same form and at the same scale in the United Kingdom.

To find why the right product finds the right market at the right time it is necessary to look at the designers', manufacturers' and primarily the consumers' contemporary response to the product. In addition it is essential to appreciate the motives of those who supplied the finance, in this instance central government. To this end extensive use has been made of the public side of government, through Hansard, and of contemporary periodicals and books.

Brenda Vale
Nottingham
June 1995

1

THE PREFAB AND ITS PEOPLE

'It had a built-in fridge – a real luxury in them days.'[1]

INTRODUCTION

In comparison with today's architectural aesthetics the prefab is small, boring and probably unworthy of extensive study. Nor in terms of housing statistics is the impact of the prefab in the post-war world very significant. It is the tenacious nature of the prefab which is the first surprise. Some 156,623 temporary bungalows[2] were produced for rent under the aegis of the 1944 Temporary Housing Programme, each with a design life of 10–15 years, though many have lasted much longer.[3] The last temporary bungalow was handed over in March 1949 (see Chapter 6), so the country should theoretically have been cleared of them by 1964. However, by this date in England and Wales there remained some 67,353 prefabs still in use as temporary accommodation under the arrangements of the Programme, and a further 21,014 which had been purchased by the local authorities and were still occupied. By the middle of 1964, of the original allocation of 124,455 bungalows in England and Wales only 29 per cent, or 36,088 had been removed.[4] By the end of the period 1945–1966, in Scotland of the 32,176 bungalows completed 13,585 were still in occupation under the Programme, 671 had been transferred to the local authorities, and 56 per cent, or 17,920, had been removed.[5] By the end of 1971, in Scotland the remaining bungalows, some 3,505 or 11 per cent of the original allocation were no longer considered temporary dwellings and were treated as permanent houses for statistical purposes.[6,7]

The prefab, however, was not one design, but rather a series of different methods of framing and cladding a basic set of accommodation stemming from a prototype by the Ministry of Works (commonly called the Portal Bungalow after the Minister, Lord Portal). This prototype was an all steel product and incorporated a combined prefabricated kitchen and bathroom unit, also the brainchild of the Ministry of Works (see Chapter 5). From the beginning of May 1944 the Portal Bungalow was on exhibition daily, except for Sundays, at the Tate Gallery. Tickets were necessary for admission. These were issued initially to local authorities for further allocation. Provision was also made for a similar exhibition in Scotland.

From the start the prototype was seen as experimental, and comments were invited from the world at large as to any improvements and modifications that might be thought necessary. The Portal bungalow was designed to be exposed to public gaze: one was even exhibited in Cairo for inspection by the armed forces:

> Five thousand years later, a number of British warriors found themselves in a similar position to the ancient Egyptian monarch, except that they required homes. Representations were accordingly made on their behalf. Although some 300,000 workers were eager to start, it was only after considerable delay that plans were eventually made. With the applied experience of five thousand years, the modern version of prefabrication took shape in the form of a 'Portal'. One was erected in the vicinity of the Pyramids.[8]

The Portal prototype was never put into production although a revised version was again exhibited in London in the autumn of 1944. However, a number of manufacturers were asked to supply bungalows based upon the prototype. Again, three of these (the steel framed Arcon house clad in asbestos cement with its own plan; the Uni-Seco which adapted an existing system of timber framed, asbestos cement clad panels to the revised Portal plan; and the Tarran which adapted an existing reinforced concrete panel and light timber frame construction to the revised Portal plan) were included in this further exhibition at the Tate Gallery, which was open to the public.[9] The aluminium bungalow was exhibited separately in the summer of 1945.[10]

These four new bungalows used materials that were in short supply because of the war (for example, timber) in the most economical way possible or, alternatively, used materials that were available but which had not previously been associated with housing (for example, aluminium). Of all the various types of bungalow produced under the programme only these four were made in any quantity – the Arcon (38,859), Uni-Seco (28,999), Tarran (19,014 for three types using the same system) and the Aluminium (54,500).[11] Not only do the four differ in their materials but also in their methods of design approach and manufacture. The quantities in which these four types were produced are also sufficient to be described as mass-produced. Most of the other types never exceeded the size of run that might be thought suitable for a prototype (see Chapter 6). In terms of a visual representation of the Temporary Housing Programme, it is these four types of bungalow which are most likely to be found in use.

THE ARCON BUNGALOW

Ultimately, the most sophisticated arrangement of the standard two bed-room accommodation was probably that of the Arcon Mark V bungalow (figure 1.1). The two-bedroom Arcon had all rooms, apart from the kitchen,

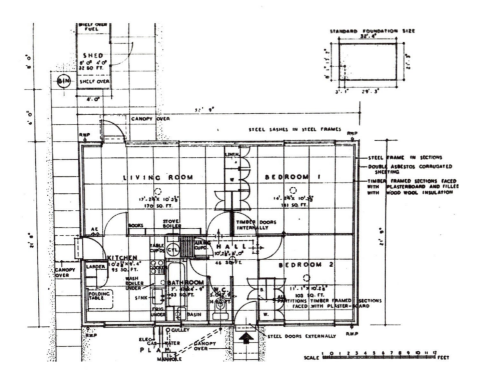

Figure 1.1. Arcon Mark V bungalow plan. (*Source*: Ministry of Health/Ministry of Works, 1944*a*)

leading off a hall which contained the WC and a built-in meter and coat cupboard. The airing cupboard, which was part of the prefabricated bathroom/kitchen unit, also gave into the hall. Partitions between the living room and bedroom 1 and bedroom 2 and the hall were partly composed of cupboard units. The kitchen, apart from its cooker, sink etc, which were combined with the bathroom plumbing and wiring, also contained a larder with ventilation direct to the outside, and a folding table. A separate shed was to be provided in the garden space for the storage of bicycles and tools. All the bungalows were variations of similar accommodation.

A complete Arcon Mark V exists at the Avoncroft Museum of Building at Bromsgrove, (figure 1.3) but the bungalow has survived in use well beyond its design life as is evidenced by the large estate of Arcons that still exists at Newport, Gwent (figure 1.2). Other Arcons can also be seen recycled for a variety of purposes. The corrugated asbestos cladding and curved ridge at the gable ends gave the bungalow a distinctive outline that made it the typical prefab in many eyes (figure 1.3).

Figure 1.2. Arcon bungalow in Newport, Gwent, 1994.

Figure 1.3. Arcon bungalow preserved at Avoncroft Museum of Buildings, Bromsgrove. (*By courtesy of* Avoncroft Museum of Buildings)

The Arcon group included a firm of architects, a group of industrialists and a building contractor.[12] From the beginning the architects of the group were interested in houses:

> In April, 1943, Arcon formed the opinion that a minimum-area demountable house, susceptible to mass production, would be required in order to take the 'razor edge' off immediate post-war demand. The work of developing such a house fell clearly into two sections: the structure or covered space; the service or mechanical core.[13]

The Arcon group first began work on the development of prefabricated construction for permanent housing, together with the development of a mechanical core where the kitchen (figure 1.4) and bathroom units were placed back to back.[14] In fact the Ministry of Works prefabricated bathroom/kitchen unit was exhibited in Spring 1944, before the Arcon version had been completed (although the former was, perhaps, less sophisticated as it failed to combine the WC in the prefabricated plumbing unit). Simultaneously Arcon had started work on a demountable house using data obtained from their investigation of prefabrication. At this

Figure 1.4. The kitchen of the Avoncroft Museum Arcon bungalow. (*By courtesy of* Avoncroft Museum of Buildings)

point, for Arcon, the 'temporary' nature of the house was not seen as being a matter of limited life but only of limited life related to location, with the demountable house being moved on once other accommodation was available. This initial approach to a temporary house may in part account for the variety of Arcon bungalows that now exist in other guises.

The development of the Arcon temporary house was known to Lord Portal and Arcon were consequently invited to exhibit their house, based on the tenets above. The Arcon Mark II was, therefore, put up in the spring of 1944 amidst flying bomb attacks. The fact that any available building labour had been redirected to repair bomb damaged buildings meant that by the Saturday evening prior to Lord Portal's inspection on the Monday the bungalow was up but not painted. The general atmosphere surrounding the development of this new house from the factory is revealed by the following description:

> The Arcon staff rallied round and mobilised their wives and friends, and on that Saturday painted relentlessly while the sirens wailed in the June sky. It was on this Sunday that the bomb that fell on St. Thomas's Hospital – three hundred yards away across the river – found us painting busily on the roof. There was no time to reach the ground and the safety of our blast wall, so we dropped flat on the asbestos cement we had just painted. In spite of all, the house was ready for the Minister's inspection. The small garden, laid overnight to give some relief from the harsh concrete of the site, glistened with recent watering. The roses, precariously pinned to the pergola, competed with the more pungent scent of new paint.[15]

Even at this early stage the house from the factory was both dependent upon hand craft labour and romanticized with roses round the door.

Following this initiative Arcon produced further designs and a prototype and by September 1944 the result of this activity was an order placed with Taylor Woodrow Construction Ltd. (the building contractor member of the group) to proceed 'with the production of 86,000 Arcon Temporary Houses'.[16]

Given the date of this contract and the fact that the first family moved into their bungalow during July 1945,[17] the process of design, manufacture, transportation and erection had been accomplished in a commendably brief time, especially as: 'During the production drawing period it was found necessary to re-design every one of the 390 separate components and sub-assemblies.'[18] Such a redesign was complicated by the nature of the factory produced bungalow. Because all components were manufactured prior to site erection any alteration to a single component had to be checked for ramifications throughout the whole built product. As in any industrialized process the architects produced drawings for the revised components, but these had then to be translated into tasks for the separate manufacturers and the whole organized through the contractors. The experience of the latter in supplying material to the United States Air Command for the construction of some thirty-six airfields had to be drawn on and expanded to meet the demands of the temporary bungalow:

> To cope with the Temporary Housing Programme it was necessary to expand this staff enormously and where before one man had sufficed, now an entire department had to be created. For such a staff, considerable office space had to be found and this was finally located in the upper floors of one of London's Department Stores. The space available was divided up and allocated to various departments – production; planning; storage; accounts; personnel and welfare.[19]

Rather than erecting a 'prototype' of purpose made and existing manufactured parts, as is still the practice of the majority of those engaged in providing new housing, the Arcon group, like others involved in the programme, were forced to design each of the components for the factory-made house anew. To produce the single standardized product from the factory demanded more in terms of overheads and organization than the traditional masonry house. The experience of the war, however, had necessitated the development of such factory organization for the production of the machinery of war. It is, therefore, perhaps less surprising that the Arcon moved from exhibition prototype to inhabited production model in less than a year.

Essentially the bungalow consisted of a steel frame with asbestos cement exterior cladding. Because of the problems of steel supply to the Temporary Housing Programme, which caused the demise of the Portal prototype bungalow, 'Arcon had been urged by the Ministry of Works to reduce the weight of steel required for each Mark V house to the very minimum . . .'[20] To avoid, therefore, the use of standard structural steel sections which were too heavy for the needs of the single-storey form, Arcon turned to the use of tubular steel, and the welded roof trusses, purlins and braces of the Mark V were the first large-scale peacetime use of the structural tube.[21]

The wall structure was formed of purpose designed hot rolled steel sections made in co-operation with Darlington Rolling Mills, a manu-facturer of metal window sections. The steel panels that incorporated the doors and windows were finished with 'stove paint' applied in a mechanized way. The size of the single pane windows was claimed to be 'far larger than any previously adopted in the small-housing field',[22] and the metal doors also had welded panels in the lower part to ensure rigidity, another new application for housing. Elsewhere, steel was used as cold rolled sections which formed skirtings, architraves, picture rails and vertical corner cover strips. These sections had a dual purpose as they acted as cover strips for the inevitable tolerance gaps between floor, wall and ceiling panels and 'since they are hollow, also form a path for electrical wiring'[23] to switches and sockets integrated into architraves and skirtings. The asbestos cement sheeting used as cladding to wall and roof structure and made by Turners Asbestos Cement Co. Ltd was also finished to a new design which incorporated curved cladding:

> The roof sheeting incorporated spaced corrugations with a flattened crown which not only emphasized the line of the corrugation, but also provided a flat bearing for the special washers and fixing bolts employed. Instead of the normal ridge capping the apex of the roof was covered with a gently curved crown sheet, which provided a neat finish and eliminated the steel supports required at the apex of more conventional roofing.[24]

The walls were also asbestos cement sheet with the wide corrugations that became characteristic of the Arcon bungalow, with a double sheet used (the roof was a single sheet) to increase strength, thermal insulation (by creating a cavity between the sheets), and resistance to rain penetration. Internally the walls and ceiling were lined with panels of plasterboard to which thin timbers were glued on a jig creating a frame work which was then filled with glass fibre quilt. Overall, 'The thermal insulation value of this construction is equal to that of an 11 inch cavity brick wall,'[25] the standard for traditional house construction at that time.

The Arcon production model was first tested on a pilot run of 100 houses in 1945, constructed on two sites, a flat site at Croydon and a difficult sloping site at Crayford in Kent:

> Time showed that the decision to advance the pilot-run ahead of main production was the right one. Any weak points in the design for mass production showed up, and details were redesigned accordingly. Taylor Woodrow Construction Ltd. were able to shoot their training films and organise their transport. The Ministry found theoretical calculations on steel work deflection confirmed by field tests. The component manufacturers' requests for modifications were reduced because they acquired a better understanding of the design as a whole.[26]

Such comment illustrates well the untried nature of the project with people moving into the first Arcon bungalows in the summer of 1945 before the field trials were even complete.

THE UNI-SECO

Unlike the Arcon bungalow, the Uni-Seco, another of the four main prefab types, received much less attention from the contemporary press even though the Seco system aimed to produce a panel that could form the basis of a 'kit-of-parts' approach to design, rather than the specific mass-produced unit. The Selection Engineering Co. Ltd. had earlier in the war produced a system of small timber frame panel construction for the erection of emergency huts. At this stage two forms of construction had been developed[27] based on timber prefabricated in the factory and assembled on site on a pre-prepared foundation after which the structure was waterproofed with 'Seco-mastic' applied to all external surfaces. Because of this experience, the first Uni-Seco temporary bungalow was no more than a dressing of the Portal prototype bungalow plan in a Seco type construction system.

The bungalow developed further, and in the 1945 version a central hall was introduced giving independent access to the two bedrooms (figure 1.5), although the overall circulation area was greater than for the Arcon Mark V. The Uni-Seco Mark 3 (figure 1.6), as it was known, incorporated the possibility of a narrow or wide frontage through exchanging the windows in the bedrooms from the long facades to the otherwise blank rear wall.

The construction of the Uni-Seco bungalow derived from the firm's experience of building huts. Once the slab was laid a timber cill was fixed around the perimeter to take the storey height wall units and the timber frame and tongued and grooved boarded floor panels. The wall panels were also of a timber frame covered both sides with flat asbestos cement sheets

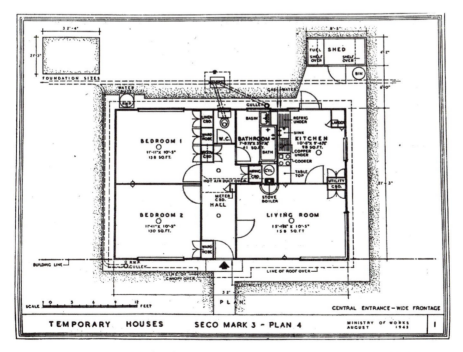

Figure 1.5. Uni-Seco Mark 3 bungalow plan. (*Source*: Ministry of Health/Ministry of Works, 1944*a*)

Figure 1.6. Uni-Seco bungalow in Kirkconnel, Scotland, 1986.

which were grooved into the edges and filled internally with wood wool in a wet cement matrix as an insulator. 'This filling, while wet, adheres to the asbestos cement sheet, considerably strengthening it and reducing brittleness.'[28] The edges of the timber frame to the panel were grooved and a loose timber tongue inserted at the vertical joint through which screws held the two panels fixed together. A Secomastic compound was then used to form an external weathering to the vertical joint and a covering strip of asbestos cement applied, giving the bungalow its characteristic external appearance. Internal partitions were formed of the same storey height panels. In terms of thermal performance, 'The panels have been tested . . . and are better than either 9 in. or 13½ in. brick, but not quite so good as 11 in. cavity, walls.'[29]

The shallow pitch roof, the shallowest of all the bungalows developed in Britain, was formed of timbers flat on the underside and sloped on top spanning across the bungalow. The ceiling of plasterboard was then nailed to the underside and the roof covering was formed of panels framed in timber with asbestos sheet to both sides and wood wool insulation between, similar to those which formed the walls. These were fixed on top of the roof beams and the joints between panels were first sealed with strips of roofing felt before the whole roof was covered with two layers of felt in hot mastic. The windows used were standard metal casements with a variety of glazing bar configurations and the internal doors were plywood flush doors in timber frames, hung on site.

Although the Uni-Seco bungalow was, therefore, less of a mass produced purpose designed artefact than either the Arcon Mark V or the Aluminium bungalow, the approach of the manufacturers to the problem of prefabricating the temporary bungalow is interesting in the decision taken to develop a panel that was one unit of a 'kit of parts'. The very fact that the Uni-Seco was the only bungalow to be supplied in narrow and wide frontage versions emphasizes this point. Moreover, the same panel and jointing technique is found in both the emergency huts at Poplar, introduced in 1944 as an immediate response to the damage inflicted on housing by the V1 and V2 attacks,[30] the temporary bungalow, and a demonstration permanent prefabricated house at Chobham. The last was in the form of a pair of semi-detached cottages 'based on a plan chosen at random, one of many suggestions for suitable accommodation for agricultural workers'[31] and was of two storeys. The house was also built on concrete piles so as to be readily demountable, and was widely publicized as an exercise in the use of a co-ordinated and prefabricated kit of parts. One commentator, although critical of the external appearance of the house, observed:

> The main tenet of the creed of the advocates of the basic modern style is that the form of the elevations shall proceed naturally from the plan and its vertical expression the section, and the structural content . . . The conviction is borne upon me that the modular planned, prefabricated building is the very medium for the attainment of this ideal[32]

THE TARRAN BUNGALOW

Unlike the Arcon and the Uni-Seco, the Tarran system of prefabrication, as applied to the third main type of prefab, was not seen to have any particular architectural merit, although of the three it was the Tarran system that was to be sucessfully adapted to a permanent prefabricated house.[33] Tarran Industries Ltd. of Hull (and also Edinburgh, Leeds and Dundee) had been involved in the provision of prefabricated huts during the war. However, the involvement of the firm, and its founder Robert G. Tarran, with prefabrication had a much longer history. As Bowley, historian to the construction industry, comments:

> Tarran started his working life as an apprentice joiner, but after the First World War set up in business as a builder on his own. He built up a fair-sized business based on Hull. In August 1934 this was registerd as a private company under the name of Robt. G. Tarran Ltd, but changed its name to Tarran Industries Ltd the following December. The next year it was converted into a public company. Some time during the thirties Tarran became interested in, and it seems really enthusiastic about, prefabrication in housing. This resulted in the formation of another private company, Solid Cedar Homes Ltd., in 1938. Tarran himself held all but two of the 20,000 £1 shares. It was this company which was responsible for the timber houses erected in Dundee in 1940 under the auspices of the Scottish Special Housing Association. At the end of the war Tarran was still an enthusiast for prefabrication.[34]

Tarran's enthusiasm for prefabrication may have led to the firm's involvement with prefabrication at Quarry Hill flats in 1935 which were to use the Mopin system of site factory prefabricated concrete panels fixed to a steel frame. However, because the firm's tender for the job was lower than the architect's estimate, it may be that enthusiasm for prefabrication at that time outweighed any real experience. The project was fraught with disagreement between R.A.H. Livett, the architect and Leeds Director of Housing, and the contractor over delays in the supply of information and poor workmanship to the extent that the scheme was only completed once the war was over. However, this scheme did represent the largest single UK experiment in prefabrication for housing before the war began.[35]

In a contrast in scale, during the war Tarran continued his involvement in prefabrication through the production of war time huts. A dry construction prefabricated timber system was used to supply clear span structures on a two foot module. Some 9000 of these parabolic section timber huts were supplied to the War Department in the first years of the war.[36] Shortages of timber probably led Tarran back to reconsider the firm's experience with prefabricated concrete panels and a new type of hut, the Mark 3, was developed which formed a direct forerunner to the Tarran temporary bungalow. This hut had vertical walls 'with "Lignocrete" panels 7ft. 3in. in height at 18-in. centres, with a timber roof.'[37] The Lignocrete panel was made of Portland cement concrete with an aggregate of chemically treated, and therefore organically inert, sawdust.[38] These panels were to form a further demonstration by Tarran of the possibilities of prefabrication, this time in the context of post-war housing. In the summer of 1943 a bungalow with walls made of Lignocrete panels was exhibited at the Conway Hall, London:

> The bungalow was on show in London for over a week, after which it was taken down and loaded onto five lorries in eight and a half hours by twelve men. It was unloaded in Hull three days later, re-erected on new foundations and completed within four days . . . Mr. R.G. Tarran stated that within a year he could have twenty-two factories in the country producing 100,000 dwellings per annum of many varied types of elevation and plan as a contribution to the 400,000 dwellings per annum which it is officially stated are needed for the next ten years.[39]

It was claimed that of the labour in the bungalow 'over 50% of total hours are in factory production'.[40] In this, the early exhibition of the Tarran Lignocrete panel bungalow was to foreshadow the arguments about the transfer of labour from site to factory that were to surround the announcement of the Temporary Housing Programme in the spring of the following year. Given that Arcon were also working on prefabrication as applied to housing in 1943, the emergence of the Temporary Housing

Programme as a phenomenon nurtured by these experiments appears to be less at the instigation of government but rather as an inevitable architectural outcome of the concerns of the times.

Tarran's enthusiasm for both his system and the application of prefabrication to post-war housing produced other demonstrations. *Picture Post* featured a Tarran stunt early in 1944. Here photographs showed the progress of a prefabricated bungalow, with concrete wall panels and plywood roof panels, which was put up in Hull by twelve workers in six hours.[41] Tarran also ran a competition to design a house or bungalow, each with either two or three bedrooms, using the Tarran system of construction, which received 131 entries.[42] The winning two-bedroom bungalow, announced in July 1944 forms an interesting comparison to the Tarran temporary bungalow as it has the same types and numbers of spaces and is also wide frontage. However, the winning design by Frederick Hill, is shown terraced, something never achieved by the temporary bungalows.

During the same summer Tarran also arranged a demonstration of a two-storey house, designed by himself, using the same system of prefabrication:

> The house . . . was erected in Hull, on prepared foundations, in eight hours on May 2 last by eight men and four women, the majority of whom are stated to have had no previous experience of the erection of this type of structure. Decoration, furnishing and completion were ready by 2.30 p.m., on May 5, when the house was officially opened by Mr. A.C. Bossom.[43]

These efforts to publicize prefabricated houses led to Tarran's opportunity to participate in the Temporary Housing Programme. The bungalow that was developed for this was a modified version which, like the Uni-Seco, provided a simple rectangular form and, internally, a hall to separate circulation to bedrooms, bathroom and living room (figure 1.7). A corner window was also introduced into the living room in this version.

From observation of the survivors of the Temporary Housing Programme it would appear that larger numbers of the Tarran bungalow are found in the north of England and in Scotland, close to the sites of production (figure 1.8). This may be partly due to the fact that, because of the concrete panel construction, the Tarran was the heaviest, and therefore most costly, bungalow to transport weighing 14 tons in total compared to an average weight of 8 tons for the others.[44] Indeed, without Tarran's persistent interest in the field of prefabrication it is, perhaps, doubtful whether a prefabricated concrete panel would have been commissioned for a programme of temporary houses that were to be distributed throughout the country. Nevertheless, because of the experience of the firm and the continued and various means of promoting the Tarran system the firm formed one of the major providers of the temporary bungalow and were

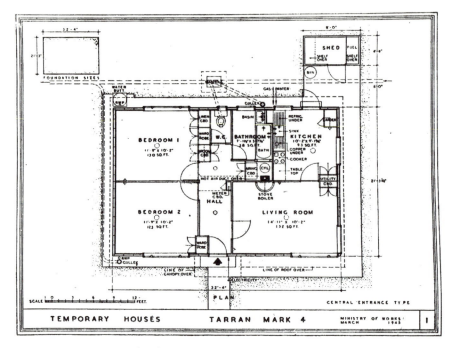

Figure 1.7. Tarran Mark 4 bungalow plan with central entrance. (*Source*: Ministry of Health/Ministry of Works, 1944*a*)

Figure 1.8. Tarran bungalow with corner window to the living room, Eckington, Derbyshire.

even featured on the Home Service: 'The B.B.C., recognising the general public interest in the rapid provision of houses, has included in its programme under the seductive title of "Building a Cottage in One Hour", an outside broadcast by Victor Smythe and Gilbert Harding descriptive of the Tarran system of construction.'[45] It must have made interesting radio.

THE ALUMINIUM TEMPORARY BUNGALOW

However, of all the temporary bungalows, the Aluminium prefab appeared to the British commentators as most representative of the ideal of a factory produced house, and was manufactured in the greatest numbers, although it also always remained the most expensive. Both at the time and since, the Aluminium bungalow has been regarded as the most important phenomenon to emerge from the Temporary Housing Programme: '. . . the aluminium bungalow, which proved to be the most successful aspect of the aluminium industry's diversification into building.'[46]

The prototype aluminium bungalow was exhibited in the summer of 1945 behind Selfridge's store in London as part of the Aluminium Development Association's 'Aluminium from War to Peace Exhibition' (figure 1.9). The exhibition prototype more or less corresponded in size to the other

Figure 1.9. The Minister of Works, Duncan Sandys, opening the Aluminium bungalow behind Selfridge's Department Store at the Aluminium War to Peace Exhibition, 1945. (*Source*: *Architects' Journal*, 21 June, 1945)

temporary bungalows approved for the programme, but the unusual expertise and labour that had gone into its development did not go unnoticed. Rather than traditional building labour, it was 'the aircraft workers and technicians, lent by these firms to produce the prototype, who carried out the work with such excellent craftsmanship and keenness.'[47]

In fact the production model aluminium bungalow was made initially in five factories: the Bristol Aeroplane Co., Weston-super-Mare, which built the prototype; Vickers-Armstrong at Blackpool and Chester; Blackburn Aircraft, Dumbarton; and A.W. Hawksley, Gloucester. The house was prefabricated in the factory in four sections, together with all the internal services, fittings and final decorations. Each section was lifted on to the prepared slab by a 5 ton crane, the units being temporarily supported on hydraulic jack trolleys which allowed units to be brought together and levelled prior to permanent fixing. Only one joint was required to each of the site services (waste, water, electricity and possibly gas) and it was held that 'Complete site erection requires 30 to 40 man-hours, depending on the experience of the crews.'[48]

It was the form and manner of production of the aluminium bungalow

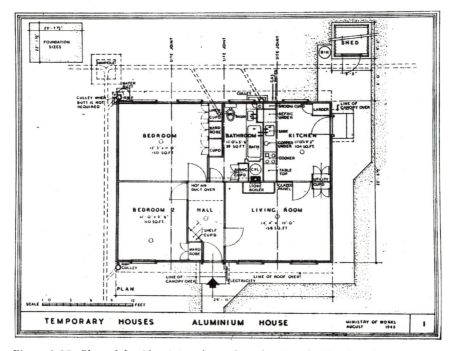

Figure 1.10. Plan of the Aluminium bungalow showing division into four segments. (*Source*: Ministry of Health/Ministry of Works, 1944a)

that excited interest both at the time and since. In plan (figure 1.10) the overall disposition of the rooms was the same as for the production models of the Tarran and Uni-Seco bungalows. However, in order to allow complete factory production of the house in four segments, each of which could be transported to site on a lorry (figure 1.11 and 1.12), the room sizes were matched to the segmental module, each module being 7 ft 6 in wide (the maximum then allowed for road transport) and 22 ft 6½ in long. The kitchen and bathroom occupied two modules in width and this meant that the WC had to be situated in the bathroom rather than being provided separately as in the other bungalows (apart from that imported from the USA: see Chapter 3). Circulation space was also reduced as the airing cupboard was in the bathroom rather than the hall. The living room and larger bedroom also took up two modules but the smaller bedroom shared part of a module with the hall. The levels of equipment and fittings were directly comparable with the other bungalows, although all fittings were installed in the factory and all finishes applied before delivery to site.

The bungalow was constructed in the factory of extruded aluminium alloy sections which formed the frame of floor, walls and roof, with other materials applied. The floor was of tongued and grooved boarding on timber joists bolted through to the aluminium frame, all involving hand labour within the factory conditions: 'It is interesting to note that as yet no better method of doing this has been developed than the traditional one of

Figure 1.11. Factory production of Aluminium bungalow segments. (*By courtesy of* the Aluminium Federation)

Figure 1.12. End bedroom segment of Aluminium bungalow being craned into position on brick foundations. (*Source*: *Architects' Journal*, 21 June, 1945)

nailing and punching, though the ends of the boarding are trimmed with a hand power saw.'[49]

The wall sections, the width of each module, were framed in riveted extruded sections on jigs and an outer cladding of aluminium sheet was riveted on. Insulation was provided by an internal filling to the wall panel of aerated lightweight concrete, with an internal finish to the panel of plasterboard. Other rigid insulation materials had been investigated but 'none . . . was available in sufficient quantity to satisfy the production programme.'[50] Internal partitions were similarly constructed, also filled with the lightweight concrete but lined both sides with plasterboard. The roof was assembled separately of extruded aluminium with two trusses, one framing each side of the module, and two trussed aluminium purlins. Externally the roof sections were finished in aluminium sheet in panels 2 ft 6 in wide made in a double layer with an inner corrugated sheeting covered with a bitumen layer and faced externally with 20 g aluminium sheet. Internally the roof sections were lined with plasterboard held in aluminium sections spanning between the trusses and with a layer of insulating quilt above.[51] At the Bristol factory where the Beaufighter had been produced, the roof sections were made up in a gallery that had been formed across the end of the factory. The completed roof sections, which could also be lifted by six men, were then 'lifted by a travelling crane and dropped over the edge of the gallery to the houses being assembled on the floor below.'[52] Windows were also of aluminium and were positioned centrally in each of the four prefabricated sections, giving an external elevation that appeared far more standardized than the bungalows made of a system of prefabricated materials and panels. All the rainwater goods were also of aluminium but the doors and frames were of timber. In the prototype, the kitchen/bathroom unit was formed of aluminium alloy framing and aluminium door fronts but all was designed to be interchangeable with the standard Ministry of Works prefabricated plumbing unit.

The aluminium bungalow was a standardized product, instantly recognizable by the cover strips over the joints between the four factory produced sections (figure 1.13). However, even as a standardized product it was recognized that a similar factory-produced permanent house was also a possibility:

> The makers claim that this house, although in the Temporary Building Programme, can be expected to have a life of at least forty years and they see no reason why it should not be used for permanent two-bedroom dwellings, where these are required, provided they are properly laid out'.[53]

In fact permanent aluminium two bedroom bungalows were constructed on exactly the same four section principle and were approved for a life of 60 years.[54] However, whether temporary or permanent there were still some for whom the visual imagery did not go far enough.

> Some will complain that the result has little in its appearance to recall the taut lines of the Spitfire or of the Beaufighter. It must be conceded that the design has not yet in outward expression fully found itself. That is not the point. What is much more significant is that the minds which have created the modern aircraft have turned their attention to the solution of an almost equally urgent problem. In doing so they have produced a design which is more completely prefabricated than any which has so far appeared'.[55]

Figure 1.13. Aluminium bungalow in Hereford, 1988.

REACTIONS TO THE PREFAB

Whatever the actual constructional type, for the first time the Temporary Housing Programme gave the public detached bungalows that could be rented through the local authorities. Moreover, the fast construction times gave the bungalows a special appeal:

> on an early trial run, the erection of one of the houses was started at six o'clock one morning and the Mayor of Croydon had lunch in it the same day.[56]

As well as the method of factory manufacture, the form of the housing, with each bungalow on its individual plot, represented a new type of working-class housing. For a number of reasons (see Chapter 5) the houses were to be temporary and this, together with the non-traditional materials of which they were constructed, meant that their appearance was considerably different from both the inter-war local authority cottage and the inter-war speculative bungalow. Despite this, however, the public appear to have retained a respect and affection for the temporary bungalows which lasted many years. The very word 'prefab' suggests a familiarization of the revolutionary prefabricated nature of their construction.

> I moved into a prefab in 1947 and it was marvellous. I'd go back into one tomorrow if I could. The design quality was far above what working class people were used to. It had a built-in fridge – a real luxury in them days – and a boiler, both fitting neatly under the work tops. It had two big bedrooms with fitted wardrobes, a lovely big bathroom with a heated towel rail and a good sized lounge – all for 14/7 a week. Of course we had the usual condensation problems but the prefab's efficiency far outweighed them. We lived there for 18 years and when we moved to our first council house there was no comparison. We'd to start buying bedroom furniture for a start.[57]

Between the years 1945 and 1949 the prefabs appeared on derelict sites, vacant land, parks and public open space in both cities and rural areas in an attempt to provide housing to meet the post-war shortage. The anxiety generated by the housing situation after the war was considerable. A survey conducted in 1950 found that of the 249 housewives interviewed, for 50 per cent the prefab was the first home that they had run for themselves, having previously been forced to share accommodation.[58] This fact alone would make the prefabs a welcome phenomenon as the following quote shows.

> Mr. Joe Linsell, who in 1984 was still living in the prefab he was allocated in 1947, had nothing but praise for its comfort and convenience. At the end of the war he and his wife Mary and two children were living in a single room at the home of his wife's mother. Having taken his case to the London County

Council he received a fortnight later a letter inviting him and his wife to view a prefab in Royal Street. He takes up the story:

'After we looked round Mary was worried, and meself – would it be our luck to get one? When we came on the Friday, there was the council people outside with a table, there was nine families lining up. 'Course, Mary's got my hand and says, "Oh, there's only eight prefabs." 'Course, well, someone was going to be unlucky and as number two went, then number three, number four, so the tension was getting worse, but when it came to number eight he called my name to the table, I said, "Yes I'll have it" . . . And of course we took it and we moved in a week after but I did feel sorry for the person who was left out and she even cried. But it's the happiest day that ever happened'.[59]

Not everyone, however, was overjoyed at the appearance of the prefabs. They were thought by many to provide sub-standard accommodation and to be a waste of money, since it was felt that the same technologies and finance could have been used to provide permanent housing. Some proposed unconventional methods to ensure the sub-standard accommodation would not be endured for longer than necessary.

It's a good thing that temporary houses are to be publicly owned so that it won't be necessary to force private individuals to abolish them; but for my part I shan't feel really happy about the temporaries unless one of the fixtures in each of them is a fifteen-year-time-bomb guaranteed not to be a dud![60]

Moreover, once the temporary bungalows eventually began to appear, criticism was made both about their looks and the way that they were erected in unlikely places. There was the feeling that the image put forward by the designers did not match the reality of the bungalows on the ground (figure 1.14). The public were made aware that this need not be the case. An article in *Picture Post* in March 1944 made it clear that prefabrication did not necessarily imply poor accommodation that was visually unattractive, citing the success of prefabricated homes in Sweden.

People have got the idea that it [prefabrication] means jerry-building, tumbledown shacks, caravans, shoddy work, ribbon development, draughts and leaks and everything that's bad in building. The Government itself seems to hold the confused opinion that prefabrication means something temporary.[61]

From the start, therefore, the public were exposed to the conflict between prefabricated permanent and temporary houses, even to the extent of anticipating the eventual outcome of the programme: 'What does matter is that, through lack of policy, people should not be put into temporary houses – and left there for good.'[62]

Perhaps the greatest mismatch, however, resulted from the difference between the reality of the bungalows and the images that factory production of houses had conjured up in the hands of the theorists of the Modern Movement. The machine aesthetics had become associated with

THE ARCON BUNGALOW

as envisaged by the designers in October, 1944

as seen by our photographer in October, 1945

Figure 1.14. Images of prefabs – the top illustration is by Rodney Thomas, a partner in the firm, Arcon. (*Source*: *Architectural Design and Construction*, December, 1945)

simple plain surfaces stripped bare of unnecessary decoration, with the flat roof and the free plan, even if such aesthetics were not the genuine creation of the factory but had to be constructed in a far more traditional manner (see Chapter 4). The bungalows, however, with pitched roofs, metal windows and corrugated cladding were, perhaps, closer in appearance to the hen house than:

> The house of cement, iron and glass, without carved or painted ornament, rich only in the inherent beauty of its lines and modelling, extraordinarily brutish in its mechanical simplicity.[63]

However, if the prefab did not represent a paradigm of factory produced houses for the architect and designer, there was every intention that the general public should be prepared for the unusual methods of production. The Army Bureau of Current Affairs devoted a number of its discussion leaflets to the question of post-war housing. In 1943 the idea of prefabrication was introduced for discussion.

> Certain materials will be difficult to find: what is the answer? One possible answer is the pre-fabricated house. These are houses that can be made in factories and assembled on the site . . . Try to keep an open mind. If pre-fabrication will produce for ex-Service men and women houses which are *both* better *and* cheaper, no one ought to put obstacles in the way of their development.[64]

Although prefabrication is here discussed in terms of the production of permanent rather than temporary houses, the public had been presented with the idea of the prefab before the programme of temporary bungalows had ever been announced by Churchill. Initially this announcement concerned the provision of emergency (temporary) houses to meet immediate needs at the end of the war.

Although much was made at the time of the economies that could be achieved through the mass-production of this housing in the factory, the Temporary Housing Programme was as much tied up with the absorption of surplus industrial plant and labour at the end of the war as it was with the provision of housing to meet an emergency. Churchill admitted as much when he first announced the programme to the public during a Sunday broadcast on 26 March 1944. He first promised that:

> the soldiers when they return from the war and those who have been bombed out and made to double up with other families shall be restored to homes of their own at the earliest possible moment.[65]

He then continued to outline two approaches that would be adopted to achieve this. The first concerned the repair of damaged houses, and this work was to progress during the war, and the second concerned 'prefabricated or emergency houses . . . I hope we may make up to half a million of these.'[66] Even at this initial stage he went on to say that, 'These houses will make a heavy demand upon the steel industry and will absorb in a great measure its overflow and expansion for war purposes.'[67] The Temporary Housing Programme was thus, from the first, seen as a double benefit; it would both house the returning serviceman and his family and provide the necessary employment to support them. These ideas were taken up in a further discussion document of the Army Bureau of Current Affairs towards the end of 1944. Discussion was centred on the changes that had occurred while the serviceman or woman had been away from home. The decline in numbers of those working in the building industry

from a prewar level of over a million to the then current 300,000 workers
was noted.

> So the Government is working on a new scheme. The idea is to 'prefabricate'
> temporary houses out of steel and other novel materials which can be partly
> built in factories and assembled in a few days. And the plan is that the
> landlords of these prefabricated houses – also called 'Portal' houses after the
> Minister of Works – shall be the Government. And the Government has
> power to remove them, as soon as the ordinary building programme catches
> up.[68]

Or, as *Picture Post* proclaimed in an article less than two months later on
the coming change over of industry from war time production to making
peace time products:

> In this Home Counties factory, orders for bomber wings are nearing
> completion. Meantime, prototypes of wooden bungalows are being made,
> embodying principles adapted from aircraft work.[69]

It seems, therefore, that it was public knowledge that the temporary
bungalows had the dual purpose of allowing the production lines,
expanded to meet war time needs, to continue and provide work in peace
time and to deliver a product that would be of immediate use to the post-
war population.

Despite their unconventional and apparently impermanent materials the
bungalows quickly became homes, not least because their layout on the
ground enabled each garden space to be given the mark of the individual
tenant. Visited and approved of by royalty (figure 1.15), they perhaps
came very close to an ideal house at a time when the people expected the
state to be implementing ideal solutions. In fact, the 1950 survey found that
housewives not only thought the daily tasks of cooking and washing-up,
cleaning, child care and laundry were easier in the prefab than in their
previous accommodation but that, when moved into permanent housing,
about half those interviewed found cleaning the house more difficult and
that this and laundry were also more time consuming.[70] The feeling was
that if technological progress had aided the favourable outcome of the war
through the development of improved factory production (for example,
aircraft) and scientific discovery (for example, radar) then the expectation
was that such technology would change the *status quo* in peace time in
terms both of providing an efficient mode for living and of creating a more
efficient mode of production. *Picture Post* even ran an article on
assembling a prefabricated tug in four days whilst announcing that this was
the way that the reader's new home would be assembled after the war.[71]

The first result of the application of war time organization and
technological development to housing was the temporary prefab. The fact
that many still survive both as housing and in a variety of new uses suggests

Figure 1.15. Queen Mary admires the garden, created by the WVS, around an Arcon bungalow. (*Source*: *Illustrated London News*, 31 May, 1947)

firstly that the construction of the bungalows was sufficiently good to last beyond the programmed life of fifteen years and, secondly, that people valued them enough to ensure that they did last and were still used even when no longer required for housing. (Prefabs have been recycled for animal housing, garages, site huts, shops and cafes.)

Nevertheless, the scale and cost of the operation, coming as it did at the end of an expensive and debilitating war, raises the question as to why the government should have spent upwards of 200 million pounds on a housing programme with a restricted life.[72] In a book published at the time, Hugh Anthony suggests that temporary housing might satisfy two distinct needs:

(a) to provide quick and removeable housing accommodation on 'blitzed' sites, in large towns or on their outskirts, so as to give the citizens of that locality the shelter they require while permanent housing is being rebuilt for them either in the form of houses or flats.
(b) to provide accommodation which can be quickly built and as quickly taken to pieces again and moved if necessary to another site for re-use. Such

accommodation would be of value in the case of the urgent movement of workers from one part of the country to another for such works as 'blitz' repairs, or wartime factories, and in peace time for major construction works, trunk roads, hydro-electric stations and the building of the new towns which are being proposed at the present time.[73]

In fact the Temporary Housing Programme neither resulted from nor met either of these needs. There was a short programme of emergency housing in London following the 1944 flying bomb attacks and hutments and hostels were constructed to house war workers both in industry and on the land, but temporary houses for families were not provided for these needs. The British Temporary Housing Programme arrived in a seemingly unconsidered rush and overspent its budget, the account being finally wound up without comment in 1956. The purpose of this book is to set out why and how the temporary bungalows came into being after the war and the way in which they became assimilated as an ideal housing type for those fortunate enough to live in one.

All these emergency houses will be publicly owned and it will not rest with any individual tenant to keep them in being after they have served their purpose of tiding over the return of the fighting men and after permanent dwellings are available. As much thought has been and will be put into this plan as was put into the invasion of Africa . . . The swift production of these temporary houses is the only way in which the immediate needs of our people can be met in the four or five years that follow the war.[74]

NOTES

1. Hubbard (1985), p. 91.

2. The standard text of British prefabrication by White (1965, p. 139) gives the number of temporary bungalows delivered by the programme as 156,667. This was the figure anticipated by Cmd. 7304 in 1948. The actual figure given at the time the account was closed in 1956 was slightly lower at 156,623. In fact the numbers appearing in the housing statistics for England and Wales and separately for Scotland give a total allocation of 156,631. This would suggest that the lower figures give a more accurate assessment of the numbers produced.

3. Prefabs have been purchased under the Housing Act 1980: 'In Newport, Gwent, is one of the largest remaining spreads of prefabs: 640 in all, of which 117, so far, have been bought by their former tenants from the council . . . It is here that a prefab can be yours for that £18,500.' (See Marks (1987), p. 50.)

4. Ministry of Health and Local Government (1964), p. 8.

5. Scottish Development Department (1970), p. 7.

6. Scottish Development Department (1971), p. 7. In England and Wales temporary bungalows ceased to be singled out in the housing statistics in 1967 when the *Housing Returns for England and Wales* were replaced by *Local Housing Statistics*.

7. It is hard to be absolute about the numbers ot prefabs. During the period of research the largest single remaining group of prefabs, over 1000 in Hull, was scheduled for demolition and replacement, the work starting in the summer of 1987. Elsewhere, prefabs have been so renovated that little of the original prefabricated nature of the buildings remains. In addition, undiscoverable numbers of prefabs have been relocated and used for other purposes.

8. Readers' Letters, *Picture Post*, 23 June, 1945, p. 3.

9. *Architectural Design and Construction*, November, 1944, p. 251.

10. *The Architect and Building News*, 8 June, 1945, p. 151.

11. Minister of Works (1948), p. 2.

12. The name Arcon comes from the original group of three architects (Edric Neel, Raglan Squire and Rodney Thomas, later to be joined in partnership by Jim Gear), formed in Spring 1943. Because no joint name could be agreed, the composite Arcon was used, which stood for Architectural Consultants. (See Squire R. (1984), p. 96). The name of the practice was later to cause trouble with the RIBA; Arcon was applied to the 'Arcon bungalow', 'Arcon house', 'Arcon classroom' and was, therefore, being used as a trade name and contravening the code of the RIBA. The industrialists in the group included Stewarts and Lloyds Ltd (responsible for the tubular steel framework in the roof), Williams and Williams Ltd (the steel framework of the walls), Crittall Manufacturing Co. (the metal windows) and Turners Asbestos Cement Co. Ltd (the exterior sheeting). The building contractor was Taylor Woodrow Ltd.

13. 'The Arcon Mark II' (1945) *Building*, Vol. 20, October, 1945, p. 262.

14. The Arcon prefabricated service core was manufactured in conjunction with Fisher and Ludlow Ltd. of Birmingham. (See Arcon, Chartered Architects (1948*a*), p. 78.)

15. *Ibid.*

16. *Ibid.*, p. 80.

17. Arcon, Chartered Architects (1948*b*), p. 148.

18. Arcon, Chartered Architects (1948*a*), p. 80.

19. *Ibid.*

20. Arcon, Chartered Architects (1948*c*), p. 115.

21. Tubular steel was developed for scaffolding in the 1920s.

22. Arcon, Chartered Architects (1948*c*), p. 116.

23. *Ibid.*, p. 118.

24. *Ibid.*, pp. 116–117.

25. Sheppard (1946), p. 81.

26. Arcon, Chartered Architects (1948*c*), p. 148.

27. One Uni-Seco system used lightweight beams and columns so that each structural member could be easily handled by two men. Such construction was used for single volume hutted buildings. Rigid wall, door and window units were then fixed between the structure. The second system was cellular in format and used standard partitions and corridor units which effectively carried the outer cladding of the hut. (See 'Hut construction', *The Builder*, 18 July, 1941, p. 61.)

28. Gloag and Wornum (1946), p. 74.

29. Greenhalgh (1944), p. 76.

30. 'Emergency accommodation', *Architectural Design and Construction*, November, 1944, p. 271.

31. 'Seco demountable factory-made cottage', *The Architect and Building News*, 2 November, 1944, p. 112.

32. Leathart (1944), p. 79.

33. The first post-war prefabricated houses developed using the Tarran system of construction were called the Kingston and the Newland. Later the Myton house was developed in Scotland. (See Scottish Office Building Directorate (1987), pp. 13–14. The 'Myton' was a two-storey precast reinforced concrete panel house where, 'All precast units to be manufactured under continuous expert supervision in properly equipped and heated factories . . .' (See Myton Ltd. *Permanent Houses in the New Tradition* (undated) (a specification covering essential details and services).)

34. Bowley (1966), p. 212.

35. A full account of the story of Quarry Hill flats and the problems faced by the contractor can be found in Ravetz (1974).

36. Rankine (1942), p. 218.

37. *Ibid*.

38. Sawdust concrete was not unknown but was thought to be dimensionally unstable because of the organic nature of the aggregate.

39. Neel (1943), p. 212.

40. 'The Tarran Factory-produced Bungalow', *The Architect and Building News*, 3 September, 1943, p. 140.

41. *Picture Post*, 4 March, 1944, pp. 18–19.

42. 'The "Tarran" house', *The Builder*, 11 August, 1944, p. 110.

43. 'The "Tarran" two-storey house, Hull' *The Builder*, 14 July, 1944, p. 26.

44. Minister of Works (1948) Cmd. 7304, London: HMSO, p. 7.

45. *The Architect and Building News*, 2 June, 1944, pp. 131–132.

46. Finnemore (1985a), p. 60.

47. The prototype of the aluminium temporary house, *The Architects' Journal*, 21 June 1945, p. 461.

48. Madge (1946), p. 215.

49. 'The prototype of the aluminium temporary house', *op. cit.*, p. 462.

50. *Ibid*., p. 463.

51. 'Production of prefabricated aluminium houses', *Journal of the RIBA*, July, 1946, p. 402.

52. *Ibid*.

53. *Ibid*., p. 404.

54. Scottish Office Building Directorate (1987), p. 101.

55. Madge (1946), p. 206.

56. Squire (1984), p. 100.

57. Hubbard (1985), p. 91.

58. Women's Group on Public Welfare (1951), p. 23.

59. Addison P. (1985), pp. 57–58.

60. BBC (1944), p. 17.

61. *Picture Post*, 4 March, 1944, p. 17.

62. *Ibid.*, p. 20.

63. Sant'Elia (1914), quoted in Banham (1960), p. 129.

64. Army Bureau of Current Affairs (1943), pp. 10–11.

65. Churchill (1944), p. 359.

66. *Ibid.*

67. *Ibid.*, p. 360.

68. Army Bureau of Current Affairs (1944a), p. 14.

69. 'Industry's Problem: the coming change-over', *Picture Post*, 6 January, 1945, p. 8.

70. Women's Group on Public Welfare (1951), pp. 36–37.

71. *Picture Post*, 22 April, 1944, p. 13.

72. When the scheme was first announced the total expenditure on the half a million Portal Bungalows promised by Churchill was of the order of 275 million pounds. The passing of the Housing (Temporary Accommodation Act) in October 1944 only authorized the expenditure of up to 150 million pounds on a reduced target of 250,000 bungalows. The final cost of the 156,623 bungalows supplied up to March 1949 was 207 million pounds (see Chapter 6).

73. Anthony, (1945), p. 30.

74. Churchill, (1944), p. 360.

2

BUNGALOWS BY THE SEA

*'. . . for every one person who said she would like to live in a flat,
ten said they would like to live in a small house or bungalow.'*[1]

THE EMERGENCE OF THE BUNGALOW

Churchill in his announcement of the Temporary Housing Programme saw
the prefab as an expedient answer to the problems of industry and housing,
yet the bungalow form appears to have met the needs, whether implicit or
explicit, of those who were to live in them. The majority of local authority
houses provided in the inter-war period were two-storey cottages, with
flats, except in cities like London and Liverpool, only appearing in
numbers in the immediate period before the war as an answer to the
provision of high-density new housing to replace the slums in inner-city
areas. The bungalow, it would appear, was a form of housing that was
associated with the middle classes who were to buy rather than rent their
housing.

> The middle class have to shift for themselves in the matter of housing, and
> many are turning eagerly to the bungalow as a hopeful solution of their
> difficulties.[2]

The prefab was the first bungalow to rent produced in any quantity and,
as such, its success may have depended at least partly on the fact that a
middle-class housing form, associated with the seaside and the countryside,
was suddenly available for all.

To understand something of the acceptability of the bungalow form it
may be useful to look at its development. Nevertheless, to talk of the
development of the single-storey house or bungalow is a contradiction in
terms as the primitive single-storey hut came long before the primitive two-
storey hut:

> The 'savage' hunter sought shelter in rock caves, the earliest form of
> dwelling, and learnt to build huts of reeds, rushes and wattle-and-daub or
> tents of saplings, sheathed in bark, skins, turves or brushwood. The
> counterparts of these can still be found in use today . . . When towns
> developed, houses had to be adapted to urban conditions; more solidly built,
> crowded together and rising to two or more storeys.[3]

However, in England and Wales the urban single-storey form is in some respects a far more recent introduction. Brunskill suggests that, 'the story of vernacular architecture is one of modification and adaptation based on ground floor living'.[4] The single-storey house with the space enclosed by the structural envelope open to the underside of the roof was, initially, all that could be easily constructed. However, it had the disadvantages of limited accommodation for the many activities that needed to take place and the difficulty of dispersing the smoke from the open fire in the living space. Inserting an intermediate floor originally improved the ground floor living and sleeping space, making it a smaller volume and easier to keep warm. The upper floor, still often open to the roof and of a limited headroom, was where the less important in the family would sleep. This idea of the least favoured sleeping quarters happening immediately under the roof was retained as houses came to be two storeys and more. In Victorian times, for instance, the attic bedrooms were where the maids slept[5] and were finished internally to a lower standard (no coving between ceiling and wall, plain rather than moulded skirtings etc.) than the remainder of the house. As a Victorian commentator on manners remarked, 'The ordinary female domestics are usually provided with Bedrooms on the uppermost stor(e)y . . .'[6] In general, however, the single-storey form open to the roof, which had once been universal, was left to a decreasing portion of those less fortunate in society until by the end of the nineteenth century it was only the rural poor who built and lived in such dwellings.[7]

Although the single-storey form in its more refined version with a ceiling between the occupants and the roof timbers survived in rural areas, particularly in the north of England,[8] and was even recommended by the reforming movement of the Chartists as a roomy and suitable rural dwelling for what they believed was to be a new way of living for the ordinary working man or woman,[9], with one exception the widespread use of the single-storey form in an urban or suburban setting was to be a twentieth-century innovation.

The exception was again in the north of England, particularly in Sunderland, where single-storey terraced houses were built in the late nineteenth century and into the early twentieth century (figure 2.1). These houses still survive and are lived in. Known locally as 'cottages' to distinguish them from two-storey houses they have a wide frontage (approx. 20 feet), a double banked plan, an outshot containing additional accommodation and a generous yard which was designed to include wash-house and WC. It was possible to make use of the attic space but the 1867 bye-laws gave dimensions so that the difference between the Sunderland single-storey cottage and a two-storey house was very clear.[10]

Despite this example, the emergence of the bungalow as a twentieth

Figure 2.1. Street of single-storey terraced bungalows in Sunderland, 1994.

century housing form appears to have received impetus from two directions. Firstly the creation of leisure time for the relatively wealthy produced new settlements of temporary and permanent residences along the south coast, usually single-storey in form. These bungalows became associated with healthy living. Secondly, the 'cottage' form (a simple rectangular plan with the upper floor partly within the roof space) was developed as the correct housing model for the working classes around the turn of the century. The single-storey vernacular house had some influence on this, although, as noted earlier, the working-class cottage was the consequence and not the bungalow.

In his history of the bungalow, Anthony King outlines a development that began as a middle-class venture into building or renting a second home that was itself specifically concerned with leisure activities such as sea bathing or the rural pleasures of golfing and walking. These bungalows were large with rooms in the attic space or even a full upper storey. The name bungalow at this time signified something other than a dwelling having only a single storey. A bungalow was rather a dwelling of simple form under a single simple roof. As a dwelling it was also arranged for convenience of use and admitted plentiful light and air, with windows or openings on four sides, hence the association with a healthy lifestyle. Verandahs were a common feature to provide covered outdoor space. Most importantly, however, the bungalow was a building concerned with relaxation and recreation and not for work or for working from. The connection with India comes from the published experiences of mid-nineteenth-century expatriates from the Indian sub-continent. These demonstrated a contrast in life-style with a Britain that was becoming increasingly industrialized, with the work concentrated in large cities from which the middle classes were attempting to escape by building in the new suburbs.

> More important . . . were the images now attached to the bungalow style of life. In the 1860s and 1870s, life in the country or hill station bungalow was seen as a positive experience, far from the madding crowd and waited on hand and foot. Like other facets of Indian and Anglo-Indian life it seemed to represent something which had been lost in England, increasingly industrialised and urban, and offering an opportunity to escape from social changes which some people were beginning to deplore.[11]

The transfer of a housing form from the Indian hill station to the south coast of Britain marked the introduction of the bungalow to the suburban south. Originally these dwellings were constructed by the speculative builder for the rich. However, the small seaside bungalow for rent or even purchase as a second home became increasingly popular in the early years of the twentieth century. This popularity coincided with the availability of railway travel that made the coast accessible, the creation of the weekend with its opportunities for leisure, and the mass production of building materials that enabled the enthusiast to construct his or her own basic accommodation that could be added to as finances allowed.[12]

A typical seaside development of this type took place on Shoreham Beach. It began in the 1890s when a local entrepreneur hauled some disused railway carriages across the muddy bay to form the start of 'Bungalow Town'. These meagre abodes were to be rented to those looking for a cheap holiday on the south coast. Shoreham also had a

Figure 2.2. Bungalow at Pagham Beach where the original carriage is visible, unaltered externally apart from the addition of a verandah, 1990.

traditional wooden ship-building industry which withered at the turn of the
century and, 'Building bungalows proved to be a timely opportunity for
unemployed joiners . . .'.[13] This also suggests that the bungalows were
neither purposely prefabricated nor built by unskilled labour. Rather it
seems to have been the low land costs and primitive and sub-standard
conditions which were to bring them within the reach of the ordinary
person on holiday.

> We rented 'Titwillow' for one experimental August, and in 1908 my father
> signed a 35-year lease of 'Rosemary' with the Shoreham and Lancing Land
> Company at a yearly rental of 17 pounds and 4 shillings. That was another of
> Bungalow Town's attractions – it was easy on the pocket; and once you'd
> settled in, there was little to make the holiday money fly; there wasn't even a
> tavern in the Town. And no shop until the Bungalow Stores eventually
> opened up . . .[14,15]

Although it began at the end of the nineteenth century, the colonization
of parts of the coast by those in search of a cheap and simple holiday was
largely undertaken during the 1920s and 1930s. The bungalows built at this
time usually offered very simple shelter. Their form in part derives from
the simplicity of their purpose and the fact that some were built by their
owners, and others extended and added to from primitive beginnings. At
Pagham Beach redundant carriages of the Chichester and Selsey tramway,
which closed in 1935, still form the basis of an estate of bungalows on the
beach (figures 2.2 and 2.3). Forming the 'prefabricated' starting point of
any individual development, the carriages are more or less explicit
according to the ambitions of the owners. Such buildings still have
considerable value as housing.[16]

For those who rented or were lucky enough to own holiday housing of
this type, whether in Sussex or on the east coast, at places like Jaywick
Sands and Canvey Island, or further north at Withernsea, or in north
Wales or on the Lancashire coast, the bungalow was to have particular
associations. It became part of an outdoor, healthy and carefree life, where
people co-operated to help each other with the fetching of provisions and
necessary services in accord with the pioneering spirit of the place. It
formed the basis of a community very different from the squalor that still
existed at the heart of many British cities.

Much the same spirit existed in similar colonies of bungalows in the
countryside. In the same way that railways had opened up areas of the
coast, so the development of the car, coinciding with the agricultural
depression, suggested a new use for the countryside as a resource for
leisure rather than just a factory for the production of food. Those who
ventured to establish new second homes, and later permanent homes, in
the countryside took the bungalow form with them.

Initially this migration was by the rich, with the establishment of

Figure 2.3. Two railway carriages with a pitched roof added across them form this bungalow at Pagham Beach (the tumble-home of the carriage is clearly visible).

bungalows in areas like Bellagio near East Grinstead.[17] However, the railways were also to open up the countryside to the poor, especially the lines to the east. The lines to Essex opened up a farmland that was heavy and only suitable for growing corn, then a cheap import, and was within reach of those living in the unhealthy and overcrowded east end of London. Hardy and Ward consider the motives of the working-class settlers on what were to become known as the Essex plotlands to be as follows:

> They ranged from people who intended to settle and commute to London by rail; people who wanted a weekend retreat and who could finance the purchase by renting to others; people with back-to-the-land and simple-life ambitions; and would-be smallholders who were attracted by the larger sites offered very cheaply in the areas more than two miles from the railway stations.[18]

Plotlands were developed in Essex around South Woodham Ferrers and at Pitsea and Laindon. The latter two areas were to become incorporated into Basildon new town after the Second World War. However, whether in the country or by the coast, the plotlands with their single-storey bungalows or shacks which were usually built by their owners were the only way that the working classes, without the earning power of the middle classes and their ability to afford mortgage repayments on one of the inter-war speculative suburban estates, could become the freehold owners of property. Some people settled on their plots immediately despite the lack of piped services, properly made roads, and facilities such as shops and schools. Others used the ownership of their plotlands to provide holiday or weekend accommodation. After the Blitz many of these Essex weekend homes became permanently settled by those who had lost their rented homes in the bombing. Others settled in their weekend country or seaside home after retirement, also becoming permanent plotland bungalow dwellers.[19]

In suburbia the bungalow was also to be a success. They were constructed by the speculative builder on the fringes of any development where the land was the cheapest. King declares this to be, 'often the cheapest form of house'.[20] It could be built at low cost because the single-storey walls required a minimum of scaffolding and, therefore, suited the smal builder with the minimum of overheads.

However, in a straight comparison, the bungalow would appear to be more expensive. Edwin Gunn looked at the cost of the same accommodation provided in a bungalow and a two-storey cottage with all the first floor rooms within the roofspace, the results being published in 1920. Overall, there was a 9 per cent additional cost for the bungalow, at least half of which was attributable to increased foundations and surface concrete. The cost of the example bungalow might have been reduced by using a simple roof form without the two valleys (the type of roof that was to cover the prefab) but the bungalow still remained the more expensive form. The comment that accompanied this study may be pertinent to the development and acceptance of the temporary bungalow as an appropriate housing form.

> Opinion no doubt will continue to be divided as to the relative desirability of the cottage and bungalow forms. Some people will consider a 9 per cent. excess little enough to pay for the convenience of a stairless home . . . but of far greater importance is the saving in labour effected by all the rooms being on one floor, and for this there are many who would think an extra initial expenditure of £60 (in the cases under review) to be far outweighed by the additional convenience secured.[21]

Apart from convenience, which was to be one of the attractions of the bungalow for those interviewed in surveys during the war, the detached bungalow had the advantage of standing alone on its plot, affirming its owner's title to his or her piece of land and affirming its owner's control of his or her own housing.

CRITICS OF THE BUNGALOW

It was this assertive isolation that gave the bungalow form at once its success and its critics. In the mid-1920s it became apparent that the rapid increase in speculative house building was encroaching on the countryside. Although the critics, often professional people trained in visual design, deplored the ribbon development and the streets of suburban semis with their broken skylines,[22] particular opprobrium was reserved for the bungalow: 'Every one who loves the character of the English countryside must be appalled by the rash of squalid little bungalows which disfigures even remote beauty spots'.[23]

The cause was taken up by the Council for the Preservation of Rural England (CPRE) who produced the forerunners of contemporary design guides. These incorporated suggestions for correct designs of houses for areas with differing vernacular traditions. Illustrations were also included to show the horror of the bungalow.

Although the bungalow had begun life as a recreational building for the rich, for a period it had appeared that the bungalow might be equated with home ownership for poorer people. However, this was soon to be denied by the pre- and post-war planning legislation[24] which put control of the environment back into the hands of those trained to be experts. However, it was recognized that it was not the single-storey form that was necessarily at fault, or even the materials used for the construction of such dwellings:

> The appearance of a building does not depend primarily upon expense. Good planning, pleasant proportions and a careful choice of site and materials are far more important than cost. A capable architect can use even the cheapest materials with fine effect.[25]

The fact remained that the average bungalow was not designed by those trained in the visual arts but by those closest to the desires of the users. Although the temporary bungalows were initially to be the products of trained designers, at least in terms of overall layout of plan and fittings, they contained within them a quality of shelter created whilst making the best of the available materials after the war. This had a mirror in the pioneering spirit of those who had built their own bungalows on the plotlands. This, together with the association of the bungalow form with that which the working classes had aspired to own, probably gave the temporary bungalows an acceptable image from the beginning. As Weaver paradoxically commented: 'There is in some people's minds a real feel for the word "bungalow" and all it means, even when they are not quite clear what it does mean'.[26]

If the bungalow form was acceptable to those who were to be the recipients of the Temporary Housing Programme, then perhaps its success as a housing form might, in part at least, be due to a realization of the dreams of the people with regard to the post-war house. Was living in a prefab in post-war Britian distantly equated with the idea of the 'holiday bungalow', or other elusive dreams?

> By 1948 almost 125,000 'prefabs' had been built. Residents' satisfaction with them was very high, perhaps because they combined the two essential

qualities of the universally desired country-cottage type, namely compact inside and a large garden. Many people were sorry to leave their prefabs.[27]

THE VALUE OF SURVEYS TO DETERMINE
THE DESIRES OF USERS

The question arises as to how closely the prefab represented the ideal post-war home of the mass of people who participated in various surveys during the war. It must be realized that there are two views of public participation through surveys. The first follows the methods of Mass Observation where data are collected from a wide variety of opinions and some method of distilling the variety into a consensus is undertaken mathematically. The second method may again seek to discover original opinions from the public but these are represented by a single individual who then sits on a committee of more or less similarly informed individuals. This committee analyses the problem of the post-war home in the light of its members' expertise and research and comes to a set of recommendations. The expectations of the public with regard to the type of post-war home that they might wish to live in may differ from what is built because of this system of committee recommendations by experts, who in turn are supposed to represent public opinion. An example of this can be seen from the work of the Council for Research on Housing Construction and their promotion of the post-war flat (see note 32).

Despite the eventual success of the prefab the single-storey house was not to form a major part of the post-war housing stock, at least not in the form of the detached cottage. Single-storey housing was, however, to be provided in flats, which, rather like the bungalow, were offered to the public as a far more convenient alternative to the two-storey house. A dramatic change in the housing stock occurred after the war with the increasing provision of the flat as the ideal authority owned dwelling. Between the wars the flat formed only 5 per cent of the subsidized dwellings.[28] The majority of the people surveyed during the war about the type of ideal house that they might like to live in were, therefore, familiar with the two-storey house form and would not have had the experience of living in flats. This inevitably influenced their opinion of what the ideal home should be like, as discussed below.

> A number of 'surveys of opinion' have been made . . ., but their results are almost meaningless. Hundreds of people must have recorded their opinion without a knowledge of the facts that would enable them to form a balanced view. This balanced view requires not only a consideration of how the advantages and disadvantages of houses and flats affect (a) the individual at home, but also how they affect (b) the town as a whole with its citizens.[29]

After the war, however, flats formed a far larger proportion of subsidized dwellings. By 1964 in the statistics for housing tenders approved, 'The proportion rose to a maximum of 55.2 per cent'.[30] The impetus for the development of flats as opposed to houses is argued to have come from architects and planners influenced by the ideals of the Modern Movement,[31] with higher rise buildings being both less wasteful of land and able to take advantage of industrialized building methods. These were, however, not the industrialized building methods of the 'house out of the factory' prefab but rather the economies of scale that were gained from large-scale building operations with a great deal of repetition of components.

Flats were also seen as the solution to the clearance of inner-city slums. If the replacement buildings rose to several storeys then more of the original tenants could be rehoused on the same site. As the Council for Research on Housing Construction reported in 1934:

> We are forced then to the conclusion that the greater part of the slum population of London and the other largest cities must be rehoused on the spot, at higher densities than cottages can possibly provide. Multi-storey tenement flats are the only solution.[32]

However, the Council felt that it was not only the issue of density in the inner cities that made flats an appropriate housing form. Savings would be made on the provision of an infrastructure if that which already existed could be used rather than developing virgin land on the outskirts. The total cost of dwellings provided was also thought to be less for flats since the land cost per dwelling was much less. The Council, however, had to admit that, '. . . up to the present tenement flats have cost in general some 50% more to build than cottages of equivalent accommodation . . .'.[33] This high additional cost was attributed to the fact that both the design of flats and their methods of construction had, at that time, not been sufficiently studied in order to effect savings through efficiencies. It was felt that the cottage dwelling was cheaper just because its construction had been standardized and made efficient through study and through the numerous examples built. Because the public liked cottages and because they were cheaper, the Council felt that architects were not encouraged to build flats. Once they did so, then a similar volume of research would be available for flats to make them cheaper and encourage others to design them. The continental apartment block developments were held up as an example of the types of flatted dwellings that could be achieved once architects turned their hand to the task. The fact that the people did not ask for their post-war housing in this form seems hardly to have been considered:

> Flats remain unpopular with the masses despite the most persistent propaganda by architectural playboys who want larger boxes of plasticine with which to indulge their creative fancy. Town-dwellers at last realise the importance of agriculture and consciously desire contact with country life.[34]

The literal demise of the post-war flat with today's emphasis on Housing Association provision of low rise 'cottage' homes may only represent the disparity between views such as those expressed by the Council for Research on Housing Construction and the image that the public may have had of post-war housing. In the magazines and discussion documents of that period the word 'house' is found repeatedly.

> Why should English prefabricated houses look like wooden huts while the Swedish ones have the appearance of pleasant homes.[35]

> The Coalition Government recognised that traditional methods of building would be unable to give us the number of houses that are required. As a result it applied itself first to the idea of building temporary houses; and then, to the idea of supplying prefabricated houses.[36]

> After the war there will be an increased demand for small houses, as a very large number of couples will wish to set up house at once.[37]

If the public expected houses rather than flats, the fact that the prefabs represented some kind of public ideal may equally be viewed in hindsight as a fortuitous accident rather than as the result of any painstaking research into the wishes of the public.

GOVERNMENT REPORTS ON HOUSING

As discussed above, publications concerning the possible form of post-war housing fall into the two categories; government sponsored reports and reports of specific surveys. Looking initially at the former, the most important report was the *Design of Dwellings*, produced under the chairmanship of the Earl of Dudley in 1944. This was then embodied in the *Housing Manual* of 1944 which was intended for the guidance of local authorities. The report was prepared by a sub-committee of the Central Housing Advisory Committee and drew upon urban and rural local authorities for evidence as well as local authority associations, voluntary organizations and some twenty-six individuals of whom 50 per cent were architects.[38] As such, public input into the discussion was severely limited, though the report was presented as a discussion document by the Army Bureau of Current Affairs, but not until 1945.[39] The report limited its field of activity to 'permanent dwellings commonly built by local authorities'[40] and despite the formation of the Committee early in 1942 no reference is made to temporary accommodation. Its concern is with the estimated 3 to 4 million houses that would be needed and constructed 'in the ten to twelve years following the present war'.[41]

The Report attempts a serious analysis of potential housing needs, recognizing that the three-bedroomed house is not ideal for all family situations and that a mixture of housing types, including flats, would need to be provided. Local authorities are recommended to provide a plan outlining detailed housing needs along these lines. Interestingly, the high standard of interior fittings that may have influenced the popularity of the prefab is recognized as desirable in all housing:

> Moreover, the experience gained by the vast number of women now in industry and in the services will influence their attitude to housing; for war-time factories and hostels often provide high standards of services and equipment, which will make such women intolerant of inferior conditions in their own homes. In the same way, both men and women have become conscious during the war of the potentialities of modern scientific developments and will expect to enjoy the benefit of these discoveries at home.[42]

The single-storey detached cottage is not, however, recognized as a potential permanent housing type. In fact the report stated that since a large proportion of the houses that were built before 1914 only had two bedrooms, and since in many areas this type of housing made a considerable contribution to the overall housing stock, the emphasis for the new housing after the war should be on, '. . . the provision of the three-bedroom house interspersed with a proportion of other types.'[43] Writing about the demographic distribution of the population post-war, Block suggested that this view was not a total reflection of the situation and that the mis-match between family size and the provision of the three-bedroom house as a standard between the wars had led to under-occupancy, which had in turn provided a cushion of accommodation to help absorb those made homeless through bombing during the war period.[44]

When considering the house on its plot, the Report spent more time discussing the quality of the sheds and outbuildings than the quality of any private outdoor space. Gardens were thought to be important for rural cottages so that the tenants could grow food. Although a need for gardens in the cities was recognized so that those whose hobby was gardening could continue this pursuit, even where they were to live in flats, the practical problem of providing the land was never tackled. Indeed, for flats the recommendation was that any central area should not be divided up into individual plots, however much the tenants might have wished for this, but that the area should be landscaped as a whole. Interestingly, at Quarry Hill flats in Leeds, individual plots were provided at the start and a tenant won the 'Gardens for Leeds' award for a number of successive years.[45] However, these plots disappeared when the area became a building site after structural renovation began in 1960. At the end of the work the plots were merged into a single landscape scheme, much of which was hard surfaced. The garden, therefore, which formed another popular attribute of the prefab, was not thought to be particularly important in the post-war house.

The report anticipated the development of prefabrication without seeing it as any kind of panacea. It was also felt that prefabrication would not necessarily produce monotonous and repetitive design, 'provided always that a competent architect is in charge of the scheme'.[46]

Although the Report aimed to produce guidelines for local authorities and, therefore, concentrated on such issues as the need for adequate storage space within dwellings and the areas required within dwellings to allow for different activities (i.e. the size of room required for a kitchen where meals are taken), there was no deliberate attempt to recommend any particular house type that might have been identified as desired by the tenants. Tenant needs were implied rather than being specifically set out and there is at times in the Report a sense of the committee's 'superior wisdom' producing recommendations on untried and unsubstantiated grounds:

> We are attracted by the blocks of 'maisonettes' . . . which have been built in place of flats on central sites in some towns. We do not think that the merits of this convenient form of development have been sufficiently appreciated and we should like to see it more widely used.[47]

In contrast to the *Design of Dwellings*, the sister Report prepared by the Scottish Housing Advisory Committee, and also published in 1944, attempted a far greater involvement of the public in gathering evidence for their recommendations. Through the press, the public were asked to send in their ideas about housing after the war, and, 'very many letters were received from the public, containing numerous valuable suggestions'.[48] In addition, questionnaires were circulated to both men and women in the armed forces and to those working in a number of Scottish factories and directly involved with war work. The replies from the questionnaires were analysed for the committee by the War-Time Social Survey. Some 15,634 individuals were estimated to have taken part in the survey.[49]

Although the single-storey form was far more common in Scotland, both as the rural cottage and the tenement flat, the overwhelming response to the question about preferred house form demonstrated the supremacy of the bungalow whether built in town or country, over both the two-storey form and the flat (table 2.1).

In addition, 97 per cent of those in the forces and 95 per cent of those in industry questioned stated that they wanted a private garden in their post-war house. Communal gardens, maintained by a small group of tenants for the private use of the group, were rejected by 95 per cent of those questioned in the forces and 94 per cent of those questioned in industry. Moreover, a public garden maintained by the local authority and associated with a particular block of flats was again rejected by those questioned the percentage rejections being 81 per cent of those in the forces and 85 per cent of those in industry.[50]

Table 2.1. Scottish house type preferences, 1944.

| | In a Town | | In the Country | |
	Forces %	Industry %	Forces %	Industry %
Bungalow-detached	21	29	41	42
-semi detached	11	7	8	8
-terrace	3	2	3	2
Two-storey house				
detached	30	13	19	11
semi detached	12	7	7	3
terrace	2	2	1	1
Flatted houses*	4	6	1	4
Block of modern flats	14	15	1	2
Not answered	3	19	19	27

*Flats in two-storey blocks, mostly in blocks of four houses – each house having separate entrance from ground level.
(*Source*: Department of Health for Scotland, 1944)

With these results from the survey the report still recommended the construction of flats, both for families and for special category groups such as single people, although two members of the committee published their dissension from this recommendation. Flats were justified because:

> . . . there is limited emphasis in our evidence on one obvious advantage of the flatted house, namely, that it continues the Scottish tradition of having the whole dwelling on a single floor.[51]

Thus, despite the overwhelming public preference for the single storey bungalow, the single storey flat was to be offered as a fulfilment of both public demand and Scottish tradition. The single storey prefabricated bungalow probably came far closer to the public ideal, and the fact that its construction was unconventional was a continuation of the delivery of prefabricated houses in Scotland between the wars: 'In 1927, for the first time since the First World War, the number of houses completed in one year passed the 20,000 mark: 1,110 of these were steel houses.'[52]

In fact the questionnaire in *Planning Our New Homes* had asked for opinions under the heading 'Standard of Construction' but the three questions were concerned with the detail of finishes and window types only.[53]

The Scottish Report, unlike its sister Report for England and Wales does concern itself with the foreseen shortage of houses immediately after the war and came to the conclusion that some form of temporary accommodation would be required. Based on examples in the USA, the Report recommended the following room areas for such temporary accommodation:[54]

Living-room	160–180 square feet
First bedroom	130 square feet
Second, third etc. bedrooms	100–120 square feet
Kitchenette	70 square feet

In fact the original two-bedroom prototype steel Portal bungalow had a floor area of 465 square feet (discounting bathroom and hall) which is exactly comparable with the minimum floor areas suggested above. The Scottish Report also examined alternative ways of meeting the post-war housing shortage (see Chapter 6).

In England and Wales, however, the official view of the post-war home did not see the bungalow as a possible housing form except *in extremis* for temporary dwellings, or except for special category persons such as old people.

From this limited look at contemporary research it would appear that the public saw the bungalow as a housing form that met their ideals, especially in Scotland. Moreover, the other attributes that went with the temporary bungalows, that is, private gardens, better equipment and more storage space were seen as desirable. Nevertheless, the official view of the post-war home was primarily a view produced by experts for the people. A number of reports, however, also presented the people's own view and particularly the view of women.

THE PUBLIC VIEW OF POST-WAR HOUSING

People were encouraged by the press to be interested in what was going to happen after the war. If opinions were strongly expressed before the war was over then it might be that those in power would take notice and act on them once peace was restored. As a populist architectural publication stated:

> When the days of reconstruction come you and I will not be asked to take over the government. On the contrary, decisions will be made by the high-ups . . . over whom, expect through Parliament, you and I have absolutely no control.[55]

Through organizations such as the Army Bureau of Current Affairs, people were specifically asked to think about the future. Consideration of how much better things were to be after the war was won was essential to maintaining the idea that the war could and would be won at all. As housing continued to be destroyed and emergency conditions prevailed in terms of requisitioning and billetting, and as workers and those in the forces were transferred to temporary camps, the idea that society could plan the type and numbers of houses that would be needed after the war and where and what these houses should be, became widespread. The Bureau itself sent out the following statistics towards the end of 1943 to form the basis of discussion.[56]

1939–1943   About 135,000 new houses have been completed.
             Nearly 3,000,000 houses in England and Wales have been damaged in air raids.
             Of these, 2,500,000 have been given first-aid repairs, and are now occupied.

Discussion about the post-war home was encouraged. There was a feeling that opinions were going to be given effective consideration. However, how much this represents the attitude only of the educated middle class is debatable. Mass Observation, in its survey of people's housing, found that people were surprised to be asked whether or not they liked their home and were sometimes surprised that it was possible to have aspirations about their ideal home.[57] Without the structure and support of an organization like the Army Bureau of Current Affairs, even in war-time the individual housewife must have felt that her opinion counted for very little.

Like the survey material mentioned above in *Planning Our New Homes*, the approach of the direct questionnaire produced a high proportion of people in favour of the conventional house and garden. During a survey of the attitudes of men and women in the forces, the following proposition was put forward: 'Assume that you live in an area that has been bombed, and the whole district (including remaining houses, etc.) is to be rebuilt. You can either stay and live in a good modern flat and be near your work, or you can move to the outskirts and have a house and garden and be away from work'.[58]

In response, of the 2407 persons questioned, 5 per cent remained undecided (120); 2 per cent wanted a flat (51); and the remaining 93 per cent opted for a house with a garden. As the person conducting the survey commented, '. . . nearly everybody wanted the house and garden, and were willing to sacrifice quite a lot to get them.'[59]

The same general conclusion was arrived at in a different way by the Mass Observation Survey. Rather than asking for specific preferences in the method of the traditional survey, the Mass Observation unit aimed to listen to people talking about their housing and about what they did and did not like. This meant that rather than ask the question, 'do you want to live in a flat?' when the flat dweller might well reply 'yes' and the house-holder 'no' with the answers thus reflecting the *status quo*, Mass Observation set out with the idea of encouraging people just to talk about their own housing, about housing issues and about what their ideal house might be. Housewives made up the bulk (90 per cent) of the sample observed.

What Mass Observation found was what others had found before them, people wanted to live in houses rather than flats, they prized their privacy and they liked their gardens:

> There can be no doubt, however, that flats are unpopular with the great majority of English people. In the present survey, for every one person who said that she would like to live in a flat, ten said that they would like to live in a small house or bungalow.[60]

To some extent findings like this have to be qualified. Mass Observation commented that people liked their flats or liked their houses often because they were new and very obviously different from the slums from which people had been moved. So even housing with disadvantages would be liked because it was fundamentally better.[71] Conversely, details which could be rectified within the housing form often meant that the whole housing form was dismissed. One women discussing her flat said:

> There's no space . . . I have to put all the rubbish in the bathroom, brooms and wood and my husband's tools. And I'd like a coat rack. There's nowhere for the children to hang their coats and mackintoshes when they come home from school.[62]

Nevertheless, as the following table[63] shows, the small house was far more popular than the flat.

Mass Observation took special notice of the numbers of people wishing to live in a bungalow, just over 10 per cent of the sample, which they considered to be a high proportion and much larger than the proportion of bungalows in the housing stock. The reasons for this anomaly were suggested as:

> People are attracted to this type of home by the absence of any stairs and the compactness of the living quarters. Many imagine that a bungalow would be more economical to run than a small house, particularly from a cleaning and heating point of view.[64]

Table 2.2. Preferences expressed in the Mass Observation Survey, 1943.

	Percentage wanting to live in				
Living in	Small house	Bungalow	Flat	'Here'	Unspecified
Old houses	48	12	6	22	12
Garden cities	49	15	1	24	11
Housing estates	40	16	3	25	16
Flats	60	4	12	15	9

The compactness and convenience of the bungalow in the form offered by the prefab was, therefore, going to coincide with the ideals of many people of just what bungalow living should be. It was not just that they wanted a bungalow, but that they wanted it for the more convenient and labour-saving lifestyle that it would offer and this is exactly what the prefab provided.

A house that was easy to run was also correlated with more fittings within the house. People commented that they would like cupboards within kitchens rather than shelves which quickly became dirty. A built-in kitchen table was also considered desirable so that, 'then it wouldn't matter if the kitchen was a bit small'.[65] Even something as simple as boxing-in the bath was commented upon as, 'The pipes under the bath are a job to keep clean.'[66] This emphasis on improved fittings within the home can also be found in the letters pages of women's magazines of the period. Of six letters found in the *Weldon's Ladies' Journal* (a monthly magazine very much for the homemaker) that followed a series on the 'Homes of Tomorrow', all concentrate on features that would make the home easier to run. Suggestions range from more storage space and a pram space to central heating and a room for children with fitted storage, all features that were to be provided in the prefab.[67]

Mass Observation also found that the desire to have a garden was strong and that communal gardens were disliked. The garden was desirable as a place to grow vegetables and flowers, dry washing and 'to sit after work and at weekends'.[68] A survey in Birmingham conducted in 1937–38 reached a similar conclusion with regard to gardens: of those who had gardens 96 per cent stated that they were pleased to have a garden.[69] Checking on the state of these desired gardens, the researchers found that in the outer ring of suburbs only 13.5 per cent of the gardens could be described as badly cared for.[70] Therefore, not only did people wish to have gardens but the majority looked after them. The same survey found that out of all the people in the city of Birmingham who had no garden 78 per cent would have liked one.[71] Whether by chance or intention, the nature of the temporary prefabricated bungalow required it to stand detached on its own plot of garden. Its popularity may have owed much to this feature alone.

The garden even entered into political propaganda immediately after the war. In a Conservative pamphlet encouraging women to use their vote in 1945 the garden was singled out as one of ten results that women 'would like peace to bring, besides, of course, a good rest and a bit of gaiety.'[72] (Other issues were: cheap and varied food; better education; a steady job; a nursery school; water laid on; another baby; a house that's home; a little fun; a modern kitchen.)

One other published survey purported to represent the views of women and the home they wanted after the war. Although claiming to represent the views of some 4.5 million women through the women's organizations that were involved in consultation and questionnaires,[73] the survey dismisses any indecision or helplessness found by Mass Observation and presents a united view of what women wanted after the war and, moreover, a view led by an educated middle class. The conclusions reached are similar but perhaps more extreme in that 90 per cent of those surveyed wanted a house or bungalow[74] and 99 per cent wanted a private garden.[75] The report discusses the interior of the post-war home and its possible fittings in great detail. The labour saving kitchen is illustrated in various forms, all with built-in fittings and a minimum of extraneous surfaces to keep clean.

Of the women asked, 95 per cent wished to have a refrigerator although not at the expense of a conventional larder.[76] Bathrooms were to be as built-in as kitchens and, 'Most women who have given evidence on the matter seem to require built-in wardrobes in the bedrooms'.[77]

The report also mentions the emergency factory made house. Although there is no record of the attitudes of the women to the prototype Portal bungalow exhibited in 1944 apart from the comment, 'Since the specimen house was opened for inspection, many criticisms have reached the Ministry of Works and alterations are to be made to the original plan,'[78] there is discussion on the problems of constructing temporary housing rather than permanent housing.

> The natural inertia of people who have got used to their surroundings, as well as the lack of better accommodation, helps to explain why the 'temporary' dwelling has so often become a permanent one in the past.[79]

This is a prophetic statement in view of the prefabs that were still inhabited long after their proposed ten year life was over.

The surveys that were undertaken during the war suggested that the ideal home for the majority of the people was the familiar two-storey house, preferably sited in its own gardens at front and back. However, the bungalow was also seen as a desirable housing form and one particularly associated with being both convenient and cheap to run. The other desire for fittings and finishes within the house that made it easier to run and thereby reduced the toil of the housewife were also attributes that the prefab possessed. The unusual construction of the prefab did not appear to make it less attractive to those using it. The war had, itself, exposed people to a rapid development of technology and it was only reasonable that the benefits of this technology should be carried over into the period of reconstruction. If this meant that houses both looked and were factory made then that was acceptable. It was to be the form of the factory made bungalow, sitting on its individual plot, and with a high level of built-in labour saving fittings that so accorded with the dream of the post-war home. *'You're on your own, your dirt's your own.'*[80]

NOTES

1. Mass Observation (1943), p. 46

2. Randall Phillips (1920), p. 9.

3. Fletcher (1967), pp. 2–3.

4. Brunskill (1978), p. 114.

5. Burnett (1980), p. 195.

6. Kerr (1972), p. 250.

7. John Burnett (1980, p. 120) cites a single room cob and thatch cottage at Mudtown, Walton-on-Thames as 'representative of low-quality building widely prevailing in late nineteenth century.'

8. The Scottish crofts offer an example. Weller (1982, p. 44) states that 'The dwellings remaining at the clachan of Auchindrain (Argyll) show how families lived well into this century'.

9. Darley (1978), pp. 167–171

10. Muthesius (1982), pp. 103–104. Muthesius also suggests that there are similarities between the Sunderland cottages and single storey urban housing in parts of Scotland.

11. King (1984), p. 70.

12. Bowley (1960, pp. 118–119) states that asbestos cement tiles and sheets were introduced into the UK in the ten years prior to World War I. After the Great War three firms started manufacture of the materials 'in a serious way'. The asbestos cement sheet and the asbestos cement roof tile were lightweight, weatherproof and inexpensive materials, ideal for the small builder or self-builder.

13. Hardy and Ward (1984), p. 92.

14. Rice (1973), pp. 1099–1100.

15. 'A survey in 1938–39 showed that 64% of those earning above £250 annually (a rough measure of the middle-class income threshold) were either buying or owned their own homes' (Hardy and Ward, 1984, p. 16).

16. A bungalow constructed of two railway carriages with additions, on the front at Selsey, was for sale for £75,000 in spring 1990.

17. Briggs (1901), Preface.

18. Hardy and Ward (1984), p. 195.

19. The idea of the retirement bungalow at the seaside was most fully exploited at Peacehaven on the south coast where plots were sold to those, 'who had retired from business and wanted a healthy home by the seashore,' (King, 1984, p. 173).

20. *Ibid.*, p. 170 and pp. 164–165.

21. Randal Phillips (1920), p. 16.

22. Critics such as: Sharp (1932); Williams-Ellis (1928, 1938).

23. Weaver (1926), p. 2.

24. The following legislation illustrates the point:
(a) Town and Country Planning Act 1932: Development in rural and urban areas had to be authorized under the act.
(b) 1935 saw legislation to control ribbon development.
(c) Town and Country Planning Act 1947: All new development was brought under the control of the local authorities.

25. Peak District Advisory Panel (1934), p. 9.

26. Weaver (1926), p. 33.

27. Short (1982), pp. 42–43.

28. Burnett (1980), p. 241.

29. The Association of Building Technicians (1946), pp. 20–21.

30. Cooney (1974), p. 151.

31. *Ibid.*, pp. 156–157

32. The Council for Research on Housing Construction, p. 73. The chairman of the Council was The Earl of Dudley.

33. *Ibid.*, p. 74

34. Osborne (1942), p. 13.

35. *Picture Post*, 18 March, 1944, p. 3.

36. *Picture Post*, 14 July, 1945, pp. 16–17.

37. Army Bureau of Current Affairs (1943), pp. 10–11.

38. Ministry of Health (1944a), pp. 53–54.

39. Army Bureau of Current Affairs (1945).

40. Ministry of Health (1944a), p. 8.

41. *Ibid.*, p. 9.

42. *Ibid.*, p. 11.

43. *Ibid.*, p. 12.

44. Block (1946), pp. 6–8. The disparity between dwelling and household size is illustrated by the following table of data for new estates in Liverpool.

| Dwelling type | Proportion of types of dwelling per 1000 | |
	Found in Norris Green, 1938	Applicant Families 1936
1 bedroom	0	210
2 "	15	260
3 "	984	450
4 "	1	102

Elsas states that from a 1944 survey the proportion of three bedroom dwellings in Liverpool was about 90% of the total. This was similar to cities like Birmingham and Southampton but Leeds was unusual in having only 58% three bedroom dwellings. (Elsas, 1946, pp. 24–25).

45. Ravetz (1974), pp. 147–148.

46. Ministry of Health (1944*a*), p. 27.

47. *Ibid.*, p. 23.

48. Department of Health for Scotland (1944), p. 7.

49. *Ibid.*, Appendix 3, p. xix.

50. *Ibid.*, Appendix 3, pp. xxix–xxx.

51. *Ibid.*, p. 13.

52. Scottish Office Building Directorate (1987), p. 4.

53. Department of Health for Scotland (1944), Appendix 3, pp. xxvii–xxviii.

54. *Ibid.*, p. 67.

55. *Your Inheritance: The Land: An Uncomic Strip* (1942). At the back of this booklet encouraging people to consider the future of both urban and agricultural land, there was a competition for schools to study the land use in their existing communities. This competition was designed to arouse the awareness of the young about the planning issues that would need to be considered after the war. The closing date for the competition was 1st October 1942.

56. Army Bureau of Current Affairs (1943).

57. Mass Observation (1943), p. 53.

58. Whittick and Schreiner (1947), pp. 202–215.

59. *Ibid.*, p. 203.

60. Mass Observation (1943), p. 46.

61. *Ibid.*, p. 61.

62. *Ibid.*, p. 151.

63. *Ibid.*, p. 220.

64. *Ibid.*, p. xxiii.

65. *Ibid.*, p. 151.

66. *Ibid.*, p. 147.

67. Weldons Ladies' Journal, 4 February, 1944, p. 53.

68. Mass Observation (1943), p. xviii.

69. Bournville Village Trust Research (1941), p. 84.

70. *Ibid.*, accompanying figs. 29, 30 and 31.

71. *Ibid.*, p. 85.

72. Eccles *et al.* (1945), pp. 4–5.

73. Pleydell-Bouverie (1944), p. 15.

74. *Ibid.*, p. 19.

75. *Ibid.*, p. 29.

76. *Ibid.*, p. 51.

77. *Ibid.*, p. 58.

78. *Ibid.*, p. 125.

79. *Ibid.*, p. 123.

80. Mass Observation (1943), p. 171.

3

OVER THERE

'We saw a square box with grubby looking walls . . .
However, going through the gate, down two steps,
into a small garden, we entered a different world.[1]

BACKGROUND

Although the relationship between the prefab and the holiday bungalow
may have had a bearing on the acceptance of the former, the influence of
the United States at a time of total war and the bright non-rationed world
that appeared to exist on the other side of the Atlantic may also have
helped to promote the image of the prefab as something new, modern and
desirable. Indeed the prefabricated house industry of the States was also
presented to the public through magazines such as *Picture Post* as a
possible model for the post-war world.[2] This was despite the uncertain
relationship that had existed between Britain and America during the early
years of the war. The Army Bureau of Current Affairs prepared discussion
documents to explore the distrust that existed in this relationship and,
later, the disruption that was caused as American troops waited in Britain
for the eventual invasion of Europe.[3] This latter produced an article by
Margaret Mead setting out the differences between the Americans and the
British, and attempting to explain why the Americans might express
surprise when they arrived: 'The first time they do this it is genuine surprise
that a nation which has such a world position could be grounded in such a
small green space.'[4]

However, one institution, the cinema, may have had an influence on the
acceptance of American invention, for American films offered images of a
different society and, moreover, a society that did not appear to feel the
effects of a war. If 30 million cinema seats were sold each week during the
war to the British public, then approximately 80 per cent of the time they
sat in these seats would have been whilst watching films produced in
America.[5] The effect that this might have had was well realized at the time.

> Miss Thorp gives, to our knowledge, the best survey of the effects of films on
> American society that has yet appeared. British audiences are shown a
> preponderance of American films, which must consequently affect and
> influence the outlook of the British Public.[6]

The real effect that such influence may have had on the acceptance of the prefab has, at present, to be left to speculation. However, if the average American looked both different and brighter to a Britain made grey by war, then the comment made by a prefab resident could be seen as a faint echo of this phenomenon, 'I have had a completely different and brighter outlook on life since I have lived in the bungalow.'[7]

The prefabricated bungalow in the USA was neither a new nor a particularly innovatory idea. At the time of the UK Temporary Housing Programme it was an accepted part of American life. In their *History of Prefabrication*, Bruce and Sandbank acknowledge the relationship between prefabrication techniques and the American timber frame house, but relate the emergence of the prefabricated house from the factory to the 1929 stock market collapse, when the area of low-cost housing was first viewed as a large and neglected market for commercial opportunity.[8] This was an aspect of the UK Temporary Housing Programme that Churchill had emphasized carefully in his first announcement of the programme to the public. Whether Churchill had actually hoped that the stimulus offered by the government order for prefabricated bungalows could produce an active privately owned industry may only seem a feasible proposition when viewed from a post-Thatcherite position. At the time, the influence of Beveridge and the war effort itself suggested that national planning was more important than private enterprise. However, the authors of the American history of prefabrication emphasized the contribution of the US two government agencies, the Farm Security Administration and the Tennessee Valley Authority, to, 'the actual use of prefabrication in direct efforts to provide and erect low cost homes.'[9] In Britain it was the efforts of the latter agency that, through the writings of those like Huxley and Casson, were to popularize the prefabricated American house, particularly to the educated middle class.

HOUSING FOR THE TENNESSEE VALLEY AUTHORITY

The Tennessee Valley Authority (TVA) was initiated in 1933, three months after Roosevelt took office as President of the USA, and it became one of the earliest of Roosevelt's 'New Deals'. The TVA was to oversee a vast reworking of the Tennessee River which drains an area of land almost the size of England, the Tennessee River being a tributary of the Ohio River which is itself a tributary of the Mississippi. At the time the Tenessee River was shallow and fast flowing and liable to flood. This damaged the valley and contributed to the flooding of the Mississippi, the effects being felt for some thousand miles and as far away as New Orleans. The valley had originally been forested but by 1933 the land had been cleared for farming. Many small farmers occupied the land without the resources to maintain the fertility of the soil. The valley was badly eroded and the farmers were becoming poorer. Although the problem had been known about and discussed for many years President Roosevelt decided that he was to be the man to act through the establishment of the public corporation of the TVA.

Over the next ten years the TVA project manifested itself in the construction of eighteen dams to control flooding on the Tennessee River and its tributaries. These dams helped to promote navigation and to produce hydro-electricity. Because this electricity was cheap it, too, helped to raise the standard of living of the communities in the valley. To build the dams also entailed the establishment of new communities for the construction workers and those who serviced them, with housing, shops, schools, roads etc, some being permanent communities and some temporary. More importantly perhaps, the project contained within it the notion of the planned use of resources and this planning was to be undertaken on a national scale. As President Roosevelt said in a message to Congress:

> Many hard lessons have taught us the human waste that results from lack of planning. Here and there a few wise cities and countries have looked ahead and planned. But our Nation has 'just grown'. It is time to extend planning to a wider field, in this instance comprehending in one great project many states directly concerned with the basin of one of our greatest rivers.[10]

The scale of the undertaking and the underlying notion of planning to meet problems meant that not only did the project generate large numbers of construction workers that had to be housed near a place of work with no existing housing,[11] but also that this problem would be anticipated, and new strategies of community planning and house production would be developed to house the TVA workers and their families. These new forms of housing were also designed to cope with the fact that the place of work of the construction workers was changing, as the time taken to build each dam varied between three and six years. Because of this requirement, the TVA project is remembered in particular for the contribution that it made to the relationship between factory production and demountability and portability. This interest in factory production also stemmed from the need to produce a considerable quantity of new houses quickly. However, the experience gained from the fast production of permanent houses for TVA workers, although equally relevant to housing in Britain post-war, seems to have been largely forgotten.

At Norris permanent houses were constructed of cinder block and were originally rented to the workers in an unfinished state with the block merely painted on the inside surface. The floors were self-coloured preformed concrete slabs on precast beams and wall and ceiling finishes were of plywood. The intention was to upgrade the houses at the end of the construction period when the workers had moved on, by spending further money on fitting them out internally. At Pickwick a different permanent house type, made of timber, was let with the upper floor unfinished for conversion by the tenant at a later date. Both types suggest an alternative strategy for meeting housing needs in emergency situations. What the mythical British housewife of the women's magazines could describe as a house that could be planned for such luxuries as a refrigerator, built-in wardrobes etc. once either the appliances or the materials were available in sufficient quantities, was a lesson of the TVA that was never exploited in post-war Britain.

> P.A.: 'I begin to see what you are driving at. Though your house may not be perfect at the beginning, it must be perfectible.'
> M.: 'Yes, that's my idea. And now that I've told you, will you please pass it on to some of your fellow architects?'[12]

Despite such innovations in speeding the production of permanent housing it is the contribution of the TVA to prefabrication in housing, both permanent and temporary, that is remembered. When the Ministry of Works' Mission to the USA to investigate methods of building reported back in 1944,[13] its visit to the TVA project produced a report on the TVA plywood prefabricated houses and no mention of the permanent TVA houses (figure 3.1). In fact the permanent and unfinished block house could have had more relevance to the British situation after the war than the prefabricated house of plywood; concrete blocks were available whilst plywood for building was very scarce.[14]

It was, however, the idea of the demountable house that caught the eye of the architectural press. For the TVA project the argument for the demountable, reusable house was persuasive. Because the dams were built sequentially and because some communities had to be purely temporary it would be advantageous if the housing could be moved cheaply from a finished dam to the site of the next.

> The idea of moving houses from one construction project to another has always been a favourite topic of discussion in TVA. In 1938 the discussions bore fruit. Seventy-two houses originally built and used at Pickwick Landing Dam were moved from their foundations to barges, floated 200 miles downstream to the mouth of the Tennessee River to the construction village being built to house workers on the Kentucky Dam.[15]

Various types of prefabricated houses which met this specification were developed, mostly made of timber, although three years elapsed between the first cumbersome experiment and the production of a totally mobile house (figure 3.2):

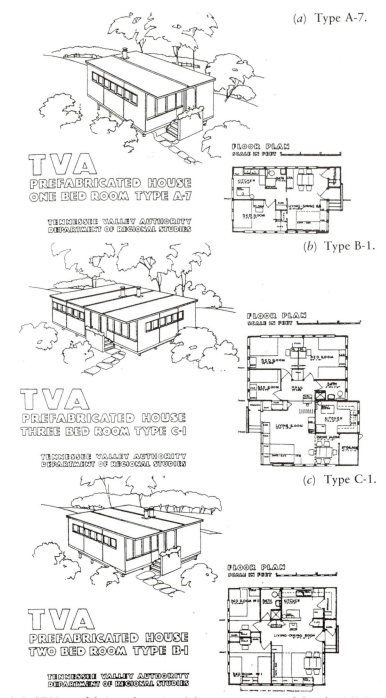

(a) Type A-7.

(b) Type B-1.

(c) Type C-1.

Figure 3.1. TVA prefabricated sectional houses as reported by the Ministry of Works' Mission to the USA in 1944. (*Source*: Ministry of Works, 1944a)

Figure 3.2. Sectional TVA houses being transported to site by lorry. (*Source*: Ministry of Works, 1944*a*)

The basic scheme adopted for making a house mobile was very simple; it was built in large sections, each of which was a load of width, length and height that would permit its safe transportation over a highway. Section lines bore no particular relationship to the floor plan of the house, except to avoid door and window openings.[16]

The first sectional houses of this type were built 60 miles from their place of erection and this first experiment showed that it was possible to do much of the interior finishing work, including plumbing, wiring and fixtures, before the houses were sent to the site. The house sections were also pre-painted, thereby reducing site work to a minimum (figures 3.3 and 3.4).

On arrival, the trailer is drawn up alongside the prepared under-staging and removable dollies, or wheels, are attached to cleats fastened to the underside of the floor panels. The sections are then rolled off the trailer on special tracks and are lined up and bolted together. The whole house is then jacked up and the dollies and track are removed. The roof joints between the sections are covered with half-round fibre pipe, set in mastic, and screwed to the roof panels. Vertical joints between the sections are covered with timber fillets. When porches and steps have been added and the connections to water, electricity and drainage and services made, the house is ready for occupation.[17]

Although starting from the concept of demountability, the TVA project had produced a house that required little labour to erect on site, transferring most of the labour of building the house to the place of production of its sections. It was this transfer of labour to the factory that

Figure 3.3. A two-section TVA house assembled on site. (*Source*: Ministry of Works, 1944*a*)

Figure 3.4. The finished sectional TVA house. (*Source*: Ministry of Works, 1944*a*)

was to provide a crucial stimulus to the development of the bungalows produced under the British Temporary Housing Programme. However, the alternative concept of producing basic shells which could be upgraded later, or even finished by their occupants, would also have cut the labour per house produced, but would not have produced the jobs in the factories that were needed for the promised full employment post-war.

The TVA continued to develop the sectional house, producing one-, two- and three-bedroom models made up of three, four and five sections respectively. Originally the sections were produced by hand in a primitive outdoor plant in a vacant field, but for later projects, including twenty-two section dormitories for construction workers, industrial construction techniques were introduced with the building elements of floors, walls, roof and partitions being first formed of sub-assembly panels. The panels were then put together into sectional units on an adjacent assembly line after which the sections were wired, painted etc. and stored before shipment. Another contribution made by the TVA to the development of the portable temporary house was the trailer home, which was produced in two sections in the factory with even the curtains at the windows factory hung.

Although the TVA projects produced innovations in the design and construction of prefabricated permanent and temporary houses it was the overall central planning for housing needs that, perhaps, remained the major contribution of the project to housing development. The USA did, after all, possess a prefabricated house industry[18] even before the spur offered by the TVA project and later by the Federal Works Agency in its effort to provide homes for defence workers during war time.

Centralized control of the housing of a whole region was, however, not the norm in either the USA[19] or Britain. In Britain government finance towards housing had been in the form of subsidies administered through the local authorities who, themselves, were responsible for assessing housing needs in their local areas. Under Conservative administrations, following the introduction of state subsidies for housing, the tendency had been to reduce subsidies and leave housing to market forces. Under the Liberal, and later the Labour, regimes the tendency had been to promote the local authorities as providers of housing. At no time in this period, apart from the Temporary Housing Programme (as will be shown), was there any attempt at national planning for housing needs.[20]

The TVA project provided a foretaste of what could be achieved with this type of planning and when the war brought with it the particular circumstances that promoted national organization (in defence, industry, labour etc.), the TVA was cited as a precedent of what could be expected if the same approach were to be applied to housing.

HOUSING FOR US WAR WORKERS

However, just as government in the UK were to be the first clients for the 'house out of the factory', so in America it was again government who were to stimulate the prefabricated housing industry to meet the demands of war.

> The Federal housing agencies, through their purchase in less than two years of almost 75,000 prefabricated dwelling units for war workers, have brought the prefabrication movement out of the stage of an experiment and into the stage of actual mass-production. The Government has become the pre-fabricator's best – and virtually his only – customer. It has also become an arbiter of standards which many fear are so low as to have the long-term effect of retarding the industry's development.[21]

This work was again reported in the British architectural journals, although the journals made no mention of the organizational problems of the American emergency housing programme and rather concentrated on the innovative techniques for housing that had resulted from it.[22]

In its turn the American war time emergency housing programme of 1940–45 drew upon the housing work of the TVA. As part of the emergency housing programme some 8 million Americans were rehoused within four years, 'more than half in new communities'.[23] These communities were built near the newly created or expanded centres of industry, themselves developed to supply materials and armaments to the allied war effort. However, wherever it could be shown that the new housing would also be required after the war, permanent housing was provided. This latter was privately financed through the Federal Housing Administration which had been set up in 1934 to undertake similar housing provision. Loans were allocated for building new houses and if the local housing authority took charge of the house building programme or private developers did the building, then the design of the housing was based on government standards of accommodation, equipment and construction. Otherwise the government became the client, selected the site and appointed an architect to execute the design. This process again illustrates the fact that the extraordinary circumstances produced by war can lead to a very different pattern of housing provision with a high degree of government intervention.

In the United States, where a community of permanent homes could not be justified, temporary houses were used for war workers. Again the experience of the TVA formed the basis for the design of these temporary houses. However, whereas the TVA had a legitimate justification for temporary and demountable homes because of the need to move their construction workers from dam to dam, and through the need to transfer labour to the factory, allowing the construction workers to build dams rather than houses, these arguments could not be justified to the same extent for the emergency housing for war workers. In fact the decision to provide temporary homes for families, rather than permanent homes or provision for single workers in hostels, produced the same counter arguments that were to surround the Temporary Housing Programme in Britain. These focused on the apparent waste of money building temporary homes when permanent homes could be built for little extra cost, and the fear that the temporary homes of today would soon become the permanent slums of tomorrow (see Chapter 5).

Nevertheless, the desire to be seen to be using a new technology triumphed and the temporary and demountable house was built in some quantity. Between 1942–44 some 1,627,290 family houses were constructed of which approximately 40 per cent were temporary and a further 4 per cent demountable.[24] The reason given for the temporary house in this context was that it could be taken down and used for other purposes or that the materials might be easily salvaged at the end of the war when the home was no longer required. It was left to the house prefabrication industry in the USA to supply these dwellings, an industry which was only too happy to expand with the prospect of a guaranteed market. Of the 101 firms illustrated in 1942 in *Architectural Forum* under the heading 'Snapshot of an infant industry',[25] less than a quarter of the firms could be said to have long-term experience of manufacturing and marketing prefabricated houses. One or two firms had been producing prefabricated garages, farm buildings etc. and were now offering houses in response to the war time emergency demands. It was an industry that had been led to expand by the offer of new defence contracts rather than the other way around.

Given the American tradition of timber construction the temporary houses of this period were largely made of wood and to save cost and speed production time, this timber was in the form of standard timber panels. Some firms developed plans on a standard grid where the dimensions could be related to a panel of width and height such that it could be easily handled i.e. the 8 ft high panel between 3 ft and 4 ft wide.[26] This experience gave rise to the lesson that, 'standardisation of parts is a solution, but standardisation of the whole is doomed to failure.'[27] Those who saw a future for the prefabricated house after the war envisaged an architecture of standard parts, prefabricated, which could be arranged to produce a plan suited to the individual's needs (see Chapter 4). In war time no such luxury was possible and the standard panels for emergency defence housing were arranged to standard plans. However, the fact that the standard panels could be economically produced in factories and assembled on site, reducing on-site craft labour, visibly linked the three issues of mass-production, prefabrication and standardization which were to echo through the debates around the British Temporary Housing Programme.

THE USA BUNGALOW FOR THE TEMPORARY
HOUSING PROGRAMME

In one respect, however, the British programme drew directly upon American experience by contracting to import some 30,000 packaged and prefabricated houses under the lend-lease agreement, although only 8,462 were ever sent (see Chapter 6). Samples were brought over and erected in Summer 1945 when the bungalow received publicity in both the national[28] and architectural press (figures 3.5 and 3.6). Initially, it was expected that these houses would have a life of 10 years compared to the 15 years of the British bungalows.[29] The plan of the house was selected as, 'one of the best of the smaller prefabricated houses designed in the USA,'[30] and consisted of two bedrooms, a living room and kitchen and bathroom, with circulation via a central roof ventilated lobby and entry from the porch and hall to the side of the bungalow into the living room (figure 3.7). In plan the bungalow was 24 ft 2½ in square but with the projecting porch area to one side and with a total floor area of 600 ft^2, making it smaller than the average British bungalow of around 635 ft^2.

The hall was intended for the storage of a pram, the living room contained a solid fuel stove, the bedrooms both had built-in cupboards, although these were closed with a curtain rather than doors, the bathroom

Figure 3.5. The prototype temporary bungalow imported from the USA in 1945. (*Source*: *Architects' Journal*, 10 May, 1945).

Figure 3.6. Exterior view of the USA temporary bungalow. (*Source: Architects' Journal*, 10 May, 1945)

had a low flush syphonic WC, bath and basin, and the kitchen was equipped with sink, draining board, gas cooker, hot water cylinder with an immersion heater, a space for a wash-boiler with a draining board over, a dresser and shelving, and the back porch outside the kitchen contained a ventilated larder and broom cupboard. These fittings were provided with the house from the USA, but the UK supplied the washboiler and an immersion heater for the cylinder to give hot water in summer. There was also a linen cupboard, heated by a loop from the hot water cylinder, which contained the cold water tank in the central hall. In this respect the bungalow was fitted out much as the British types. However, the cost of transporting the houses from the USA meant that British fittings were later substituted to bring down the cost.[31]

In terms of construction the American bungalow was essentially timber framed, as might be expected, with the floor arriving in seven prefabricated panels of tongued and grooved boarding on softwood framing, factory finished, so that the packaging of the house was designed to be used to protect the floor during erection. The walls arrived as timber frame units, 8 ft long, faced externally with some type of insulating wallboard (e.g. fibreboard) or with asbestos cement sheets backed with an insulating quilt. The wallboards had to be protected by external painting. Fibreboard or asbestos cement was also used as an internal cladding. Internal partitions were of softwood studs faced with wallboard. The roof was also pre-fabricated in sections, there being twelve for the main roof and two smaller

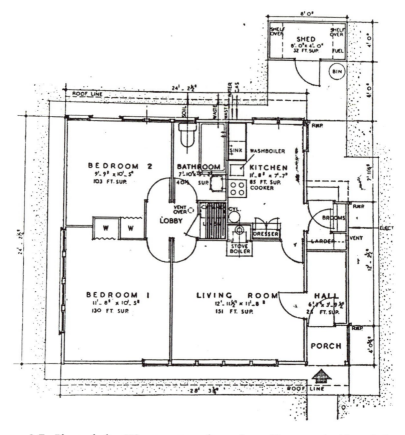

Figure 3.7. Plan of the US temporary bungalow. (*Source*: *Architects' Journal*, 10 May, 1945)

sections for the porch. Framed in wedge shaped timbers to give a very shallow pitch, the ceiling was faced with wallboard, the exterior of the units was clad in flat asbestos cement sheet covered with three layers of roofing felt, and each unit incorporated an insulating quilt. All the timber was 'treated with a toxic dip against woodworm and termite'.[32] The packaged home, once shipped from America, was supposed to require only unskilled manual labour to put it up on a prepared slab.

In many ways the American bungalow did represent a true temporary, prefabricated and factory produced home, such as the programme had intended to provide. This was obviously achieved by drawing on the experience of the Americans in this field of housing and much might have been gleaned from them. An external wall cladding for a limited life could be made of a material that relied on a waterproofing layer such as paint for its weatherproofing, rather than using a truly weatherproof material, such as absestos cement, which might have been more readily associated with permanent dwellings. Compact planning with internal circulation, such as is found in the TVA dwellings, is more appropriate to limited life housing than the daylit hall of the other bungalow types. Even the replacement of cupboard doors by curtains suggests that the housing is seen as not permanent, as well as reducing both the weight and amount of materials in the dwelling. All the British bungalow types failed to realize the potential of a true temporary dwelling and rather sought to produce a substandard hybrid between a temporary and a permanent bungalow.

SWEDISH PRECEDENTS

It would be unwise to suggest that the USA formed the only precedent for the prefab, although the 1944 mission of the Ministry of Works to look at prefabrication in America demonstrates the importance that government attached to this precedent. Swedish experience was also cited in the press (see Chapter 2) and the prefabricated timber house in Sweden had received publication in Britain before the war,[33] especially the partially self-built garden city estates around Stockholm. So noteworthy were the houses and their method of production that they were prefixed by one author by the term 'Magic' to denote the change from the city slums to the wooden cottages in the country.[34] As one commentator was to note:

> The story of prefabrication in Sweden is a simple and happy one. Despite the fine record of achievement, it is a recent story, for it only goes back to 1920. Before that date, Sweden already possessed the advantages of high architectural standards, a tradition of building in timber and a plentiful supply of that material.[35]

Standardization and mass-production of materials enabled costs to be kept down, although architects were employed, 'to control the placing of houses, the exterior colour schemes and fencing . . . and horticultural experts for the gardens.'[36] Before the war some 50,000 people lived in the owner-built garden suburbs around Stockholm (figure 3.8), between 2 and 8 miles from the city but linked to it by subsidized buses.[37] The quality of construction was also high (figures 3.9, 3.10 and 3.11):

> Although the average floor area of small Swedish houses is less than in England, far more attention is paid to thermal insulation, to double windows and proper heating . . . House equipment, too, such as stoves, cookers, plumbing, built-in cupboards, etc., has been more highly and rationally developed and is better designed than in this country.[38]

A smaller scale version of the same approach existed in the allotments surrounding Stockholm where cabins were built by the tenants to five

Figure 3.8. Swedish house assembled by tenants. (*Source*: Denby, 1938)

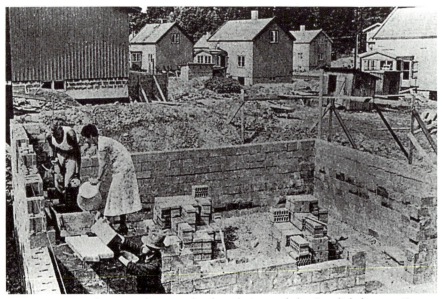

Figure 3.9. Work proceeding on the foundations of the Swedish house. (*Source*: Denby, 1938)

standardized plan types and where those who could not afford to go away for holidays could enjoy recreation in the country and cultivate a garden.[39]

The advantages of the Swedish housing experience were also obvious to those forced, through war, to live in such countries.

During the past two months I, too, have taken an interest in prefabricated houses, but not Portals. Here in Norway we see many houses prefabricated by numbered logs; in fact like log cabins. I am billeted in one, and, what a billet! Central heating, h. and c., and all conveniences. On inquiring from a Norwegian friend, I was assured that they are cheap and quickly-built, and will last 30–40 years. He is an architect.

Homeless paratrooper, Norway.[40]

Figure 3.10. Raising the prefabricated timber walls of the Swedish house. (*Source*: Denby, 1938)

Figure 3.11. Typical interior of the Swedish house. (*Source*: Denby, 1938)

It was not just the quality of Scandinavian prefabricated houses that failed to appear in the prefab. The architectural press also noted the opportunities for home ownership that prefabrication might offer. The Swedish 'Magic House' was not so much predicated on prefabrication as a process but as a way of allowing people to help build their own houses in Sweden's equivalent of the garden cities:

> In 1927 the city [Stockholm] decided to experiment in making the houses themselves as cheap as the land – through partial standardisation of designs, quantity production of materials and through labor supplied largely by the prospective owner . . . The city had in storage the lumber all cut to the required lengths, the materials for walls prefabricated in handy sections, likewise forms for the concrete foundation walls, and a press for making concrete blocks on site . . . With this set up, an able bodied workman putting in his week-ends, holidays and daily after-works hours in the long northern summer days, with the aid of family and friends, can build the greater part of his own house.[41]

This venture demonstrated that prefabrication offered possibilities other than reduction of cost and transfer of skilled labour from site to factory. It offered the chance for the occupier to have a real stake in the home through contributing 'sweat-equity'. Such a technique was published in *Picture Post*[42] but at no time did it appear to enter into any discussion of the UK Temporary Housing Programme.

Although in appearance the form of the UK prefab, standing in its own plot, was similar to the 'Magic' house, what is missing is the creation of specific communities, for the prefabs as a temporary measure were placed on any land that was available, and the link between prefabrication and the possibilities of self-build. Nevertheless, the publication of the Swedish work in a number of sources both before and immediately after the war would suggest that it formed some precedent for the temporary bungalow.

UK PRECEDENTS FOR THE PREFABRICATED BUNGALOW

Some precedents can be found from within the UK itself. Experiments had been undertaken in this area after World War 1, but these could not have promoted great confidence in the possibilities of such techniques. The conversion of an army hut to a family bungalow, exhibited 1919, at Horse Guards Parade, London does not appear to be more than a rather homespun temporary emergency measure. Of more interest, perhaps, is the fact that, as part of the emergency measures of the First World War, a number of timber prefabricated houses had been imported from the USA for workers at the Austin Motor Company. Two hundred had been erected in 1917 at a cost of around £750 per dwelling inclusive of roads and sewers. This compared with housing costs of £606 for conventional housing built at that time but excluding site costs.[43] The bungalows were raised off the ground on brick piers infilled with trellis, and were of timber frame construction, finished externally with weatherboarding and internally with plasterboard and roofed in shingles. The bungalows were centrally heated and in 1944 the comment was made that, 'after 27 years of service they remain popular with their tenants, and . . . if properly cared for they will last for 80 years.'[44] Such schemes did not offer any contemporary precedent, for the majority of building after the Great War – under the slogan 'Homes for Heroes' – was of a strictly conventional low-rise masonry construction with one or two skirmishes into prefabrication.[45]

Some limited experience in the field of prefabrication and dwelling was gained during the Second World War in Britain. Whereas it is commonly thought that house building ceased during the war, much new housing was provided in the form of hostels, camps and dormitory accommodation associated with both the armed forces and those drafted into the industrial workforce.[46] Whereas war time accommodation for American workers concentrated on the family house, those drafted away from home to work in Britain were largely single people although some married quarters were built for key workers who had to be transferred.

> In important industrial centres, such as Coventry, where lodgings are very hard to find, and in connection with large factories in remote districts where there is no accommodation, it has been necessary to build hostels . . . They vary in size, but generally offer accommodation to between 500 and 1,000 workers; and some are for men, some for women, and some for both sexes.[47]

Early in 1941 when the ordnance and aircraft factories were expanding rapidly, 35,000 workers had to be accommodated in some forty-five hostels built by the Ministry of Works for the Ministries of Supply and Aircraft Production.[48] The hostels had a central 'welfare centre' with hall, canteen, games room, reading rooms, lounges etc., surrounded by single-storey dormitory blocks. Air raid shelters were also provided. However, the prefabrication industry did not exist in even the embryonic form of that of the USA and most hostels were constructed of conventional materials using traditional methods.

Some early experiments were made with a system of prefabricated timber for camps labelled 'for peace or war' which were, 'planned to accommodate 350 children . . . but since the camps are to be used as evacuation camps in time of war, and may be used by adults in the holidays,'[49] they were also planned for adult occupation. The separate units, which were laid out to minimize the spread of fire and designed by Tait (of Sir John Burnet, Tait and Lorne), were made of western red cedar and roofed with cedar shingles. The buildings which were, 'constructed in standardised units which are pre-fabricated and delivered on to the sites,'[50] had a module of 6 ft wide by 8 ft or 10 ft high, depending on the use of the unit. This differs from the American approach of a panel dimension designed to be handled by one man.

Even the permanent housing built during the war exhibited none of the experimental tendencies that were to underlie the Temporary Housing Programme and creep into the permanent housing programme after the war. Experiments at this time were confined to permanent structures which attempted to minimize the use of timber, usually by substituting reinforced concrete in such elements as first floor structures and staircases, such as the Ministry of Supply houses of 1942 which incorporated concrete lintels, precast concrete stair treads, precast concrete first floor joists and roof joists, and precast concrete eaves. The cost of the scheme varied between approximately £800–£900 per house, exclusive of roads and sewers.[51]

The chief area of experiment with prefabrication techniques in Britain began with the war-time programme of hutments. The use of prefabrication in these structures formed a precedent for the later Temporary Housing Programme and firms such as Tarran and Seco, later associated with the temporary bungalows, were involved in the design of huts from the start (see Chapter 1). To begin with the materials used were traditional brick and timber but these were replaced with precast concrete, plasterboard and later asbestos cement sheets. Eventually the standard Ministry of Works hut was constructed of precast concrete uprights and roof beams with wall infilling of brick, clay block or other available material. Some of these techniques were used for single-storey sleeping quarters for hostels, and also for dormitories and other buildings for the newly established camps for the services. Hutments were also built to house Land Army Volunteers when, by the winter of 1940, it was obvious that there was not enough accommodation for those engaged on land reclamation or even for those contracted to work on existing farms.

During the early years of the war journals, and especially *The Builder*, contained plenty of suggestions for huts that either used unconventional materials or were of a prefabricated and demountable form and often constructed of concrete in order to save on scarce timber.[52] The idea of prefabrication related to the war effort in this field was also discussed in a lecture that Dennis Clarke Hall gave at the Architectural Association in 1940.

> Existing [building] methods are the result of years of practical experience. New methods of construction, such as prefabrication, cannot be based on such experience, nor can they be based on pure theory. Every successful practical realisation of prefabrication has been preceded by research and experiment involving many failures. The present crisis shows the extent to which the building industry is subject to economic constriction. The fact that in this and preceding crises the industry has turned to alternative systems points to the fact that building can continue if satisfactory systems of construction are evolved.[53]

Despite knowledge of the USA experience with prefabrication, and despite the wartime opportunity in the UK to experiment with a programme of prefabricated huts and hostels, an opportunity was missed to establish the industry to support the permanent post-war factory made house. Whereas in the USA permanent prefabricated buildings had been the goal, in the UK experiments with prefabrication were associated with temporary structures or structures designed to meet emergency needs, and there was a sense that building would return to its 'normal', or traditional, methods, once the immediate crisis was over. This attitude may have had a bearing on the development of the temporary prefabricated bungalows after the war.

However, the same ideas of standardization and mass-production of parts in one factory for assembly elsewhere did find their way into other areas of wartime production, particularly into the expanded aircraft industry after 1941. To avoid damage from German bombing the process of manufacture was broken down into manufacture of components and, for every stage up to final assembly, manufacture of each stage or component proceeded in at least three different places, so that it would always be possible to rely on a supply of components if one or even two factories were stopped because of bomb damage.[54] The fact that images of production lines were to appear in both the architectural and popular press[55] forged a connection between the changed techniques of production evolved as a result of the war and the potential applications to the building industry once peace was established. As Sheppard was to claim, seeing the dwelling as a technical rather than a social phenomenon, 'A house is much less complicated than an aeroplane or a ship.'[56]. The story of the temporary bungalows was to prove him to be mistaken.

NOTES

1. Rooney, Lewis and Schule (1989), p. 42.

2. See, for example, 'Fifty Thousand Brides Envy her', *Picture Post*, 27 October, 1945, pp. 16–17. The article suggests that 'Prefabrication has cut down America's housing problem'. Or see, *Picture Post*, 21 September, 1946, pp. 12–13. This article shows the American husband putting up a plywood prefab in California in a day, though the editorial comment suggests that the house would be 'Not such a certain protection against Britian's storms and fogs'.

3. See Army Bureau of Current Affairs Nos. 22, 26, 52, 59. The Forces Wavelength also broadcast a programme 'America and Ourselves' every Thursday starting 2 October 1941.

4. Army Bureau of Current Affairs (1944*b*).

5. Cinematograph Film Council (for the Board of Trade) (1944).

6. Thorp (1946).

7. Women's Group on Public Welfare (1951), p. 16.

8. Bruce A. and Sandbank H. (1944), p. 7.

9. *Ibid.*, p. 14.

10. Huxley (1943), pp. 5–6.

11. Not all the communities associated with the TVA project were temporary. In some places such as Chickamauga there existed sufficient housing in nearby Chattanooga. New permanent settlements, such as Norris, were constructed where they would be within commuting distance of an existing town, in this instance Knoxville. See Huxley (1943) and also *Architectural Forum*, **71**, August, 1939, pp. 99–108.

12. FitzGerald (1944), p. 21.

13. Ministry of Works (1944*a*), Appendix 7, pp. 27–28d.

14. The shortage of plywood after the war is exemplified by the following quote: 'At the present time there is a desperate shortage of materials that can take the place of timber in joinery, partitions and fittings. There are all sorts of wall-boards and plastic and metal sheet materials, while steel cabinets are used in place of wooden cupboards and kitchen units. Most of these cannot be said to have displaced timber permanently. They are used because plywood is unobtainable.' from Bateson (1948), p. 6. Professor Bowley also refers to post war timber shortages for housing in Bowley (1966), pp. 199, 217. The use of timber was derestricted in 1953.

15. Towne (1942), p. 50.

16. Towne and Purnell (1946), p. 178.

17. Ministry of Works (1944*a*), p. 28.

18. 'Prefabrication gets its chance', *Architectural Forum* 1942, **72**, February, pp. 81–88. This article gives a resumé of the firms producing prefabricated houses. The oldest, E.F. Hodgson Co. began producing sectional houses in the USA in 1892.

19. As in Britain, housing in the USA had been provided as a mixture of private enterprise and public intervention through a variety of agencies when public outcry about the slum conditions in some places meant that action had to be taken. A critique of the muddled and often overlapping way in which these agencies worked can be found in Abrams (1946).

20. The history of the local authority housing in Britain has been well documented, see Swenarton (1981); Daunton (1984); Gaskell (1987); Burnett (1980); Orbach (1977).

21. Bruce and Sandbank (1944), p. 15.

22. To begin with the effort to house war workers was hampered by the number and cross interests of the various agencies entitled to provide housing. These agencies were only reorganized in 1942 in an effort to provide planned housing for the workers. The majority of the 722,000 units provided by the Federal Public Housing Authority, some 550,000, were temporary or demountable. Privately financed new construction continued to be built (Abrams, 1946, pp. 296–307).

23. Casson (1946), p. 3.

24. Gray (1946), p. 226.

25. 'Prefabrication gets its chance', *op. cit.*, pp. 81–88.

26. Anthony (1945), p. 54.

27. *Ibid.*, p. 56.

28. *The Times* reported that the first batch of American bungalows was being erected at Tottenham as a training measure to familiarize the British builder with bungalow construction. See *The Times*, 9 July, 1945, p. 2. A prototype had been erected earlier at the Building Research Station.

29. Scottish Office Building Directorate (1987), p. 97.

30. 'Temporary houses from the U.S.A.,' *Architectural Design and Construction*, June, 1945, p. 143.

31. Scottish Office Building Directorate (1987), p. 97.

32. 'Temporary houses from the U.S.A., *op. cit.*, p. 144. Presumably termites were not likely to be a problem for bungalows in the Temporary Housing Programme. The article does not discuss the properties of the 'toxic dip' in relation to wet rot.

33. Denby (1938), pp. 48–95.

34. Gray (1946), p. 88.

35. Cox (1945), p. 22.

36. Lock (1939), p. 923.

37. *Ibid.*

38. Anthony (1945), p. 56.

39. Lock (1939), pp. 924–925.

40. 'Readers' Letters', *Picture Post*, 28 July 1945, p. 3.

41. Gray (1946), p. 88.

42. 'A House Goes up in a Day', *Picture Post*, 21 September, 1946. 'It comes to you in a truck; and you can erect it yourself with the help of a hammer and some nails and a book of words, in a day.'

43. The cost of £606 refers to the unit cost of a three-bedroom house at the Well Hall Estate, Woolwich, with living room, parlour, scullery and hot and cold running water. Adding 20 per cent for the costs of the serviced site would bring the Well Hall house cost to £727. See 'The Inter-Allied Housing and Town Planning Congress', *The Builder*, 18 June, 1920, p. 727.

44. 'Events and Comments', *The Architect and Building News*, 29 December, 1944, p. 190.

45. British prefabricated systems were surveyed by the Ministry of Works see, Ministry of Works (1944*b*).

46. When it was realized that by the end of 1941 another 1.8 million men and women would be required for the services and civil defence and that the munitions industry would have to expand to meet the needs of the new conscripts by 1.5 million personnel, it became obvious that there would not be enough men to do the job and women would have to substitute. At the end of 1941 conscription of unmarried women was introduced, with a choice of joining the women's services, civil defence or industry. Women up to the age of 40 also had to register for war work, although heavy domestic responsibilities would exempt them. A full description of women's role in World War 2 can be found in Lewis (1986); Summerfield (1984).

47. Ministry of Information (1944), p. 45.

48. Kohan (1952), p. 372.

49. 'Camps for Peace or War', *Journal of the RIBA*, 14 August, 1939, p. 933.

50. 'Events and Comments', *The Architect and Building News*, 11 August, 1939, p. 160.

51. 'A Midland Wartime Housing Scheme', *The Architect and Building News*, 20 March 1942, p. 214.

52. An exhibition of novel design and construction for huts was held on Coombe Hill Golf Course in 1940. See *The Builder*, **158**, 5 January 1940, pp. 5–8.

53. Hall (1940), p. 539.

54. Kohan (1952), p. 319.

55. *Picture Post*, 6 January, 1945, p. 10. 'At Burnley Aircraft Products, a progressive Northern factory, workers assemble the first prototype aluminium kitchenettes: on the right, a plane's emergency petrol tank.'

56. Sheppard (1946), p. 15.

4

THE HOUSE FROM THE FACTORY

'If houses were constructed by industrial mass-production, like chassis, unexpected but sane and defensible forms would soon appear and a new aesthetic would be formulated with astonishing precision.'[1]

THE IDEAL OF THE FACTORY PRODUCED HOUSE

However much the temporary bungalow through its form, equipment and layout could be said to represent some ideal of dwelling to its occupants, the idea that the same temporary bungalow might represent some ideal of a factory made house to designers has always been in question, as a comment of the time reveals:

> Our experience and knowledge of prefabrication is so limited in this country that it would be unwise to embark at once on a large programme of permanent prefabricated houses embodying any radical departures from well-tried methods – too many mistakes would probably be made. The wise policy seems to be to erect temporary houses, at the same time continuing research and experiment until we can produce a prefabricated house which is really superior in all respects to the traditional house.[2]

Yet, even though the temporary bungalows were not seen by designers as a model for a house mass-produced in the factory, there was still the assumption that the mass-produced house was an important goal. In the immediate post-war world it seemed that the experience of mass-production gained during the years of conflict would inevitably produce good consequences when applied to the design of houses:

> Although progress in building was arrested, war production has produced valuable discoveries in the way of new materials, plastics, plywoods, light non-corroding metals, wall surfaces, heating, lighting, air-conditioning, and improved construction practices. These are ready and waiting for the conversion of war factories to full scale peace production. There will be a new engineering approach to housing problems.[3]

Ideas about the application of new methods and materials to housing were also presented in the popular press. *Weldons Ladies' Journal* forecast the arrival of the plastics age which would itself bring as yet unconsidered possibilities for colour within the field of house construction.

Kitchen and bathroom units will be mass-produced in a variety of designs low
enough in cost for the smallest types of house, and that dream of pouring
a shining liquid into a charming, house-shaped mould and turning it out like a
jelly may be a reality in the post-war world.[4]

It would seem, therefore, that the public had been encouraged to hold
an open mind on the aesthetics of the factory made house. Certainly such
extreme examples as the all glass kitchen would not have been a surprise in
the post-war world,[5] and even before the war cartoonists, such as Heath
Robinson, were not slow to present and gently ridicule the possibilities of
the new materials and methods of manufacture with which designers were
experimenting.[6] Designers themselves also had expectations about the
aesthetics of the factory made house, as Gloag and Wornum illustrate:

Factory-made houses, even with a life expectation of fifty years, are in the
nature of consumable goods. They represent a departure from all hitherto
accepted ideas about building. They have nothing to gain from time. Age and
exposure to weather will not produce the attractive wrinkles and apple
cheeks of healthy old age.[7]

Yet, when the house out of the factory did appear in the guise of the
prefab, with aesthetics perhaps closest to those of the war time hut, it must
have appeared as a disappointment to many designers. What, therefore,
had the designers expected? At some point previously the idea had been
developed that the technologies existed to allow houses to be produced in
the factory just as cars were produced. Such a change would also allow
productivity within the building industry to increase, just as had happened
with the first assembly line in the slaughterhouses of Cincinatti in the mid-
nineteenth century.[8] For those passionate about mass-production, however
great the mechanization of the production of materials within the building
industry,[9] overall productivity was still limited by the hand constructed end
product on site. Although it may be possible to point to a 'moment' when it
seemed feasible to transfer the techniques of an automobile production
line to the manufacture of a house, what is harder to discover is the origin
of the assumption that houses, as a product, might be equated with cars,
themselves developed to meet very different parameters. This assumption
has, perhaps, more to do with architectural image than with an actual
exploration of some improvement in the way houses might be produced, or
even why the established method of producing houses might be unacceptable. (It might be possible to conceive of the house as a product which
needed to be hand built in order to meet the ever changing conditions of
site and end use). The image of mass-production may have been applied to
architecture before the practical implications of the approach had even
been considered. Indeed, unlike Ford who looked for a more productive
way of building a car, the architects seemed to be searching for a whole

new product in their quest to mechanize the building industry. As Le Corbusier, an early advocate for mass produced housing, stated:

> If the problem of the dwelling or the flat were studied in the same way that a chassis is, a speedy transformation and improvement would be seen in our houses. If houses were constructed by industrial mass-production, like chassis, unexpected but sane and defensible forms would soon appear, and a new aesthetic would be formulated with astonishing precision.[10]

If, therefore, the image of the factory produced house was developed before the technology existed to mass-produce houses in the factory, then it is understandable that the temporary bungalows may not have been an expression of this preconceived image.

As Le Corbusier's statement indicates, the hypothetical house from the factory has most often been linked visually to the factory production of cars. At most levels this parallel is difficult to understand. The car developed as a motorized carriage, initially the privilege of the rich, and was for the first years of its development a hand-built curiosity rather than a product which, from conception, had been destined for mass-production and wealth creation. Unlike shelter, which if it exists in a society is seen as a necessity for every member of that society, the car was initially not seen as a method of revolutionizing transport, nor, despite the infrastructure provided by society to support the car, is it even accepted today that every member of that society will have a car.[11] To this extent the development and production of the railways in Britain might be seen to have more in parallel with houses as the railways at least offered the chance for equal access to transport for all people.

> The 1851 Great Exhibition . . . could never have drawn the six million visitors it attracted from every corner of the country during its six months' currency had it not been for the railways. They . . . brought the trip within the scope of almost any town-dweller's pocket by offering return excursion fares from the industrial north no higher than the day-wage of a craftsman or the equivalent of two days' pay for a labourer.[12]

However, the railways were never developed with such an altruistic attitude to the users of transport but rather as a way of making money for their owners. Their success came because the railways enabled others to make money as goods and raw materials could be moved far more quickly around the country. This positive feedback encouraged the development of more railways, and more railways could give more economic growth. However, the railways were still constructed in craft based workshops.

If a comparison had to be made between the production of some form of mass transport and the production of mass housing, then comparison with the far less expensive, and hence more accessible, bicycle might seem more apposite. Such a comparison was once made by Lethaby: 'We have to aim at a standard of ordinary good quality; damp, cracked and leaky "architecture" must give way to houses as efficient as a bicycle.'[13] Indeed, the bicycle is very much a standardized object whose overall disposition of components (in terms of frame, wheels, and drive transfer mechanism) was settled very soon after its invention, differences occurring in details such as colour of paint and amount of chromium.

Lethaby's statement does no more than suggest that the factory produced product would offer more reliable and standardized performance than the craft based product. For the later theorists, who were to compare a building to a car, the purpose of the comparison is less well defined. It is, perhaps, precisely because a car shares some common characteristics with a building in terms of offering shelter from the environment and a container for human activity that its production methods have been compared to those of buildings.

It was through the work of Henry Ford that the car developed from the early craft-based product into the mass-produced item from the factory. However, Ford pointed out that the achievement of an increase in output from the first small car, built by a handful of men in a shop in October 1908, to the appearance of the ten millionth small car in June 1924 and the thirteen millionth in 1926[14] was not, ultimately, what interested him. Rather, in parallel with the economic benefits derived from the railways discussed above, Ford was interested in the growth in the American economy that would be made possible once people owned cars and could move around with comparative freedom. When discussing the purchase of Ford tractors with a delegation from Russia he said:

> 'No, you first ought to buy automobiles and get your people used to machinery and power and to moving about with some freedom. The motor car will bring roads, and then it will be possible to get the products of your farms to the cities.' They followed the advice and bought some thousands of automobiles. Now, after several years, they have bought some thousands of tractors.[15]

There is some parallel in this understanding of the national benefits that might accrue from a policy of mass-production that gave cars at a price which many could afford, and the Victorian reformers, like Chadwick, who recognized that good housing benefited not just the individual but the whole of society, since it allowed the individual to be a more effective member:

> To whatever extent the probable duration of the life of the working man is diminished by noxious agencies (neglect of sanitary measures), I repeat a truism in stating that to some extent so much productive power is lost; and in the case of destitute widowhood and orphanage, burdens are created and cast either on the industrious survivors belonging to the family, or on the contributors to the poor's rates during the whole period of the failure of such ability.[16]

However, what is remembered of Ford is less his interest in the influence of mass-production on economic growth but rather the images contained within the whole process of mass-production which thus resulted in the affordable product. These images range from the necessary subordination of the individual to the moving production line, satirized in Chaplin's film *Modern Times*, to a ridicule of the standardized product itself which was to be any colour so long as it was black. In fact the model T Ford was produced in black because this was, before World War I, the only colour of fast drying paint available. After developments in cellulose paint during World War I, the model T was available in other colours.[17] It is these images that designers transferred to the concept of the mass-produced house from the factory, whether with a belief in the benefit of the single well-made standardized product, or as a challenge to the designer to produce variety within the standardized factory made approach. These attitudes are encapsulated within the views of two architects, Le Corbusier and Gropius, who both independently campaigned for the house from the factory.

LE CORBUSIER AND THE MASS-PRODUCED HOUSE

The approach taken by Le Corbusier to the car, or automobile as he termed it, was to look for a perfect standardized product. His view of the development of the automobile showed how, visually, the car had been transformed from the hand made product, where the assembly of the parts to make the whole could be seen in the final product, to the streamlined factory made product where the necessary assembly of the parts had been shrouded within the bodywork of the whole. This approach embraces the supposition that if houses are to be as streamlined as cars then this will be as a result of a similar approach to manufacture. It is as if the 'clean' lines of engineering are not the result of design but depend upon a process that is itself seen as advanced:

> The establishment of a standard involves exhausting every practical and reasonable possibility, and extracting from them a recognized type conformable to its functions, with a maximum output and a minimum use of means, workmanship and material . . .[18]

The connection missing from this argument is the fact that it was the Model T, a car that was not at all streamlined in appearance, that had been mass-produced on the assembly line at a price many could afford because of the increase in productivity offered by the change in manufacture. Other designs of car have been and continue to be mass-produced in the same way. Although the design of the car has to be subjugated in part to the exigencies of the production line, the development of the automobile in the

USA has been more concerned with the exterior styling of the mass-produced product in order to introduce variety and choice into the market.[19] Le Corbusier, however, saw the streamlined engineered product, made in the factory, as an aesthetic object that had resulted from the process. Without, therefore, first developing the technology that might be needed to increase productivity in the building industry he proposed an architectural image that might result from such technology:

> Contractors' yards will no longer be sporadic dumps in which everything breathes confusion; financial and social organisation, using concerted and forceful methods, will be able to solve the housing question, and the yards will be on a huge scale, run and exploited like government offices. Dwellings, urban and suburban, will be enormous and square-built and no longer a dismal congeries; they will incorporate the principle of mass-production and of large-scale industrialisation.[20]

The mass-production process as envisaged by Le Corbusier to support the image was in two parts. The first concerned the production of standardized fittings and components for the house in the factory and the second looked to the introduction of reinforced concrete technology that would involve a semi-industrialized process on site, for example the repeated reuse of standard shuttering. These ideals were tested on the scale of a housing estate at the Pessac development in 1925 (figure 4.1):

> M. Fruges, an altruistic Bordeaux industrialist, told us: 'I am going to enable you to realize your theories in practice . . . Pessac should be a laboratory. In

Figure 4.1. Houses on La rue Corbusier Jeanneret at Pessac, 1963. (*By courtesy of* Alan Blanc)

short: I ask you to pose the problem of a house plan, of finding a method of standardization, to make use of walls, floors and roofs confirming [*sic*] to the most rigorous requirements for strength and efficiency and lending themselves to true taylor-like methods of mass-production by the use of machines which I shall authorise you to buy.'[21]

Despite these words the fifty-one houses at Pessac, which were completed between 1925–26, would not seem to offer particular improvement over traditional methods of building in terms of time. M. Fruges, the instigator of the project stated that, 'Shortly afterwards, more than two hundred workers were on the site and progress was made at the rate of two villas (main structures) per week.'[22] In addition, there remains a gap between the idealized method of production and the visual appearance of the estate. Reinforced concrete at Pessac is still used in the form of post and beam, just as Perret, for whom Le Corbusier had worked in 1908, had exploited it in the flats at Rue Franklin of 1902–1903, albeit that the column and beam are in part subsumed into the plane of the wall. Were the material to be truly exploited in the most efficient way, that is the maximum shelter for the minimum of material, the forms resulting might have more nearly approached Maillart's 1910 Zuercher Lagerhaus-Gesellschaft warehouse with its reinforced concrete mushroom columns, or even his later 1939 concrete shell Cement Industries hall, both in Zurich.

Thus Pessac was an example of the pre-conceived image of mass-production realized through an apparent rationalization of building technology. This example of the new architecture was to be reinforced by exhibition developments such as those at Stuttgart and Vienna where hand-made houses were given the veneer of the machine aesthetic. The very plethora of different forms for a house that looked as if it was mass-produced, coupled with the use of the same aesthetics for single projects, such as Le Corbusier's Villa Savoie which was never conceived as a potential prototype, negated any real search for a standard mass-produced house. As Banham has observed:

a historian must find that they produced a Machine Age architecture only in the sense that its monuments were built in a Machine Age, and expressed an attitude to machinery – in the sense that one might stand on French soil and discuss French politics, and still be speaking English.[23]

The irony in the relationship between Le Corbusier and the house from the factory is that, faced with the problem that gave birth to the Temporary Housing Programme, the need to produce a simple low cost house at the end of the war, he ignored factory technology and returned to a load-bearing, hand-built product, 'employing reinforced . . . cement blocks cast on site or alternatively traditional rammed earth or pise construction . . .'[24] in the form of the 1940 project for the Murondins House.

GROPIUS AND THE MASS-PRODUCED HOUSE

If Le Corbusier, in his search for the standardized house, developed an architectural image that imitated the appearance of what seemed to be the standard mass-produced car, the approach taken by Gropius was, broadly, to search for diversity within a standardized process. For Gropius, as for Ford, mass-production was seen as a vehicle for wealth creation and consequent improvement in living standards:

> But in the last resort mechanisation can have only one object: to abolish the individual's physical toil of providing himself with the necessities of existence in order that hand and brain may be set free for some higher order of activity.[25]

Gropius's interest in the possibilities of prefabrication had begun late in 1907 when he was working at AEG under Behrens (where Le Corbusier also worked for a time in 1910, just after Gropius had resigned). The architectural office of the company had been working on an estate for housing the factory workers. Stemming from this contact with housing, Gropius presented a memo to the Chairman of the company, Emil Rathenau, detailing a programme for the industrialization of building. In the memo he envisaged the production of standardized building elements in the factory, such as staircases, doors and windows, which could then be assembled into standard house types, whether cottages, houses or flats. Gropius' proposal was for the establishment of a company to undertake this work and his memo included detailed specification and costing of the component parts and finished products.[26] The emphasis that Gropius placed on the project, in contrast to Le Corbusier's vision of the perfect standardized object which brought with it the call for the creation of, 'The spirit of living in mass-production houses',[27] was the acceptance of the need for individual variety and the establishment of a method of achieving it:

> It is by the provision of interchangeable parts that the Company can meet the public's desire for individuality and offer the client the pleasure of personal choice and initiative without jettisoning aesthetic unity. Each house is in the end its own self by means of form, material and colour.[28]

This proposal may not have had an immediate effect on the workers' housing for AEG, but for Gropius it represented the start of a life-long interest in making houses from a mass-produced kit of parts, a route which would produce variety rather than the single standardized product. However Gropius did not concentrate on the design of such housing to the exclusion of other methods of construction. In *The New Architecture and the Bauhaus* he illustrates a housing estate at Dessau built in 1928, the design and construction of which involved the staff and students at the Bauhaus. In appearance the estate has more in common with the smooth plane, white, aesthetics of the ideal mass-produced house of Le Corbusier, than with Gropius's own 'Copper-Plate Houses designed for Mass-Production, 1932'.[29] The Copper-Plate House was single storey and of prefabricated copper clad panels with factory glazed windows and doors, the whole arriving on site on a lorry and trailer (figure 4.2). The sandwich panels were locked into place on a prepared slab to form an outer skin and inner partitions and a sectional flat roof were then added.

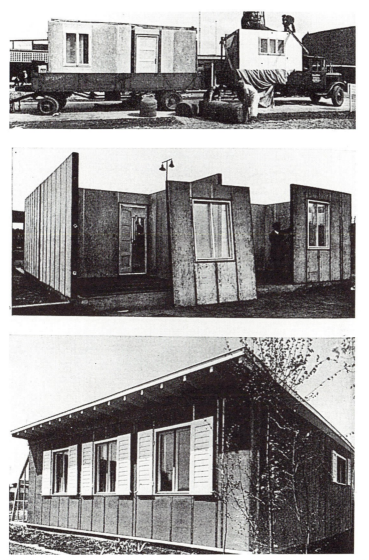

Figure 4.2. Gropius's Copper-Plate houses which were designed for mass production. (*Source*, Gropius, 1935)

It may be that the scale of the problem of producing the house from the factory and the capital required to initiate the process (other than for making experimental versions) mitigated against larger experiments in the field. Thus, the staff and students at the Bauhaus might be able to design products capable of mass-production to go into buildings, but the 'container' for such products was still traditionally constructed.[30]

The problem of the setting-up costs involved in establishing a house produced in the factory seems to have been understood by Gropius, even though such a realization was perhaps only hinted at. The Copper-Plate House was a free standing bungalow on its own plot. However, the tradition in European cities was for the worker and his family to live in a rented flat:

> The single home with a garden is more suitable for families with children in higher-income brackets who are permanently settled and do not depend on changes in place of employment and on repeated moving, while the rented dwelling in an apartment house is better adapted to the needs of the more mobile working class. The one-family house fails to meet the needs, in regard to cost or otherwise, of this largest group of housing consumers because its universal introduction is prohibited, not by the ravages of a capitalistic society, but by the very nature of cities.[31]

The problem of applying the mass-production techniques of the detached bungalow to the apartment block only exacerbated the capital costs problem. The experience of 'prefabricated' apartment blocks is that the process became one of rationalized site manufacture of components coupled with standardized fittings made in the factory as for any other building. The approach of the kit of parts, which could be altered and varied, became replaced with a standardized, repetitive product.

However, Gropius's involvement with the single house mass-produced in the factory continued after his move to the United States, where the history of such an approach had produced an industry of some substance. Into this industry Gropius, and his associate Konrad Wachsmann, first attempted to introduce their Packaged House, a system of load-bearing timber frame panels joined with metal connectors, developed between 1941–42. With backing from Wall Street, the system was reborn as the General Panel Corporation and prototypes using 'six standard panels – wall, door, window, floor, ceiling and roof units – all constructed on substantially the same standard frame' were made.[32] A demonstration house was put up in Boston early in 1943.[33] However, despite the wartime housing programme of the USA which had been expected to, 'do for Prefabrication what World War I did for the aircraft industry – raise it from infancy to adolescence in no time,'[34] the system devised by Gropius and Wachsmann failed to be effective:

Four years of intensive effort, and not one house built for sale – and this during wartime, with its incredible demand for instant housing, when the location of wartime industry involved a population shift of some 8 to 10 million workers, this at a time when the climate of urgency was highly supportive of creative initiative, particularly in the industrial field.[35]

This failure of a long standing preoccupation with the kit of parts approach at a time which could not have been more propitious for such a venture has been attributed to a division of effort amongst those collaborating on the project.[36] Perhaps of more interest to the post-war developments in the UK is not the seductive drawings that Gropius supplied to illustrate the possibilities of the system for a house that could be extended when resources allowed, but the working drawings for the General Panel House. The hut-like structure with a pitched roof is immediately familiar either as a sister to US prefabricated timber housing or to the UK temporary bungalows. The adaptation of the General Panel System to barracks closely resembles Ministry of Works war time hutting. Perhaps the standardized 'objet-type' of the mass-produced house sought by Le Corbusier was, in fact, the hut as developed by Wachsmann and Gropius.

THE DEVELOPMENT OF THE PREFABRICATED HOUSE IN THE UK

To explore further the mis-match between the expectations of designers concerning the form of the house out of the factory and the reality of the temporary bungalows it is necessary to turn briefly to the well documented field of developments in prefabrication in the UK.[37] Before either Le Corbusier or Gropius came to consider the possibilities of the mass-produced house and the relevance of such a product to a system of prefabrication, prefabricated and sectionalized buildings of timber had been developed and exported from the UK to the colonies in the nineteenth century.

The advertisements for portable colonial cottages, the prefabricated cottages for emigrants, continued regularly until 1841 . . . After 1841, however, the volume of advertising and, presumably, the volume of business transacted began to decline, following the sharp drop in emigration to Australia and New Zealand.[38]

The architectural forms of such structures are again simple pitched roof forms with more, or sometimes less, applied decorative detail. The decorative elements supply the memories of romanticized cottages – the fretted barge board, shutters and finials – but the building is essentially a hut; the extrusion of a simple section. The introduction of corrugated iron to those engaged in the business of supplying the colonies with buildings meant that a material more resistant to rot and termites could be used to clad a framing of either timber or iron. However, the discipline of the material lent itself to prefabrication within a system in a way that timber, which is far easier to alter on site, did not, and the corrugated building found a wide export market to the point where, 'During the last third of the nineteenth century the prefabricated corrugated iron building had become commonplace'.[39] Even the much cited Tipton Green lock-keeper's cottage, claimed to be one of the earliest prefabricated buildings in England,[40] constructed of cast iron wall panels, probably before 1790,[41] is a bungalow with a pitched roof. Such consistency is perhaps explicable just in terms of the technology of making a building in parts. Repetition is inherent in the approach and so the section is simply extruded into the hut-like form. A roof of prefabricated sections, which have been joined in some way, will be better able to shed rain if pitched rather flat. An on-site welded joint, necessary to make a leak-proof roof, is not an obvious part of a prefabricated joint technology.

In the UK the relationship between the mass-produced house and prefabrication had been uncertain. The possibilities of first cast iron and, later, steel frame construction suggested methods of prefabricating large frame structures, as were developed in industrial buildings like those of the eighteenth-century users of cast iron, William Strutt and Charles Bage. However, apart from the export trade to the colonies, the same technologies were not, at first, seen as applicable to housing. Before the First World War these materials of prefabrication were only used to any extent in housing for their decorative qualities, as found in the railings and verandahs of Cheltenham and other spa towns.[42] Thus, although Le Corbusier saw the mass-produced house as a search for a new standard product and Gropius saw it as the search for a suitable set of mass-produced components, prefabrication in Britain when it was applied to housing was seen as an alternative way of constructing an acknowledged standardized product, the three-bedroom house.

The initial impetus for looking for substitute methods of construction appeared after World War I, when the conditions of both housing (apart from the absence of bomb damage) and the building industry were not dissimilar to those which occurred after the Second World War.

> 1918 found the country faced with an acute shortage of houses due to the virtual suspension of building during the war, and also to a deficiency inherited from the years immediately before the war, when not more than 58,000 houses were built annually. The shortage was aggravated by the speed of demobilisation and by a large increase in the number of families wanting homes. At the same time the building industry had been seriously weakened by the war, and the local authorities, who under optional powers had built few houses before 1914, were generally ill-equipped to undertake a large-scale housing drive.[43]

To combat these problems encouragement was given to the development of building systems that could replace traditional craft labour, especially bricklaying.[44] There was no request that such systems should be based on factory labour, although the Tudor Walters Report of 1918 did encourage the use of standardized factory made components, such as grates and sinks, in order to provide higher standards at reduced costs.[45] House systems encouraged in the inter-war period used structures and claddings of concrete, timber, and metal in an effort to move away from traditional brickwork. However each manufacturer was allowed to develop and put forward a system for approval: there was no systematic analysis of what the most economical method of providing non-traditional housing might be. Some, like the Boot Pier and Panel continuous cavity wall house did attempt a measure of site mechanization with precast units manufactured on site and, 'special plant . . . for moving them and for erection.'[46] Others, like the Airey (Duo-Slab), were formed of concrete piers poured in-situ with precast concrete slabs laid without mortar joints between the piers in an effort to reduce skilled labour. The image of these prefabricated houses, however, was firmly rooted in the English cottage tradition, so much so that the potential freedom offered by the light steel frame could be crowned with a conventional tiled roof (figure 4.3), brick stack and brick cladding without drawing any comment when used as an illustration in the Ministry of Works Post-War Building Studies.[47]

This same approach to the prefabricated house also occurred after the Second World War and can be seen in the Ministry of Works demonstration

Figure 4.3. 'Typical light steel frame construction.' (*Source*: Ministry of Works, 1944*b*)

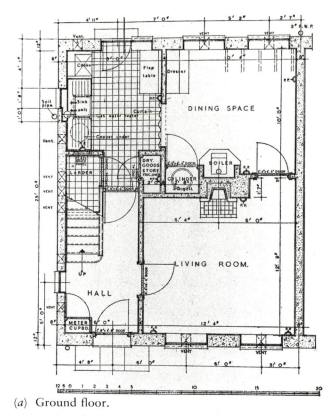

(*a*) Ground floor.

Figure 4.4 (a) and (b). The standard demonstration plan as used by the Ministry of Works at Northolt in 1944. (*Source*: Ministry of Works, 1944*c*)

houses built at Northolt, Middlesex, plans for which were published in 1944 (figure 4.4). The purpose of the demonstration was to examine the labour and materials costs involved in both traditional and prefabricated house systems for, 'the purpose of estimating probable post-war costs for methods of house building advocated in *Housing Manual 1944*.'[48] All the prefabricated systems were constructed to a plan that closely followed the standard inter-war semi three-bedroom 'universal plan'. Some plan experiments were carried out in traditional brick construction but all, except for a three-bedroom house that could be converted to house two families during the emergency period (see Chapter 6), only changed the arrangement of ground floor rooms, keeping to the three-bedroom format throughout. Apart from the prefab, the assumption that the three-bedroom house was somehow to be adapted to prefabrication rather than starting with the technology and devising the most suitable plan arrangement seems not to have been considered at any time. The example of the

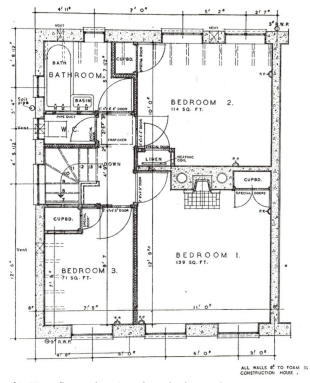

(b) First floor, showing three-bedroom layout.

TVA had shown that the production of the sectional house in the factory did have an influence on plan arrangement, just as the aluminium prefab plan was more or less aligned into the four sections to be joined on site. Moreover, contemporary evidence that the three-bedroom house was not necessarily a good match to actual housing demand seems not to have been taken into account; 'Between 1911 and 1931, one-person households increased by 63 per cent; two-person households by 74 per cent and three-person households by 61 per cent.'[49]

The opportunity existed in examining alterations to the process of producing houses to look again at the finished product. Although the temporary bungalows did offer a different product the approach taken to their design could not really be said to be a re-examination of housing. Rather, the two-bedroom detached form was seen as an emergency measure only whilst sufficient standard three-bedroom products were built. The example offered by the TVA of demountable and extendable housing made possible by the prefabrication of the sectional components seems to have been missed in the British approach. Although designers had suggested that prefabrication would bring differing aesthetics no attempt was made to relate these to the process of manufacture. If the obvious prefabricated dwelling was a hut, then the prefab provides another example of the emergence of this 'objet-type', but the prefab is a hut dressed in a number of differing outer garments, from asbestos cement sheet to prefabricated concrete panels. With the possible exception of the curved ridge of the Arcon, no attempt was made to produce a decorative expression through acknowledging the properties of the materials of construction (asbestos cement sheet can be worked wet on moulds to provide curved shapes). This situation was acknowledged by F.R.S. Yorke:

> Experiment with concrete and steel was hampered by the same narrow outlook, a clinging to forms dictated by quite different materials; and, because success did not follow immediately the attempt to use the new materials as direct substitutes for the old, the materials themselves were condemned . . .
>
> We cannot reasonably ignore the semi-temporary asbestos and corrugated iron bungalows that have in the last decade sprung up all over the country. We may dislike their design but we must admit that they provide homes at a price that those who live in them can afford.[50]

UK DESIGNERS AND 'A MACHINE FOR LIVING IN'

If, as Yorke indicated above, designers were ignoring the evidence given to the public of the mass-produced house they could afford, how did designers set about constructing the images associated with the tenet of Le Corbusier that, 'The house is a machine for living in'?[51] The evidence on the ground suggests that many houses that were built in this image were single projects and could, therefore, never attempt to involve any systematic attempt to alter the production process. The methods of building fall broadly into two categories; those that used reinforced concrete to form the exterior walls and those that resorted to traditional brick construction with an external render to complete the image. Of the former type a pair of houses at Ruislip by Connell and Ward were built, 'entirely of reinforced concrete; the beams, floor and roof-slab tie in to form a monolithic structure, and the walls above and below the windows act as beams.'[52] Even with an exterior waterproof coating the finish of such houses was not always as perfect as the image. Of Chermayeff's house at Rugby, also with walls of 4 in thick reinforced concrete, Myerscough-Walker says:

> One of the greatest disappointments in modern domestic architecture is the lack of quality of the surface. The buildings frequently photograph well, but look much less attractive in reality . . . If you look closely . . . you will see all the marks of the concrete shuttering.[53]

Nor did such an approach to constructing machine aesthetics necessarily perform well in the long term. Of Saltings, Hayling Island, a house by Connell and Ward with walls of 4 in reinforced concrete, the problem of restoration in the 1970s was, 'how to restore the clean simplified lines of the machine aesthetic to their original appearance but at the same time solve the technical problems that were posed by the aesthetic'.[54] Water penetration was eventually solved by the installation of new windows with the incorporation of a damp proof course missing in the original. The external finish was also stripped and renewed as part of the restoration.

It was possible to achieve the same appearance with brick construction, as with the Headmaster's House, Dartington by Howe and Lescaze (figure 4.5). Built in brick and timber with steel windows the house was rendered externally, 'to look like concrete'.[55] A similar construction was used for a group of houses by Herbert in Hampstead Garden Suburb (figure 4.6) where the 13½ in and 9 in rendered brickwork is exposed between the upper windows. The houses were deliberately built, 'as an experiment to cater for people looking for a soundly constructed "ready-made" house . . . (as) an alternative design to the more stereotyped speculative houses adjoining'.[56] When F.W.B. and F.R.S. Yorke came to build a group of seven houses for brewery workers in Stratford-on-Avon, complete with communal garden and separate allotments, the external rendering was dropped in favour of 11 in cavity brickwork simply expressed (figure 4.7).

Figure 4.5. Headmaster's house, Dartington, by Howe and Lescaze. (*Source*: Myerscough-Walker, n.d. (*c* 1939))

Figure 4.6. House at Hampstead Garden Suburb by G.B. Herbert. (*Source*: Myles Wright, 1937)

Thus Yorke, who was an exponent of the white walled reinforced concrete cubic house, as at Nast Hyde, Hatfield, found it more difficult to apply the same technology to working-class houses. The houses built for Critall much earlier, in 1928, for workers at the firm's new factory at Silver End garden village, Essex though having flat roofs and white walls were not revolutionary in construction either. MacManus, assistant to Tait who was given the job of designing the houses, stated that he, 'subsequently realized that they were really the traditional house styled in the manner of the new architecture that was just beginning to emerge on the Continent'.[57]

Machine aesthetics were, therefore, achieved in Britain for single house projects far more readily than for working-class houses. Even so, the aesthetics were exactly that and in no way related to improved or industrialized site techniques as Le Corbusier had proposed. The dream of the artisan family sunning themselves on the *toit-jardin* was to remain just that, while the ordinary people pottered about in the gardens of their, 'little home-made wood and pink-asbestos-roofed bungalows.'[58]

If the architectural profession had been led to expect either the machine aesthetics of Le Corbusier or the adaptability of the kit of parts approach offered by Gropius once the techniques of mass-production were applied

Figure 4.7. Terrace cottages for brewery workers, 1939, by F.W.B. and F.R.S. Yorke. (*Source*: Yorke, 1943)

to housing, then the temporary bungalows must have been a disappointment. However, like the evidence found in the USA and Scandinavia, or even that of the Victorian industry making portable cottages for the colonies, the prefab is typical in being a pitched roof dwelling separate on its own plot. In this sense it can be seen as an extension of the imaginary ideal factory produced dwelling, even if for architects it did not accord with their image of a factory produced house. Moreover, the bungalow in its separate plot had overtones of suburbia at a period in history when many designers felt at best ambivalence and at worst antipathy to such a housing form. Barbara Jones might hope that:

> . . . authority should intervene and allow only carefully designed houses in the twentieth century idiom to be made, as convenient as a pre-fab [*sic*], sometimes with scope for enlargement from a little house to a medium-sized one, and as labour saving as possible.[59]

However, the same article is illustrated with the caption, 'Gabled or flat-roofed, the suburban house proclaims its monotonous individuality'.[60] Certainly nothing could be viewed as more monotonous than an estate of prefabs photographed either from the air or before any planting had yet been established. The problem with the temporary prefabricated bungalow was that, as housing, it could be nothing but monotonous. Yet there was still a feeling that something better might have been achieved.

> Wars create the situation where side by side with permanent housing there will almost certainly grow up an architecture of prefabrication, something better than temporary housing for war-workers . . . prefabrication offers chances of evolving better equipment and design, which will benefit eventually the more permanent house which the building industry will provide.[61]

If designers felt that prefabrication techniques had worthier goals than the production of temporary bungalows it is not surprising that the latter, however much they were liked by the public, should not be seen by designers as important in other than an emergency context. The result was that designers turned to the prefabrication and rationalization of a dwelling type that more nearly fitted the machine aesthetics, the block of flats. If it had proved difficult to achieve these aesthetics in a single house, such difficulties might be removed if sufficient repeats of the standard unit could be achieved. The obvious way to do this was to pile up the units into mass housing schemes, each mass scheme differing from the next once sufficient numbers of the standardized parts had been produced to reap the economic benefits. The single bungalow on the single plot could not be tolerated, even if prefabricated, because it was not urban in form. Just as Le Corbusier had suggested an image for the mass-produced house, so the image for a collection of mass-produced houses was the city and not the suburb: 'The profile of the town seen against the sky becomes a pure line, and as a result we are able to lay out our urban scene on the grand scale. This is of the first importance.'[62]

Such a symbol seemed a true representation of mass-production in building and the result of such imagery on UK housing has been well documented. Had the possibilities of the temporary bungalow been appreciated in terms of the quality of housing it offered to the public the story of post-war housing in the UK might have been very different.

NOTES

1. Le Corbusier (1927), p. 123.
2. Cox (1945), p. 34.
3. Church and Drysdale Smith (1947), p. 6.

4. *Weldons Ladies' Journal*, March, 1944, p. 49.

5. 'The American Kitchen of the Day-After-Tomorrow is still only a dream even to U.S. housewives. The oven on the left is all glass, the cooker has its own lighting fixture, the sink tops have foot control. But there are a few disadvantages too. Those who live in glass kitchens have to keep their shelves very tidy.' Bruce Milne (1946), p. 33. The all glass kitchen was exhibited in 1944 in Toledo, Ohio.

6. Heath Robinson and Browne (*c* 1930), p. 32. This features the 'one-piece chromium steel dining suite'.

7. Gloag and Wornum (1946), p. 133.

8. Roy and Cross (1975), p. 54.

9. 'The second half of the nineteenth century saw the birth of numerous machines for the brick industry . . . Inventiveness was encouraged by a demand for bricks so great it could not have been met by traditional methods alone, with the labour available.' See Woodforde (1976), p. 110.

10. Le Corbusier (1927).

11. In 1981 44 per cent of the population had the regular use of one car, a proportion which had held relatively steady since 1971. Also in 1981 15 per cent of households had two or more cars leaving 41 per cent of households without access to a car. See Central Statistical Office (1982), p. 125.

12. Freeman Allen (1982), p. 72.

13. Lethaby (1911), p. 249.

14. Ford (1926), p. 1.

15. *Ibid.*, pp. 7–8.

16. Chadwick (1842), p. 245.

17. Setright (1989), p. 151. The development of nitrocellulose for explosives increased in World War I and manufacturers were anxious to find a new use for their manufacturing plant and product once the war was over. Quick drying paint which could be coloured was offered to the motoring industry which was quick to take it up. The parallel between industrial expansion during the war, post-war needs for employment and the Temporary Housing Programme are obvious.

18. Le Corbusier (1927), p. 127.

19. Hesketh (1980), pp. 178–179.

20. Le Corbusier (1927), pp. 217–218.

21. Boesiger and Girsberger (1967), p. 42.

22. Fruges speech given in 1967 at Pessac quoted in Boudon (1972), p. 10.

23. Banhan (1960), p. 329.

24. Frampton (1987), p. 31. In fact, Le Corbusier's approach might seem suitable for a France which had been overrun and occupied during the war. However, it has to be contrasted with that of Jean Prouve who saw the factory produced house as a way of providing much needed housing after the war: see Huber and Steinegger (1971).

25. Gropius (1935), p. 25.

26. Herbert (1984), p. 23.

27. Le Corbusier (1927), p. 12.

28. 'Gropius at Twenty-six', *Architectural Review*, July, 1961, p. 50.

29. Gropius (1935), p. 59.

30. 'The demonstration of all kinds of new models made in our workshops, which we were able to show in practical use in the building (the Bauhaus itself), so thoroughly convinced manufacturers that they entered into royalty contracts with the Bauhaus which, as the turnover increased, proved a valuable source of revenue for the latter.' See Gropius (1956), p. 31.

31. *Ibid.*, p. 122.

32. *Architectural Forum*, June, 1943 p. 94.

33. 'Prefabricated Panels for Packaged Buildings', *Architectural Record*, April, 1943, p. 52.

34. 'Building Money', *Architectural Forum*, December, 1940, p. 531.

35. Herbert (1984), p. 276.

36. *Ibid.*, pp. 270–271.

37. The standard account of prefabrication in the UK is White (1965).

38. Herbert (1978), p. 22.

39. *Ibid.*, p. 115.

40. This date ignores the medieval practice of prefabrication in timber frame structures whereby timber was cut and preassembled before marking and transport to the final place of erection: see West (1971), p. 60.

41. Sheppard (1946), p. 39 and Sheppard (1945), p. 71.

42. Sheppard (1945).

43. Ministry of Health (1948*a*), p. 1.

44. White (1965), p. 38.

45. Local Government Boards for England and Wales and Scotland (1918), p. 52.

46. Ministry of Works (1944*b*), p. 58.

47. *Ibid.*, p. 73.

48. Ministry of Works (1944*c*), p. 7.

49. Block (1946), p. 54.

50. Yorke (1943), p. 28.

51. Le Corbusier (1927), p. 10.

52. Smithells (1939), p. 63.

53. Myerscough-Walker R. (n.d.) No. 37.

54. Russell (1977), p. 582.

55. Myerscough-Walker, No. 38.

56. Myles Wright (1937), p. 51.

57. MacManus, F. quoted in Gould (1977), p. 11.

58. Yorke (1943), p. 187.

59. Jones, B. in Weidenfeld (1947), p. 47.

60. *Ibid.*

61. Robertson (1944), p. 78.

62. Le Corbusier (1929), p. 232.

5

THE NEW JERUSALEM

*'. . . we are now hearing a good deal about the New
Jerusalem which is to be built after the war.'*[1]

HOUSING NEEDS AFTER WORLD WAR II

During the period between the First and Second World Wars both the
numbers and types of housing available in Britain changed. With the aid of
subsidies from the state the local authorities had been enabled to build
houses for rent. The depression in the building industry had also reduced
house prices and given a spur to the speculative housing market. More
people were buying their own houses at the start of the Second World War
than ever before.

> Following on the gradual growth of real income since the First World War,
> this made possible a significant transfer of families from the group who
> normally had to rent houses to those who could just afford to move up into
> the social class of small house-owners.[2]

In assessing housing needs at the end of the war the Minister of
Reconstruction reported that by 1939 only 6 per cent of the population
were living in overcrowded or unacceptable houses and that, 'over 30 per
cent of the population were living in new houses which had been built since
1919.'[3] The same order of change in the housing stock was reported by
Rowntree in 1939 in the second survey of the housing of York. He found
that some 12,078 houses for working-class people (and the working classes
formed two-thirds of the total population of the city) had been constructed
since the first survey of poverty in the city which had been undertaken in
1899. Of this 2907 had been constructed in the period before the First World
War and 51 during that war which meant that 9120 houses or 75.5 per cent
of the new houses had been built since 1918. Of these 9120 houses, 52.5 per
cent had been built by the city council with government subsidy, a further
3.6 per cent had been built by private enterprise with government subsidy
and the remaining 43.9 per cent had been built by private enterprise with
no state subsidy.[4] By 1939 the city of York had a group of 423 slum houses
in one area, together with some individual slum houses in other parts of the
city.[5] In York, therefore, which was claimed to be typical of the medium
sized towns in England, the housing stock had considerably altered in

composition between the wars. Nevertheless, despite the new housing, the Rowntree survey could only claim that, 'By 1939, 30 per cent of the working-class population lived in comfortable and satisfactory houses', and the same percentage of working-class houses in York had baths.[6] From this it must follow that a considerable proportion of the working-class population was living in the older terraced housing which had been put up before the day of the indoor bathroom and WC. *Picture Post* was also to expose housing conditions where siblings were forced to share tiny bedrooms and where there was no bathroom or garden and only an outside WC, such that, 'Running hot water is a luxury to dream about. On washday, Mrs. Owen has to boil kettles in their only fire and carry them out to the tub.'[7]

However, the new housing of this inter-war period had an effect on housing expectation of particular relevance to the prefab. As Simon pointed out:

> Over 90% of the inter-war houses were built on suburban estates at about twelve to the acre. The greatest advantages of this scattered development were, firstly, the light and air which each house enjoyed, and secondly, the fact that every house had a good garden . . . We made nearly four million gardens in twenty years.[8]

The rehoused working classes, therefore, found themselves not only with new houses but with new gardens. Those who remained in the older houses would look to these new estate homes as the models of what they might themselves expect when the remaining slums and older houses were finally cleared away at the end of the war. The fact that the temporary bungalows were to fulfill this expected model, each sitting centrally in its own garden, could partially explain the welcome they were given after the war by the people who were to live in them.

During the war prior to 1941 there was little discussion of housing either as a public national issue or in parliament. This was despite the bombing of 1940–41 with its consequent destruction of homes. Only after the cessation of civilian bombing and the transfer of the German military drive towards the Eastern Front was it possible for the country to draw breath and take stock of what the war and the war effort had done. Although the rehousing of those made homeless through bombing had been achieved without building any substantial amount of additional accommodation, it was realized that both temporary repairs to houses and the requisitioning of housing together with the way in which families took in homeless relatives would lead to a worsening of the housing standards to be dealt with after the war.[9] At the time, however, when it was uncertain whether the allies would be successful, there were more immediate problems than worrying about future housing difficulties.

Some would suggest, however that the problem of the post-war housing shortage was only identified once those empowered to investigate the difficulties of post-war reconstruction became themselves more able to cope with the task.[10] From this time public interest also swung towards issues of reconstruction and housing. Since it affected everyone, it soon became a favourite topic, taken up by such organizations as the Army Bureau of Current Affairs in their booklets.[11] Official concern began with the Official Committee on Internal Economic Problems which discussed the post-war housing plans made by the Ministry of Health. These examined the provision of new permanent housing after the war.

> In their work on the long-term problem, the Ministry of Health from the first made it clear that they contemplated a very large post-war house building programme of from three to four million houses for England and Wales alone, within a period of ten to twelve years after the war.[12]

The majority of the housing indicated by this programme represented the continuation of the programme of slum clearance and the amelioration of overcrowded conditions that were in existence before the war. As has been shown earlier, twenty years of house building in York still left 60 per cent of the working-class population without a modern house with full sanitary conveniences. Moreover, the quality of the nation's houses deteriorated during the war as normal maintenance was not carried out. Between 1934 and 1939 the government claimed that the output of houses was 300,000 a year. Between 1939 and 1945 less than 200,000 were constructed.[13] The proposed new permanent housing programme at the end of the war was to continue the work of clearance and new house building, rather than just compensating for the houses destroyed by bombing. Moreover the enforced break in the programme gave a chance for the public to consider what housing they would like. As the survey by the Bournville Village Trust observed of Birmingham:

> So far, the destruction of war has made amazingly little difference to the general picture we give of how and where Birmingham lived and worked. When, therefore, we talk of rebuilding Birmingham we are not primarily concerned with the problems of war damage, but we do advocate seizing the opportunity the war has created to look at our city anew and to plan its rebuilding with a new vision.[14]

Discussions of this nature centred on the long term planning of homes after the war. In other places, however, it was realized that there might be more immediate housing problems to solve as part of the efforts of post-war reconstruction. As White summarizes:

> In the six-year war period, not more than 200,000 houses were built, mainly for war workers in new locations. As many houses as that were totally destroyed by enemy action and a further quarter of a million made unfit for habitation without major repair, while a still greater number were in need of minor repair.[15]

The rate of family formation had also dropped as a result of the war, although the rate of marriage did not. At the end of the war there would, therefore, be a population of newly married couples looking for a home in order to establish the family life with children which the war had interrupted. At the same time an industry massively expanded to make tanks, aeroplanes etc. for the war effort would find itself in peacetime with no market for its products. In addition, the servicemen returning after the war would expect to pick up their life where they had left it and part of that life would be full time employment. To keep the production lines going and create more jobs new products had to be found. If these products could be factory made houses, utilizing the techniques of prefabrication, then two post-war problems could be solved simultaneously. Moreover, transferring the skills of house building to the production line meant that the houses could be erected on site without skilled labour and it was recognized that there would be a shortage of traditional skilled building labour after the war. Those with the task of organizing the post-war world were, therefore, faced with a multi-faceted problem. The injection of new blood into the committees concerned with the issue of reconstruction after 1942 did bring the discussion of these issues into parliament and it was in parliament that the idea of a new type of prefabricated house of a temporary nature for production at the end of the war was first discussed publicly.

From the first it was recognized that housing after the war had to differ from the housing conditions that prevailed during the war. Those returning from abroad, or those who had been working long shifts in factories, often without a break from one week to the next, did not necessarily want to return to a world that reminded them of war time. If any houses made on factory production lines were to look like temporary barracks and hostels then it was unlikely that they would be acceptable to the majority. This point is illustrated by the following extract from a lecture in the 'Post-War Home' series given by George Hicks MP:

> Today working men and women are on active service, and in most cases every month of their lives spent in camp, barracks, hostel or front line adds to their appreciation of the home they have left. They have been regimented and standardised: after the war they want to regain their sense of individuality. If fittings and manufactured parts generally have to be standardised, let there be some scope for personal differences in colour or arrangement.[16]

In his 1942–43 personal survey of the country James Hodson made the following observations:

> I've attended several of these discussions in the past week [talking of the Army Bureau of Current Affairs] . . . the subject, Town Planning. In this group of twenty or thirty, we had a dozen different regiments, and different

types of men. But all were united on wanting the government to control where factories must go and where houses must go – and nobody wanted to live in a flat. They want semi-detached houses and in some cases, subsidised rents that vary with income. No slums for them.[17]

and later he notes, talking to women, 'Nearly all wanted to cook by electricity, but most were content to do without a refrigerator (probably never having had one). They will put up with utility clothes, etc., during the war, but not after.'[18]

The suggestion here, from both men and women, is that the post-war house would have to accord with the people's idea of 'home'. Any house would have to have an element of individuality, be traditionally recognizable as a home but it was also to be serviced and heated to a high standard. War had shown the public new, sophisticated products and it would not be unreasonable to assume that industrial production could produce the same sophistication in housing components. A new housing solution was required which would give the people confidence in the type of country that they were fighting for:

> Mr. Churchill, I am informed, has appointed a sort of Cabinet for Home Affairs which meets once a week – Bevin, Morrison, Brown and Anderson. But Churchill, were he really wise, would take a deeper interest in the Home Front than is apparent, and would not refrain from speaking of the Britain we ought to try to build post-war.[19]

PARLIAMENTARY DISCUSSION OF POST-WAR HOUSING

Housing first appears as a parliamentary topic in King George VI's Speech of 11 November 1942. The King did nothing more than offer a vague promise to alleviate, 'wherever possible therefore the housing difficulties consequent upon the war.'[20] From this time, however, housing formed a subject for debate in both the Houses of Parliament. The initial concern of parliament with regard to housing at this time was the immediate problem of the provision of new cottages for agricultural labourers and their families. Part of this programme appeared to involve the provision of temporary bungalows, several of which were put up in Wales. During the Commons proceedings of September 1943, the MP Mr Jackson questioned the Minister of Works as to, 'whether he is aware that a pair of prefabricated cottages are being erected in the urban area of Brecon; and whether it is the new policy of the Ministry to erect such dwellings in districts of this kind.'[21]

The complaint here was about the siting of the cottages, but the existence of these dwellings can be seen as a precursor to the later temporary bungalows. Their form and materials, however, appear to have been derived from the Ministry of Works hutting programme:

In 1942 the Ministry of Works possessed prefabricated concrete sections for some 1500 emergency bungalows which had been designed for the housing of key industrial workers and their families; they were at this time lying unused, as it had recently been decided that no more separate bungalows were to be provided. The Ministry of Agriculture made the suggestion that these prefabricated bungalows would solve one peculiarly difficult problem – the provision of accommodation for key workers, stockmen or foremen, on farms in the possession of Executive Committees; many of these farms had been acquired because they were derelict and had no living accommodation of any kind. After much negotiation and delay, fifty pairs of such bungalows were authorised as a first instalment followed by authorisation of a further thirty-four pairs, sites were found and construction was begun in the summer of 1943. After a visit of inspection to one pair in Wales, Ministers were so dissatisfied with the limited space and inadequate amenities of these bungalows that all further building of this type was suspended. It was agreed that if accommodation had to be provided on isolated holdings for a key worker, the standard brick cottage, built to last, would have to be erected.[22]

This evidence for experiments in temporary housing during the war – experiments which were, moreover, unsuccessful – leaves the question as to why the government took the decision to invest in a prototype temporary post-war bungalow during 1943. This prototype, known as the Portal bungalow after Lord Portal, the then Minister of Works and Planning, was to be made of steel.

The King's speech had made a vague reference to the possible existence of a housing problem and in reply to this speech, Lord Wimborne (seconding the motion) made the following statement:

I am also very pleased to see that the gracious Speech takes notice of the great housing difficulties caused by the war. These are, indeed, acute. I am told that in some industrial districts the night worker, returning home, has to occupy the bed just vacated by his colleague who goes back to take his place in the factory by day. We must do something, either by erecting huts or hostels, perhaps by providing prefabricated houses, to improve the housing conditions of those workers to whom we owe so much, and to whom so much of our success is due.[23]

Here the idea of prefabrication techniques is linked to the provision of housing to meet an emergency need, although only as an extension of the existing machinery for providing huts and hostels.

In the Reconstruction Debate of 16 December 1942 in the House of Lords the provision of emergency housing first became publicly linked to a discussion of post-war industry. Lord Portal, in emphasizing his inability to predict the employment position immediately after the war, pointed out the general difficulties that would be faced by industries which were at that time geared to the war effort. However, he anticipated no such difficulty with the building industry which he declared would be given a general boost as soon as the war ended.

We know there will be a vast amount of building to be done in this country after the war is over. In discussing this I put housing first . . . Not only are we assured of a very large programme of building, but nearly all the materials are at hand in this country. You have your brickfields . . . and what we are trying to do is to maintain these brickfields in a state where they can start up immediately when they are wanted. We have got concrete, cement, roofing, and that sort of thing in this country. Timber may be a difficulty, but that probably may be got over by using substitutes, or through timber imported from over seas.[24]

Apart from demonstrating Lord Portal's unfamiliarity with the building industry and building materials (since timber was imported from overseas before the war and the cessation of this trade had led to war time shortages), the statement also shows that no consideration had been given to the problem of finding the skilled labour that would be necessary to implement this increase in traditional building. However, Lord Portal did go on to make the following statement, 'we may have to have a short-view policy as well as a long-view policy . . . And we may have to do that with building.'[25] This, at least, hints at some type of different 'building' to meet immediate short-term needs at the end of the war.

THE BACKGROUND TO THE TEMPORARY HOUSING PROGRAMME AS DISCUSSED IN PARLIAMENT

It was not until the House of Commons Supply Committee debate on housing in May 1943 that any public discussion of something approaching the scope of the Temporary Housing Programme occurred. For the first time each of three separate housing problems directly attributable to the war was discussed, as the following sample extracts demonstrate.

1. Relocation of industrial labour:

> . . . there are two factories on the confines of my own constituency to which the Ministry of Labour is constantly seeking to direct more labour . . . when the labour gets there it finds a billeting situation which is already intolerable owing to a large increase of Civil Servants and compulsory and voluntary evacuees.
>
> Although I have pointed out to three of the Ministries that the situation could have been eased at once by the provision of temporary hutments for unmarried workers to house only 400 . . . nothing has been done so far. The result has been that labour is lost to those factories; workers have drifted away because they cannot bring their families with them; billeting difficulties have arisen, and nothing has been done, because . . . insufficient prominence has been given by the Minister to the question of housing in direct relation to the war effort.[26]

2. Loss of housing stock through bomb damage and the cessation of house building during the war:

May I direct attention to one or two practical considerations which will arise after the war . . . We shall, of course, have to deal immediately with the 3,000,000 houses which have suffered war damage. We shall, of course, have large arrears in that there has been no house building during the war, and that will be well over 1,000,000 houses. In addition, there should be an annual output of between 300,000 and 400,000 houses a year . . . It is clear that the building industry is going to be fully occupied for the best part of 20 years at least.[27]

3. The fulfilment of the expectations of those returning from the war:

In some ways the war improved matters. It enabled certain evacuees to see for the first time in their lives, better standards of housing and conduct . . . After the war it is essential that the people who return should not be allowed to lapse again into the conditions that were revealed by the evacuation surveys, and it is essential that my right hon. Friend should . . . take the committee into his confidence and tell us something about what his real housing plans may be.[28]

The general attitude in the debate at this time is, perhaps, summarized by the following:

After the last war we heard a good deal about homes for heroes, and we are now hearing a good deal about the New Jerusalem which is to be built after the war. I do not think that this country is likely to stand a second disappointment.[29]

Here then was public announcement of the scale of the post-war housing problem and the reasons for its occurrence. Some discussion of the use of temporary buildings, apart from the provisions of hutments to relieve the housing problems of transferred labour, also ensued. Earl Winterton suggested that local authorities should be compelled to put up temporary wooden buildings as people were living in overcrowded and substandard housing. He suggested that the country look to the American tradition of timber building to see the high standards of comfort that could be achieved.[30] He failed to mention the shortage of timber that was already leading local authorities to experiment with other replacement materials such as concrete for floors, roofs and stairs,[31] or the work of the Directorate for Economy of Design on Timber which was developing simplified roof trusses, plywood huts etc. in an effort to use what timber there was most effectively.[32]

In contrast. Sir J. Walker-Smith offered the following comment on temporary accommodation:

. . . such will be the urgent and clamant demand for houses after the war that we shall have to provide a considerable number of temporary houses . . . we may have to do it but we should keep the number to a minimum. They will have to be built to a common monotonous standard of design, by mass-production methods, with prefabrication.[33]

He goes on to cite his own experience with temporary houses after the First World War in Scotland when he was induced to sanction the building of a considerable number of houses, intended to last two years which had stayed up as slums for the next 20 years. The deterioration of temporary accommodation allowed to remain after its certified lifespan was a constant criticism levelled against the Temporary Housing Programme from this time onwards.

In conclusion the debate of May 1943 made two important revelations. The first was a public statement of the potentially critical position of housing provision after the war and the lack of any apparent government concern about this problem. As Sir G. Shakespeare commented, 'It would help if this House created public opinion and brought pressure to bear on the War Cabinet which is not showing that broad sympathy with housing that one expects from it.'[34] The second revelation was that some interim solution might be necessary to answer this problem as the building industry could not be geared up to produce the required number of houses immediately after the war. However, there was disagreement as to whether 'temporary' accommodation would be the ideal solution. Mr Silkin offered this comment, 'I hope that research will still continue in the direction of temporary dwellings. Probably the last word has not been said, though as far as present knowledge goes it is quite hopeless to expect any solution from that quarter.'[35]

The Minister of Health, Mr E. Brown, summarized the attitude of government at the end of the debate. He underlined the two housing problems of present and future provision but pointed out that since taking up office he had been more concerned with the immediate situation of providing air-raid shelters and dealing with those made homeless through bombing. He mentioned that he had reinstated the Central Housing Advisory Committee,[36] which had not met since the start of the war, and reported that this committee presided over a number of sub-committees, 'making reports on the issues we shall all have to face.'[37]

At this stage, therefore, two years before the war was to end, there was no positive assurance that anything like the Temporary Housing Programme would be initiated. A further ten months were to pass before Churchill's announcement of the bungalows (see Chapter 1), during which time a positive link had been found, and made public, between housing needs after the war and the necessity to use the nation's investment in industries tooled up for the war effort by diverting skills and plant towards a factory made peacetime product.

WHY 'TEMPORARY' BUNGALOWS?

However, why the factory made house was to be linked to the provision of 'temporary' accommodation is harder to determine. During the Reconstruction debate in the House of Lords in December 1943, Lord Barnby made the following remarks:

> It must be realised that the industrial mass production of houses by this prefabricated system, which can be brought about, for example, from the utilisation of the aircraft industry, can do something to help in the solution of the problem.
>
> There is the problem of whether such houses should be regarded as of a permanent or temporary character. That must depend upon the types, but as the volume of houses that is needed cannot be provided by ordinary methods, those which involve an admitted short-term life should be regarded as a war charge.[38]

He, therefore, hinted that the durability of the factory made product would depend upon the standard of housing offered to the general public. To be classed as 'temporary' the construction of the factory-produced house would have to be such that it would begin to decompose beyond an economic maintenance level once its design life had pass (a situation which on the whole did not happen with the individual temporary bungalow types, many of which are still in use today). Alternatively, the two-bedroom prefab might have acquired the 'temporary' label as, for families, two bedrooms had not been acceptable since Chadwick exposed the moral evils of overcrowding in his report of 1842. The two-bedroom prefab was, therefore, a temporary expedient for families until sufficient three-bedroom permanent accommodation had been constructed. The waste of resources, however, inherent in this approach did not pass unrecognized. 'It [speaking of the Portal bungalow] is also far too small for a family. The idea that it would be pulled down before the newly-married couple have a large family is a fantastically extravagant, if not an impossible one. The materials used to build the various types of the Portal bungalow can equally be used for semi-permanent and more spacious houses'.[39,40]

Additional support for the link between the temporary nature of the programme and the provision of reduced internal accommodation is given by the government's initiative for a programme of permanent prefabricated houses. Steel, the material of the original Portal bungalow, was used for permanent prefabricated houses, but these were generally of two storeys and with the conventional three bedrooms. A demonstration project was organized at Northolt under the aegis of the Building Research Station. The results were then assessed and recommendations for the systems to be used post-war were made.[41]

However, the accommodation provided by the two-bedroom bungalow, whether temporary or permanent, would not be substandard for the proportion of the population who did not need a third bedroom to accommodate children of a different sex. Overcrowding of existing housing was already accepted as a necessity of war time. It would seem reasonable, therefore, that the bungalows, if they were built with a normal life, could have provided temporarily for families and in the longer term for the newly married, married couples whose children had left home, the elderly and single people. The fact that the bungalows were a political gesture towards the victorious returning soldier, and to those newly married who hoped to pick up the threads of a normal life after the war, would not have stopped their alternative use at a later date for a section of the population for whom the accommodation would not have been substandard.

There appear, however, to be three other possible reasons for the factory produced bungalows to be given the label 'temporary': the technology used, the building unions, and finance. The first, and perhaps least important, reason for the temporary label was to make the new technology acceptable to the people. War time had produced drastic changes in both the organization of society and the technologies available to it. Normal caution in assimilating innovation and development was apparently disregarded during the emergency, making new products and methods of manufacture immediately available as the need arose. However, with this explosion of technology must be coupled the desire of the ordinary person for things to return to normal after the war. It was apparent that there were to be changes (the Beveridge Report of 1942 had assured that[42]) but permanent changes had to be seen as changes for the better. Housing was one area where traditional values had never been lost despite the experience of many of the population who had lived in prefabricated, factory produced huts and hostels. During a series of BBC discussions on housing which took plce in March 1944,[43] after Churchill's announcement of the emergency steel bungalow, the following exchange took place:

Mrs White: 'Will all the temporary houses be like huts?'

Chairman Slade: 'I don't know Mrs. White, does bungalow sound better?'[44]

The suggestion here is that the image of the factory produced, prefabricated or demountable accommodation was linked in the lay person's mind to what they already knew of the product. Since the proposed Portal bungalow under discussion bore more resemblence to hutting of this type than some of the later successful permanent prefabricated houses – (e.g. the British Iron and Steel Fabrication house designed by Gibberd (figures 5.1 and 5.2)) – the 'temporary' label remained to reassure the public that the Portal bungalow was not the only possible model for the house out of the factory but merely an interim solution that happened to use similar technology. The public would, therefore, be able to accept the new technology of the factory built house when permanent houses of this type were produced.

Figure 5.1. The British Iron and Steel Federation steel framed and partially clad house, designed for a sixty-year life and shown under construction at the Northolt demonstration site. (*Source*: Ministry of Works, 1944*c*)

Secondly, the label 'temporary' may have been used as an assurance to the traditional building trades and their unions. In light of the massive programme of house building that the government had promised after the war, most of which was to rely on traditional skills, this seems unnecessary. Nevertheless, the building trade unions were disturbed by the government referral to the factory made houses using non-building trade labour for their erection on site.[45] Attaching the 'temporary' label again ensured that the use of non-building trade labour was only for an emergency period. As Lord Portal had said in the Lords Housing Debate on 8 February 1944:

> Total prefabrication in fact means the production of something in a factory, the erection of which will require very little man-power on the site. That is the essential point with regard to temporary prefabricated houses, as the difficulty is obvious of obtaining necessary labour for permanent houses . . . after the war.[46]

Figure 5.2. British Iron and Steel Federation houses at Corby in the late 1980s.

This reinforces the point that the temporary nature of the programme was linked to a shortage of labour as traditional building skills were to be primarily directed to the permanent house building programme. Before the war there had been 1,000,000 employed in the building industry but this had been reduced to 387,000 during the war. The government was set to expand the industry to a level of 800,000 skilled personnel by the end of the first year after the war, through adult and apprentice training.[47] Thus the building unions were to be reassured that their skills would not be devalued by the introduction of the factory made house during this period by ensuring its 'temporary' nature.

The overriding reason, however, for a 'temporary' label being attached to the bungalows would seem to be linked to their method of finance. From the time of Churchill's initial announcement to the public it was the government which was to own the factory made bungalows which were to be licensed to the local authorities on the basis of housing need. The local authorities were to supply the sites and the infrastructure. In the history of public housing this was almost without exception the first time that central government had become housing providers. Since the 1890 Housing of the Working Classes Act which enabled local authorities to become owners of property, government money had been channelled into housing through subsidies to the local authorities who were the actual owners of the property. At times this subsidy could be massive, as with the Addison Act of 1919 where for local authority schemes approved by the Ministry a subsidy equivalent to all losses in excess of a penny rate was to come from central funds. Such housing was provided in response to the crisis after the

First World War when there was an estimated need for half a million new homes for the heroes returning from the war. With the shortage of labour and materials after the First World War and the consequent more than fourfold increase in the price of building a house, the huge demands made on the Treasury by this subsidy meant that the programme was severely curtailed. When it ceased in 1921 only 214,000 houses had been sanctioned. Later housing subsidies available to the local authorities never again reached the largesse of those administered under the Addison Act.[48]

The apparent failure of the Addision Act before the full programme of houses had been completed, albeit that the Act was concerned with the provision of permanent rather than temporary accommodation, may have made the government wary of again announcing a centrally funded programme of housing provision which they might be unable to fulfill. It would be far 'safer' to leave the provision of permanent housing in the hands of local authorities to whom blame could be transferred if permanent housing failed to appear and slums failed to be cleared. At the same time, the 55 years of local authority involvement in housing could not be ignored and if the government were to step in as a major owner of housing, even if in response to an emergency situation, the local authorities who owned the land could have been obstructive as they saw powers removed from them.

However, because the government was using the Temporary Housing Programme as an opportunity to direct both industry and housing provision it would not have been possible for it to relinquish total control of the factory made bungalow to the local authorities. It was essential that the bungalows were produced in the same way as, for instance, aircraft, with many different factories engaged in making parts for the whole, which were transported to storage depots from which final distribution occurred. Only in this way could the planned economies in production be achieved. All this pointed to central organization and control.

However, to avoid conflict with the local authorities and to underline their role as the owners of state subsidized housing, the label 'temporary' could be viewed as a convenient soubriquet for the government owned, emergency factory-made house.

THE FIRST EXHIBITION OF THE PORTAL BUNGALOW

The arrival of the Portal bungalow, which was given its first limited exhibition at the Tate Gallery in London, was first announced by Lord Portal in the House of Lords on 8 February 1944:

> . . . we shall have the first prototype [made by hand] ready at [the] end of April when it will be shown to the Minister of Health, the Secretary of State for Scotland, and others interested in this matter.[49]

Its mainly steel structure had been designed by the Ministry of Works with the assistance of the Building Research Station and, in particular, Dr Stradling and Mr Fitzmaurice. The architects were Mr C.J. Mole, the Ministry of Works architect[50] and Mr A.W. Kenyon, consulting architect. The bungalow was built by hand rather than by machine by the motor manufacturer Briggs Motor Bodies Ltd, Dagenham and the Pressed Steel Co. Ltd, Cowley.[51]

The bungalow (figure 5.3) was a rectangular shell which had been simply divided by a central wall under the ridge line, with subsidiary partitions formed of storage and plumbing units. The accommodation consisted of a living room of 145 ft^2, two bedrooms each of 125 ft^2, kitchen, bathroom, separate WC and shed all contained within a net floor area of 616 ft^2. The plan had been devised to minimize circulation space and, in this respect, follows the model of many of the US temporary or emergency houses, where bedrooms could open off a living room or kitchens open off a living space (figure 5.4). This arrangement was not one that was familiar to the British public. The Universal Plan of speculative builders between the wars had ensured that all rooms opened off a neutral circulation space of either hall or landing. An article in *Building* attempted to play down these unusual features by suggesting that, 'The living room and kitchen are "en suite" separated by a glazed screen in the centre of which is a glazed door.'[52]

The main feature of the plan, however, was not so much the basic standard of accommodation provided, as the level of equipment and built-in fitments that were included (figure 5.5). The partitions between the kitchen and the bedroom and the living room and bedroom were both

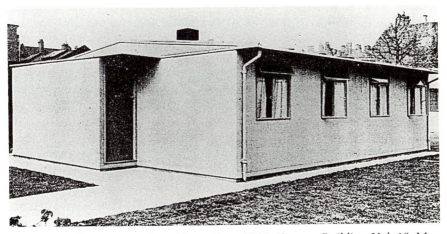

Figure 5.3. The prototype Portal bungalow, 1944. (*Source*: *Building*, Vol. 19, May, 1944)

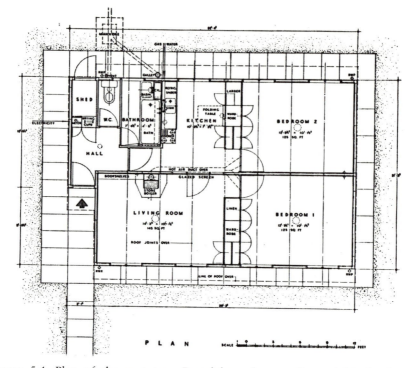

Figure 5.4. Plan of the prototype Portal bungalow as first exhibited. (*Source: Building*, Vol. 19, May, 1944)

arranged as deep cupboards. On the kitchen side these gave a larder with L-shaped horizontal shelves, the lower part of which was intended for the storage of dry goods and the upper part of which was ventilated to the outside and intended for perishable food. The second double-door cupboard in the kitchen was for crockery, brooms and other portable kitchen equipment and between these two cupboards was a folding table. On the kitchen side all the cupboards were made of steel. The second bedroom side of this deep partition took the form of a deep, full-height wardrobe with hanging rail and another shallower cupboard with shelves for storing folded clothes. On the bedroom side of this unit the doors had plywood panels but all the framing and shelving was in steel. All the cupboard partitions between the living room and the main bedroom were in steel with plywood panels to the fronts. In the living room a shallow china cupboard with shelves and three drawers at the base was provided and on the bedroom side was a duplicate of the wardrobe and shelved cupboard of the second bedroom with the addition of another deep

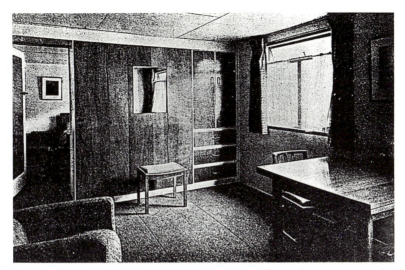

Figure 5.5. View of the living room of the Portal bungalow prototype looking through to bedroom one, 1944. (*Source*: *Architects' Journal*, 11 May, 1944)

cupboard designed to store clean linen on shelves in the top half and soiled linen in the bottom. The living room had additional built-in bookshelves.

The astonishing number of built-in fittings for a local authority rented house was only surpassed by the level of equipment provided in the prototype prefabricated bathroom/kitchen unit. On the kitchen side were a cooker, sink and refrigerator built into a steel unit with doors and there was a further drawer beside the sink and pot and plate racks above. On the bathroom side was full-size bath with a separate washbasin and space for a combined clothes washing boiler (this was not ready for the prototype) all built into the steel unit, and there was even a steel towel rail provided above the bath. All the plumbing was situated in the central area of this prefabricated service unit, together with the hot water cylinder. The hot water was to be heated by a solid fuel back boiler in the living room stove in winter and by an electric immersion heater during the summer months, the switch for which was mounted on the kitchen side of the panel. The living room fire also provided hot air to the bedrooms which was directed through two steel ducts. The WC did not form part of the heart unit but was provided separately, tapping into a cold water feed. Opening off the hallway was a drying cupboard and a cupboard for the electricity meter. (The gas meter was combined with the heart unit and positioned under the sink.) These cupboards backed on to a shed with a rack for storing a bicycle, this shed having a door opening on to the garden side. In the original prototype there was no door opening from the kitchen to the outside.

Thus, the first major piece of public post-war housing showed a considerable increase in the level of the detailed design of the interior spaces. There are several possible reasons to account for this change. The first reflects the study of American houses that preceded the programme of factory made houses in Britain. The demountable and other emergency house types that had been developed in the United States were often equipped with a heart unit similar to that of the Portal bungalow. Such houses also contained built-in cupboards and kitchens. A second possible reason is enshrined in the government title for the Portal bungalow, i.e. the Emergency Factory Made House. Because the bungalows were to be factory produced and designed for the minimum number of skilled on-site man hours, the opportunity existed to rethink the way that fittings were made and put into a building. As Gloag said in 1946, 'The putting on or fitting in of plumbing and services are incompatible with the basic idea of factory-made houses.'[53] It would seem to be more appropriate for mass-production if a partition wall of cupboards could become a standardized item in the place of the bricklayer putting up a partition, which is then plastered and on which the joiner afterwards constructs a cupboard. The opportunity given by Lord Portal as Minister of Works and sanctioned by the War Cabinet, to go ahead with the Emergency Factory Made House gave designers the chance to rethink such traditional methods.

The increased level of equipment in the Portal bungalow can also be related to a need to provide continuing employment for industries and workers no longer required for the war effort by steering industry to produce new products. In the Housing Debate in the Lords where Lord Portal announced the ideas for the prototype bungalow, Lord Barnby raised the argument that the production of new homes in this way would lead to a demand for consumer products which would again mean more production and more jobs.[54] Obviously the revolutionary step of putting a refrigerator in each emergency house as standard would lead to a further demand for such equipment when the family moved to their new permanent house. Thus it would be possible to stimulate a national demand for a product that very few people had yet seen in ordinary housing.[55]

Finally, high levels of equipment within the Portal Bungalow can also be related to the raised expectations of the population. During the same debate Lord Addison, described the results of a survey of some 25,000 people who had been asked about the housing they would like to see:

> . . . the great majority, some 90%, I think wanted a house rather than a flat . . . They want them light, dry and warm . . . They want good washing facilities and cooking facilities, and they want something much better than they have had hitherto in the provision for keeping food . . . People want a shed in which they can keep things, a place for storing coal and a place for

hanging up wet coats when they come in out of the rain. They want somewhere to keep boots and odds and ends of that kind.[56]

To a great extent the Portal bungalow supplied all these wants, although what this ideal house might have looked like is glimpsed in a contemporary *Punch* cartoon which shows a conventional brick built three-bedroom house arriving by stork (figure 5.6). In contrast, the Portal bungalow appeared as the hut made of steel, which, of course, it was. The way in which the steel frame and panels of the bungalow had been designed meant the structure was unable to offer any flexibility in planning and appearance. (Special provision had to be made within the floor panel structures to receive the partition walls and partitioning cupboards etc.) From the beginning it appears that the Portal bungalow was regarded as a 'unique solution', albeit well designed, but one that was incapable of alteration. There is a link between this approach and the contemporary Utility system, where in areas like clothing and furniture the government permitted the manufacture of a very limited range, but great care was taken to see that good designers were used for each of the products. From

Figure 5.6. 'Pre-fabricated houses are now in the air.' (*Source: Punch*, 16 February, 1944)

the inception Churchill had, in his announcement of the bungalows to the public, apparently seen them as a further Utility product since thousands of them were to be produced, all the same, and all of steel. No thought was given to possible alternative plan formations within the same prefabricated system, despite the fact that local authorities were encouraged in laying out the bungalows on the ground to face all living rooms towards the south to receive some sun.[57] The fact that there was any variety given to the bungalows at all through the number of different types sanctioned under the scheme happened more because of the demise of the increasingly expensive Portal bungalow than by design.

THE COST OF THE PORTAL BUNGALOW

At the time the prototype bungalow was exhibited at the Tate Gallery its estimated cost if it were to be put into mass-production was £550. This price was as, 'manufactured, delivered and erected with the necessary services of water, drainage, gas and electricity laid on.'[58] This figure did not include land costs but did include the cost of the concrete slab or concrete piers to support the prefabricated floor. In parliament Lord Portal announced that the total house contained approximately 5 tons of steel and another half ton of timber, mostly in the floor. The estimated cost included an £80 allowance for the cupboard and heart units and Lord Portal compared the total cost with the cost of purchasing the materials for a traditionally constructed brick house which he stated to be £510 at that time.[59] The Portal bungalow was not, therefore, a substantially cheaper alternative to a conventional house. As Lord Portal said in the same debate:

> . . . the whole object of erecting these emergency houses is to make a substantial contribution to the interregnum period, using as little site labour as possible, to enable our labour force to build itself up for the permanent building programme.[60]

In June 1943 Lord Portal had already put the increase in general building costs for housing over pre-war prices as high as 105 per cent.[61] However, given pre-war costs it seems hard to justify an estimated price as low as £550 even though factory production was supposed to reduce labour costs. Cullingworth[62] gives the average costs of three-bedroom local authority houses (including out buildings) for this period as follows:

1938–39	average area: 800 ft^2	average cost: £380
1947	average area: 1029 ft^2	average cost: £1242

This would give an average pre-war price per square foot for housing of £0.475 and a post-war price of £1.21. An increase in building prices of 105 per cent would give a mid-war price per square foot of £0.97 which would suggest that the price for a 617 ft^2 house of traditional construction would be £598.50. However, an extrapolation of Cullingworth's figures would suggest a mid-war price of nearer £750 per dwelling. Although the Portal bungalow is smaller than the traditional three-bedroom house, a smaller house does not necessarily produce a proportional reduction in costs. Moreover, the materials used for the Portal bungalow were unconventional. However, if Lord Portal's figures suggested that the Portal bungalow would be marginally cheaper than a conventional house, then the actual cost of conventional building would suggest that this estimate of £550 per bungalow was too low. This can be confirmed from the eventual costs of the programme, as the bungalows erected cost more than double this initial estimate (see Chapter 6).

CRITICISM OF THE PORTAL PROTOTYPE

Criticism was certainly forthcoming both from the public and from professional observers during the two periods that the prototype bungalow was exhibited.[63] For a while the design and building industry press was full of descriptions and responses to the Portal bungalow. Such criticism manifested itself in the names people gave the prototype: 'The Churchill Steel House' (since Churchill had announced it to the public), 'Tin Lizzie II', 'Portal's Priorities' (Lord Addison), 'Heartbreak House' (George Bernard Shaw) and, 'as one present at the pre-view called it the Damn Tin Can'.[64] As a name, history has preferred the Portal bungalow or Portal house.[65] However, any product that spawned this degree of immediate response ranging from horror to affection was probably bound to be taken to the nation's heart.

Response and criticism were broadly directed at three levels; the need for any emergency factory made house at all; the planning of the Portal bungalow; and the construction and prefabrication methods used. These will be considered separately although there may be some overlap between the subject areas in quoted contemporary comments.

Was the Emergency Factory Made House Necessary?

The critics of the emergency house programme were, in general, supportive of pressing ahead as fast as possible with building permanent houses in the immediate post-war period. The Portal bungalow was seen as a time wasting use of resources, both labour and materials, particularly since the accommodation provided was sub-standard for families compared with the average three-bedroom house. Moreover, the cost of the bungalow was such that it could not be let at an economic rent whereas a permanent house could be. In general, such critics held the view that the nation would be happier waiting for a 'proper' house rather than taking up temporary residence in one of 'Portal's Priorities'. A letter from H.B. Creswell to the Editor of *The Architect and Building News* offers a sample of such disapprobation:

> Although every one of the many persons whose opinions I have canvassed – including the high and the lowly and the technically informed – have agreed with my view of the disaster threatened by the Portal house; yet the great Dailies, the Popular Press, and the responsible Ministers of State – in person – whom I have with great expenditure of time, ingenuity and nerve-tissue, made acquainted with the enormity of the proposal, everywhere met me with a cold, rigid, immovable, voiceless obstruction which I can only compare to that of dead elephants. The one thing left is for me to put on skirts and lipstick, padlock myself to the railings in Whitehall and scream. This I do not propose to do . . .[66]

Most people, however, were aware of why temporary accommodation was necessary and rather than chain themselves to the railings were prepared, albeit reluctantly, to put up with what the government was offering. As L.H. Keay, Liverpool City Architect and Housing Director commented:

> I hate them [temporary houses], just as much as most people do, because I believe in providing the best possible homes for people who deserve them but we'll get the good homes more quickly by putting up some temporary buildings and that's my reason for suggesting them.[67]

Keay's argument was that the temporary housing programme would free all possible skilled building labour for the permanent housing programme, labour which might otherwise be engaged in some immediate makeshift arrangement to solve the housing crisis. At least the temporary housing programme would be a planned focus for this emergency activity and the country would be seen to be acting to alleviate the crisis whilst the building industry gathered itself and began the task of providing proper housing for the people. Keay, in the same broadcast, goes on to make the point that the temporary house was to be seen as a stop gap and, 'if there's any chance of the temporary accommodation being occupied for five years to ten years by the same family, I'm dead against it.'[68] He went on to suggest that if the temporary bungalows were to be put up in areas that were to be redeveloped permanently then they should be sited on land needed for road widening or for public open space so that they would be automatically removed as redevelopment occurred. It was further suggested that if the buildings were to be truly demountable then, as people were moved into their new homes which they had watched being built around them, the temporary bungalows could be taken down and moved and re-erected for the same purpose in some other city or town.

Other contemporary observers, however, proposed different solutions for ensuring that the houses did not remain beyond their declared life of ten to fifteen years, such as the incorporation of a time bomb (see Chapter 1). Other critics were quick to point out the problem of moving families on after only a short period in *any* new accommodation: people make friends, build ties in communities and might not wish to be sent to a new permanent home, miles away. Some designers recognized this problem and a solution was proposed by Walter Segal. He suggested that the Portal bungalows be sited parallel to terraces of proposed permanent houses, the gardens of which could be allotted to those renting the temporary accommodation. The occupier would thus be able to make a home in a permanent neighbourhood, watch his new permanent house being built and, 'work his garden in the knowledge that when the time came for him to move from his Portal to his permanent house, the garden would still be his and where he wanted it.'[69]

Such a constructive proposal was, however, rare. Most critics saw temporary housing as a necessary evil. As the editor of *Building* wrote:

> It seems useless kicking against the pricks. The Government has decided that about half a million houses must be quickly built, so that returning soldiers shall have homes at the earliest possible date, and the Churchill Steel House seems to be the most rapid method of meeting this demand, without interfering with the skilled traditional labour required for the permanent post-war building.[70]

Problems with the Plan

If the Portal bungalow was a necessary evil then many of the observers were keen to demonstrate how the initial prototype might be improved. Such advice was often directed to the internal layout. Probably the most gentle criticism is contained in a letter from M.H. Baillie-Scott, the Art and Crafts Movement architect, published in *The Builder*:

> Sir – I have been spending my declining years in an old farmhouse only reminded of what is happening in the building world by a friend who occasionally sends me one of the building papers showing me the latest examples of the degradation of the building art.
> With some noble exceptions these so-called modern houses have usually enormous windows which afford the rooms little protection from external conditions. There is usually an enormous window on the staircase where little light is required. The garage doors are the most prominent feature, suggesting that the most important thing in the house is the means of escape from it, while the inevitable flat roof combined with large glass areas still further fail to protect the house from the weather, with which the radiators are engaged in a losing battle. The building is 'streamlined', although it is à static structure, and so it becomes hideous and a blot in the landscape, largely because it is practically unsound.
> When, then I was sent the plans of the emergency one-storey prefabricated

house I was most agreeably surprised to find it had none of the faults I have referred to and had been planned with sound common-sense. Windows were of a reasonable size, roof was sloping, and great ingenuity had been displayed in all its fittings.

The plumbing is compact and there should be little risk of the annual tragedy of burst pipes, and everywhere one sees evidence of thought and skill. The acid test of such a building is whether one would like to live in it oneself, and that I would most willingly do. I should miss for a time the fire of wood or coal, but with my few pieces of old furniture the somewhat mechanical atmosphere of this machine to live in could be neutralised and humanised.

Then with plenty of books and some favourite pictures I should be well satisfied, and so, after the war, if I am still living, if anyone will let me one of these emergency dwellings I will be glad to occupy it.

The only fault I can see in the plan of the emergency house is that the only approach to the living-room is *via* the kitchen, but this can be easily remedied by a glazed screen with doorway to the so-called kitchen.[71]

Not all critics of the plan were, however, so mild though as one observer pointed out, 'There is no ideal plan for the small house, particularly in so small an area as 616 sq ft. There is only a balance of advantage and disadvantage.'[72] Most attempts at replanning centred around the problem of circulation discussed by Baillie-Scott above. There was little discussion of the choice of the rectangular form or the level of accommodation provided, although an article in *Building* which assessed various alternative planning proposals for the prefab that had appeared in the professional press suggested that:

> there are planned 500,000 of the Emergency Houses, and while everything speaks in favour of mass production as envisaged, the proposed quantity should be large enough to be split into two or three types of varying size without any danger to the economy of the selected method of production. Thus the general building programme of these houses might provide for say two groups, one with an accommodation of three rooms and the other with four. The same jigs and tools might be utilised throughout wherever this would be practicable.[73]

This idea was never taken up and the spirit of Utility prevailed. The task for both the actual and putative bungalow designers became the best possible arrangement of spaces within the given envelope. It was noted, however, that the existing envelope had its own problems. The service connections were at the 'back' of the dwelling or rather at the side opposite to the road frontage. A reversal of this would immediately save on site costs. Moreover, the wide frontage of 32 ft was itself a potential problem if the temporary bungalows were to be sited on land that was eventually intended for permanent housing. A traditional brick terraced house might have a minimum frontage of 16 ft,[74] so that it might just be possible to build two permanent houses on the one bungalow site. This meant that the bungalows would be expensive on land, road and service run costs unless

the local authorities could reuse these when permanent building commenced. Indeed, of all the prefab types, only the Uni-Seco had the option
of a narrow frontage even though this would appear to be a more
economical starting point for any prefab designer.

In Liverpool, L.H. Keay had used such a starting point for the design of
an emergency semi-detached bungalow. The plans provided a floor area of
635 ft^2 with an 18 ft frontage and the bungalows were intended as a
replacement for dwellings destroyed by enemy action in the high-density
areas of the city, where many of the houses had frontages of less than 16 ft
and few were greater than 20 ft.[75] The accommodation supplied was
similar to that of the Portal bungalow but failed to make use of the Ministry
of Works prefabricated plumbing and heating unit or the built-in
cupboards. The plan arrangement also produced a very narrow living
room. A prototype of the 18 ft bungalow was built in Liverpool by the
Housing Committee but despite seeking the sanction of the Ministry of
Health to build a quantity of these bungalows in Liverpool none was
authorized under the Temporary Housing Programme.

The majority of improvements to the plan and circulation of the Portal
bungalow (of which sixteen suggestions appeared at one time in the
construction press[76]) kept the rectangular envelope but transferred the
main entrance from the narrow side to the front elevation. Since this could
be assumed to face on to the street, the rooms could be economically
arranged around a small central entrance hall. The serviced rooms were
then grouped centrally, opposite to the front door. A second group of
critics grouped these service rooms against the front elevation, thereby
reducing connection costs, again providing a central entrance. This
arrangement had the advantage of shielding the WC from the direct view
of a person standing in the front doorway (a further criticism of the original
Portal bungalow plan). This revision can be seen in H.B. Cresswell's plan
and also that proposed by Walter Segal (figure 5.7). Neither of these plans

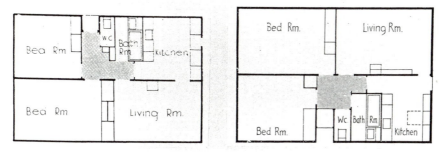

Figure 5.7. Suggested revisions to the Portal plan as proposed by H.B. Cresswell
(left) and Walter Segal (right). (*Source: Building,* July, 1944)

has the projecting porch at the side and Segal claimed that his revised and improved plan was 11 ft^2 less than that of the Portal prototype. Both of these revised plans are very similar to the plan used in the production version of the Arcon bungalow.

A third group of critics took the Portal bungalow and added a central lobby so that the bedroom no longer opened off the living room. An example of this type is the plan proposed by the Association of Building Technicians. This plan also featured a main door on the long elevation while maintaining the original door at the side as a back entrance.

As well as private critics, some local authorities responded to what they saw as the deficiencies of the Portal prototype. Possibly these same local authorities saw the imposition of a housing solution from central government as a threat to their autonomy as local housing providers. Along with the Liverpool suggestions discussed earlier, the Leeds Housing Committee attempted to devise its own temporary bungalow. At Leeds R.A.H. Livett, Housing Director (and architect of the pre-war Quarry Hill flats) put forward a proposal complete with a bay window. He made use of the Ministry of Works heart unit, and the Leeds bungalow had an overall area of 665 ft^2 compared with the 623 ft^2 of the complete Portal plan. None of these local authority suggestions met with any success when forwarded as alternatives to the Ministry of Health.

The original Portal plan was, however, revised in the light of the criticisms received. The revised version was exhibited in the autumn of 1944 (figure 5.8) alongside the three other alternative emergency houses; the Arcon; the Uni-Seco; and the Tarran. The revised Portal plan did not improve the circulation as the critics had suggested. Rather, it was based on a more compact services lay-out. The shed was removed from the overall envelope to become a separate structure, giving an enlarged hall which had room to store a pram. The living room opened off this hall. The WC had been screened from the front door by turning it and the kitchen had been increased in size and had a back door to the garden, although the kitchen was still to be entered from the living room. The bedrooms were not changed. The kitchen and bathroom combined plumbing and heating unit was altered by backing the stove in the living room directly on to the unit, thereby reducing pipe runs and making the stove part of the prefabricated package. This change was made possible by the altered hall. The warm air ducts to the bedrooms remained.

The alteration also made it possible to have two extra cupboards in the kitchen with a 'table-top' or worktop over them. The wash-boiler, or copper, was now incorporated next to the sink in the kitchen rather than under the bathroom basin and was designed to have a wringer attached, used in conjunction with the kitchen sink. An extra cupboard and a towel rail were provided above the refrigerator as the hot water cylinder had

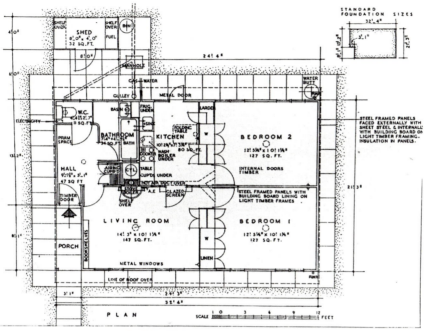

PRESSED STEEL BUNGALOW

Figure 5.8. Revised plan of the Portal bungalow exhibited in autumn 1944. (*Source*: Ministry of Health/Ministry of Works, 1944*a*)

been moved nearer the boiler. The cupboard containing the vegetable racks was moved away from the cooker as this proximity had been criticized in the original lay-out. The revised kitchen, in addition to a door to the outside, had a separate window with an opening vent so that it could be ventilated without having the back door open.

Other changes that were made in response to comment and criticism included the redesign of the porch so that it became an extension of the main roof supported on a post at the outer corner; ventilators were provided over each window; internal doors were of wood instead of steel; and the height from floor to ceiling was raised by 6 inches to give a 7 ft 6 in ceiling height. Even this modification was not sufficient to please the Manchester Housing Committee who wanted an 8 ft floor to ceiling height, 'always regarded as a minimum in Manchester'.[77] However, this latter criticism probably underlines the distrust of the local authorities of what they regarded as central government interference in housing provision. While no-one appeared to be whole-heartedly in favour of either the revised or original Portal plans, the level of service provision was praised:

Mr. J. Westwood, M.P., has told a Glasgow Labour Party housing conference that the kitchen unit in the new 'temporary' dwelling would be the envy of four-fifths of the women in Scotland, and he added . . . that once the standard of equipment for temporary houses had been set, no Local Authority would dare to put inferior equipment into permanent houses.[78]

The evidence of the recommended levels of servicing in the Ministry of Health's Housing Manuals of 1944 and 1949 would underline the truth of this speculation.[79]

The Methods of Construction and Prefabrication

In its radical departure from traditional methods of construction the Portal bungalow engendered little criticism. With little direct experience of the technology involved most observers simply accepted the approach that had been taken and the materials used. However, one critic felt that the floor construction with its mixture of wood and steel on a slab was halfway between a suspended floor and a solid floor and that, 'It would seem a sounder policy either to accept a floor finish direct on to the site concrete or alternatively to design a floor suspended on point supports only and thus limit site levelling difficulties.'[80]

The fact that the prototype bungalow had been primarily made in a car factory produced comment. Some were worried that the building trade might seek to obstruct its production, though others felt that traditional methods would be unable to rival the production promises:

Concurrently, we have Mr. Luke Fawcett, General Secretary of the Amalgamated Union of Building Trade Workers, declaring that 'we can build to the highest standards all the houses required – and that as speedily as the wretched substitutes boosted with so much ballyhoo.' Everyone will be united in wishing that this might be possible, but the experiences following the last war, when difficulties were less, cast doubt upon such optimism, and the estimated production of 'Portal houses' at 2800 per week will take some equalling if traditional methods are to be relied upon.[81]

However, the building industry was probably more concerned with the implications of the permanent housing programme rather than those of the temporary proposals. The government was talking of 300,000 houses per year once the war in Europe was over. Worries were centred around the potential 'boom and bust' in the building industry which would have to expand rapidly to meet this demand but without any promise of permanent continuing employment once the targets had been achieved. In addition, the unions were concerned that rapid training courses would be given in trade skills to those returning from the services to meet this demand in labour, thereby negating the apprenticeship system. Against these worries the temporary housing programme, limited in time and number, was almost an irrelevance.[82]

Only one editorial took the construction method to its obvious literal conclusion:

I hear that these houses are not being made by building contractors, but by a well-known firm of motor-car body builders. It is not generally known that each house is to be equipped with a jet-propulsion gadget by means of which it will be transported with great rapidity from factory to site. Neither is it realised, as much as it should be, that the windows are to be of the motor-car wind-screen pattern, complete with wipers. In the passage-like halls of these houses is to be mounted a dashboard panel bearing upon its Bakelite face a variety of dials and gauges. These will inform the lucky tenant of the pressure in the WC cistern ball valves, the depth of water in the roof storage tanks, and whether the gas is turned off at the mains before he leaves on his annual holiday.[83]

The Portal bungalow was exhibited in order to be criticized. This, in itself, was a fundamental change in the level of public involvement in housing production. As a result, some modifications were made to the original but the fundamental approach to the design remained, that of a single mass-produced product to meet the needs of all the people. For a nation still at war the Portal bungalow also had the value of providing a novel solution to a shortage of decent housing that had existed before the war but had been exacerbated by it. The fact that the Portal bungalow was a novel solution to the problem of housing should not be under-estimated. The war was going to change society; Beveridge had assured the nation of this. The Portal prototype was at last firm evidence of a new approach to solving old problems. To a nation that was mass-producing aeroplanes of advanced design the house mass-produced in the factory would seem a reasonable concept. That each Portal bungalow was to look identical to its neighbour hardly mattered; those who worked in factories understood that the mass-production of tanks and aeroplanes meant exactly that. They could, after all, be painted different colours and the bungalows were to have gardens that could be made individual. Here was, finally, something tangible that fulfilled the promises government had made about the post-war future and that was different from what had existed before. Only a few members of the architectural profession were to see the Portal bungalow as a chance missed; a chance for prefabrication and mass-production to provide a system of house building that would give individuality and flexibility at reduced cost in both materials and skilled labour.

The Churchill Steel House is a revolution in building technique forced to fruition under the glass roof of politics. In itself, the new technique is an achievement pregnant with possibilities and capable of being controlled to the benefit of mankind. The nation demands that houses be quickly built to house the home-hungry when the war ends. The fact that this new technique may be detrimental to the interests of architects, craftsmen, and builders, and that the country is about to be littered with these uniform steel houses, is not relatively important to frantic searchers for a home. But we think it is vital that this new technique should be developed and controlled by architects so that the results may be both more seemly and more economical to the nation. It can, for instance, be developed for the building of medium-life houses of varying materials and more diversified designs. If we seize it, there is at hand a newer and greater freedom; neglect it, and we are bound, for a generation at least, to the monotony of the machine.[84]

NOTES

1. Official Report House of Commons, 4 May 1943, Vol. 389, col. 81–82.

2. Bowley (1966), p. 364.

3. Ministry of Reconstruction (1945), p. 2.

4. Rowntree (1945), p. 14.

5. *Ibid.*, p. 35.

6. *Ibid.*, p. 51.

7. *Picture Post*, 1 January, 1944, pp. 22–23.

8. Simon (1945), p. 72.

9. At the start of the war Britain responded to the need to rehouse people for the war effort by a reduction in space standards, through more people sharing the same accommodation, and by a far better use of existing resources, through the requisitioning of empty or under-used properties. The normal standard to be observed in billeting was one person per habitable room. The Billeting Officer could also exercise judgement in cases of very large rooms where the standard could be exceeded. See Ministry of Health (1942), pp. 23–24.

10. Cullingworth (1975), p. 19. Cullingworth describes how nothing much happened towards reconstruction policy until Greenwood resigned the office of Minister without Portfolio on 3 March 1942 to be succeeded by Sir W. Jowitt as Paymaster General who was himself succeeded by Woolton as Minister of Reconstruction on 15 November 1943.

11. The Army Bureau of Current Affairs supplied booklets and lectures on topics that were thought to give the soldiers reasons for fighting. The post-war world, therefore, formed a favourite subject. Discussions would be led by an officer of the unit.

12. Cullingworth (1975), p. 42.

13. Ministry of Reconstruction, (1945), p. 2.

14. Bournville Village Trust (1941), p. 2.

15. White (1965), p. 121. White is summarizing the statement by the Minister of Reconstruction in Ministry of Reconstruction (1945).

16. *The Builder*, **162** January–June 1942, p. 388.

17. Hodson (1944), p. 190.

18. *Ibid.*, p. 300.

19. *Ibid.*, p. 16.

20. Official Report House of Lords, 11 November 1942, Vol. 125, col. 3.

21. Official Report House of Commons, 24 September 1943, Vol. 392, col. 558.

22. Kohan (1952), p. 377.

23. Official Report House of Lords, 11 November 1942, Vol. 125, col. 12.

24. Official Report House of Lords, 16 December 1942, Vol. 125, col. 600–601.

25. *Ibid.*, Col. 601.

26. Official Report House of Commons, 4 May 1943, Vol. 389, col 53.

27. *Ibid.*, col. 66–67.

28. *Ibid.*, col. 64–65.

29. *Ibid.*, col. 81–82.

30. *Ibid.*, col. 53.

31. For example, see housing at Canley Estate, Coventry in *The Builder* 2 January 1942, pp. 4–5. Also see, *The Architect and Building News*, 20 March, 1942, p. 209.

32. *The Architects' Journal*, 29 January, 1942, pp. 94–95.

33. Official Report House of Commons, 4 May 1943, Vol. 389, col. 83.

34. *Ibid.*, col. 70.

35. *Ibid.*, col. 119.

36. Members of the Central Housing Advisory Committee included Sir F. Freemantle (Conservative), Mr. Silkin (Labour), Miss Lloyd George (Liberal).

37. Official Report House of Commons, 4 May 1943, Vol. 389, col. 135.

38. Official Report House of Lords, 9 December 1943, Vol. 130, col. 240–241.

39. Rose (1947), p. 13.

40. Lord Portal made such a statement in The House of Lords: 'These houses are intended for the newly married primarily'. Official Report House of Lords, 1943–44, Vol. 131, col. 560.

41. Ministry of Works (1944*c*),

42. Beveridge (1942).

43. The broadcasts were later published as BBC nd. (1945)? *The Times* announced the twenty minute programmes, also called *Homes for All*, which were broadcast between Thursday 23 March and Tuesday 28 March on the Home Service.

44. BBC (1944), p. 39. Mrs. White was a serviceman's wife who was called in as an independent assessor of the housing situation and G.O. Slade was the chairman.
    Mrs. White – 'I'd like to be one of the women who are going to see the model and have their chance to express their views about it. They might do one or two up nicely for exhibition so that people can see what they look like'.
    Slade (chairman) – 'A very good idea Mrs. White and I hope the Government will adopt it.' Exhibitions of the bungalow were in fact arranged later in 1944.

45. The construction journals make reference to a possible boycott of the Temporary Housing Programme by the building trades unions, e.g. 'The Churchill House' *The Architect and Building News*, 12 May, 1944, p. 85. 'It [the Churchill House] seems to be a very good effort if it is not criticised as "building", and I hope the building operatives and their Unions will not seek to obstruct – as has been hinted.'

46. Official Report House of Lords, 1943–44, Vol. 130, col. 700.

47. Ministry of Reconstruction (1945), p. 2.

48. For a full explanation of the workings of the Addison Act see Swenarton (1981).

49. Official Report House of Lords, 1943–44, Vol. 130, col. 700.

50. C.J. Mole succeeded T.P. Bennett as Director of Works at the MOW at the end of June 1944. During the design period for the Portal Bungalow he was Deputy Director of Works. See *Architect and Building News*, 2 June, 1944, p. 132.

51. Kenyon was considering parallels between cars and housing before the war. At a talk given in 1934 he said '. . . after all small houses do not cost much more than a standard make of family motor car and not nearly so much as the higher class car, and they do not depreciate in value . . .' See: Harper (1987), p. 28. *The First Hundred Years of the Sheffield Society of Architects*.

52. 'The Churchill Steel House' *Building*, **19**, 1944, p. 122.

53. Gloag and Wornum (1946), p. 111.

54. Official Report House of Lords, 1943–44, Vol. 130, col. 714.

55. An ABCA discussion document listed the refrigerator as a luxury item, alongside motor cars, vacuum cleaners, silk stockings and double breasted suits. See ABCA (1943) *When the Lights Go On* No. 48, July 31st, 1943, p. 6

56. Official Report House of Lords, 1943–44, Vol. 130, col. 693.

57. Ministry of Health/Ministry of Works (1944a), p. 10 and p. 30.

58. Official Report House of Lords, 1943–44, Vol. 131, col. 565.

59. *Ibid.*, col. 558.

60. *Ibid.*, col. 565.

61. Official Report House of Lords, 1942–43, Vol. 127, col. 804.

62. Cullingworth (1966), p. 145.

63. The criticisms discussed here resulted from the exhibitions of the Portal bungalow in both May and October 1944.

64. Editorial in *Building*, May, 1944, p. 141.

65. For example the terminology used in White (1965), p. 139.

66. *The Architect and Building News*, 8 September, 1944, p. 152.

67. BBC (1944), p. 35.

68. *Ibid.*

69. *The Architect and Building News*, 8 September, 1944, p. 152.

70. 'Heartbreak House', *Building*, **19**, June, 1944, p. 141.

71. 'The M.O.W. Emergency House', *The Builder*, 4 August, 1944, p. 86.

72. 'Ministry of Works emergency factory-made house', *Architectural Design and Construction*, **XIV**, June, 1944, p. 126.

73. 'Plans for the Portal House', *Building*, **19** (7), July, 1944, pp. 178–179.

74. Suggested frontages for terraced and semi-detached houses in the *Housing Manual 1944* (Department of Heath, 1944) range from 16 ft 4 in for a 4-person 2-bed semi (p. 80) to 18 ft 1 in for a 5-person 3-bed semi (p. 78) to 25 ft 3½ in for a 5-person 3-bed terrace (p. 77).

75. 'Liverpool's Narrow Frontage Bungalow', *The Builder*, 9 March, 1945, p. 196.

76. 'Plans for the Portal House', *Building*, July, 1944, p. 179.

77. 'More critics of the Churchill-Portal House', *The Architect and Building News*, 2 June, 1944, p. 132.

78. *Ibid*.

79. Ministry of Health (1944, 1949). See, for example in the latter, 4–person (3-room) maisonette plan p. 91 and old person's bungalow, p. 74.

80. 'Emergency factory-made house', *Architectural Design and Construction*, **14**, June, 1944, p. 127.

81. 'Building Trade Workers and the Churchill-Portal House' *The Architect and Building News*, 2 June, 1944, p. 132.

82. BBC (1944), pp. 47–56.

83. 'Squinch', *Building*, **19** (5), 1944, p. 127.

84. 'Heartbreak house', *Building*, **19** (6), June, 1944, p. 141.

6

THE COSTS OF THE PROGRAMME

'The future of any non-traditional systems of house construction
will depend, however, on their success in competing in price
and on equal terms with traditional houses.'[1]

STARTING UP

When Lord Portal introduced the prototype bungalow to Parliament in the
Debate on Housing Provision in the House of Lords on 2 May 1944 he
estimated that a month would be required to assess the bungalow and to
sort out any improvements that might be made or even any economies that
might be effected. A further six months would then be required to tool up
for production. Allowing for the fact that the war effort had to come first,
Lord Portal estimated that once the resources became available it would
take a further three months to work up to a full production target of 2000–
2500 bungalows per week. He further stated that the Ministry of Health
was already dealing with the question of sites for the bungalows.[2] This
process had been initiated by Lord Portal and reported to Parliament
earlier in 1944:

> The Government have decided that in the late spring and early summer
> arrangements will be made for the use by local authorities of plant and
> machinery as they become available from airfield construction, for the
> preparation of housing sites, including roads and sewers and, where desired,
> electricity, water and gas services, sufficient for the maximum number of
> houses which can be built during the first two years after the war.[3]

The smooth path towards the mass-production of the Portal bungalows
was furthered by the Deputy Prime Minister (Mr. Attlee) towards the end
of July 1944 in the House of Commons. Following a review of suggestions
and criticisms of the prototype Portal bungalow during June, Attlee stated:

> The Government have approved the model of such a house . . . and are
> planning for large-scale production as soon as the necessary industrial
> capacity can be released from the war effort. The emergency houses will be
> purchased by the Government, and will be made available to local authorities
> to supplement their ordinary housing programmes.[4]

The final plan for the bungalow was the responsibility of the Ministry of
Health but the execution of the programme remained with the Ministry of

Works. The Temporary Accommodation Bill was introduced in the Commons on 19 July 1944,[5] and given a second reading on 1 August that same year.[6] However, the debate was adjourned to be resumed after the recess and the second reading was completed on 26 September 1944.[7] Royal assent was given on 10 October 1944.[8] By this time the original programme of half a million homes announced by Churchill had already been curtailed. On 22 September the Minister for Reconstruction reported to the Cabinet that little more than 150,000 of these dwellings could be provided without competing significantly for resources needed for permanent houses.[9] Publicly the Bill was to proceed through Parliament on a reduced target of 250,000 bungalows, all to be completed by 1 October 1947. The money set aside for the programme amounted to £150 million.[10]

During the Commons debate at the beginning of August it was obvious that alternatives to the all steel bungalow were under consideration. Mr. Willink, then Minister of Health, told the Commons that the Portal bungalow was a first design and, 'the possibility of adding to it [this first type] is being examined.'[11] Mr. Hicks (Joint Parliamentary Secretary to the Ministry of Works) was more explicit in reply to a written question stating that, 'Three definite proposals for an alternative type of emergency house, making use of other materials, are now being examined in detail by my Ministry.'[12] (These presumably were the Arcon, Uni-Seco and Tarran as they were to be exhibited in the autumn of 1944, alongside the revised Portal.)

During the same day's debate Mr. Willink also introduced the extent of the labour force necessary for the temporary bungalows and for permanent housing after the war. The target of 300,000 permanent houses was based on a labour force in the building industry of 350,000–380,000 persons, compared to a pre-war strength of 1,000,000. In contrast to this:

> I am advised by my Noble Friend the Minister of Works that whereas it takes 100,000 building operatives to build 100,000 houses in a year, the building labour required for 100,000 of these bungalows is not more than 8,000 to 10,000 . . . we have reason to think that something of the order of 100,000 of these bungalows can be produced within one year of going into production.[13]

A cost breakdown was also provided at this time. It included an additional £50 to cover improvements incorporated after the exhibition of the prototype. The breakdown was as follows:[14]

£100	services, erection and transport
£100	kitchen unit and cupboards
£400	carcase, roof, ceilings, partitions, lining material, doors, insulation, paint and other fittings
£600	TOTAL COST

Later in the debate Mr. Hicks broke this figure down further. He stated that £50 was the estimated cost for the provision of services and drainage to each bungalow, i.e. making the necessary connections on site (the local authority were to provide the actual roads and services to the bungalow sites). The built-in cupboards and the kitchen units, including the gas cooker and the refrigerator, were estimated at another £100. In addition, £175 was the cost of the *steel* in the carcase, roof and ceiling, walls and floor supports and the shed.[15]

The cost of the Portal bungalow was always a point of criticism both in this debate and in others that followed in both Houses. By then, however, the nation was expecting half a million temporary houses as a token of faith in the new life that was to follow the years of struggle of the war. There could be no thought of cancelling the programme and an 8 per cent increase over the original estimated cost was accepted even though some of this cost could be ascribed to inappropriate improvements, for example raising the headroom, which itself took the bungalow further away from the idea of 'temporary' sub-standard accommodation.

INTERVENTIONS BY THE GERMANS

In addition to the Temporary Housing Programme being seen as a means of providing a new peace-time product for the steel industry and, therefore, as a way of avoiding unemployment exacerbated by the demobilized armed forces, the Germans also provided a reason for the bungalow's continued survival. On 12 June 1944 the first V1[16] landed on London. These flying bombs were launched from the French coast and timed for their fuel to run out over London where they would drop unpredictably from the sky. Bombers had come in raids and then gone home but the flying bombs were an ever present menace through day and night. They caused a considerable amount of damage in London despite the concentration of coastal anti-aircraft units whose purpose it was to shoot them down as they came over. At their most successful the anti-aircraft guns shot down some 30 out of the 100 flying bombs daily sent over, but for many weeks most of the bombs found their target. The attack itself lasted for 80 days until the launching sites were overrun by Montgomery's army in September.[17] During this period out of 10,500 V1s launched, 2340 fell on London causing some 24,000 casualties. On 8 September 1944 the first V2 arrived.

> We heard this huge explosion and we thought a gasometer had been blown up . . . It transpired that it was the first rocket bomb dropped on London and it was utterly devastating. We hadn't got over the buzz bombs – they were still going strong – and now we had this to put up with. I'm awfully glad that we were just about winning the war at this point because there wouldn't have been very much of us left had it continued.[18]

The V2s, or rocket bombs, were more destructive of property than the V1s. Some 518 fell on London over the next six months, destroying 107,000 houses which represented accommodation for some 500,000 persons. In addition 170,000 houses were seriously damaged and a further 700,000 houses were in need of some repair.[19] Between September 1944 and the end of March 1945 when the attacks were stopped, the emergency housing situation in London caused by this bombing produced a new set of solutions. With the numbers made homeless rising and the winter approaching the government proposed a three part answer to the crisis:

(a) to requisition houses in the centre of London;
(b) to complete repairs to damaged property;
(c) to erect 10,000 temporary huts.

Lord Portal was to be in charge of the requisition of the huts which were to be put on sites supplied by the local authorities according to the needs in each of the boroughs. The huts were to be of two types: the Uni-Seco (figures 6.1 and 6.2) and the asbestos cement Nissen (figures 6.3 and 6.4). The huts were to be put only on cleared sites where drainage and other services were available and the proposal was to provide concrete slabs as

Figure 6.1. The Uni-Seco emergency hut, built in response to the damage caused by the V2 rocket bombs, under construction. (*Source*: The Builder, 22 September, 1944)

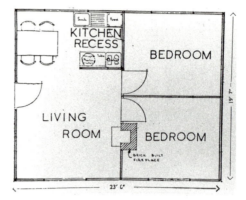

Figure 6.2. The Uni-Seco emergency hut, plan. (*Source*: *The Builder*, 22 September, 1994)

Figure 6.3. A group of emergency Nissen huts built in response to the damage caused by the V2 rocket bombs. (*Source*: *Building*, Vol 20, March, 1945)

bases for the huts which could ultimately be extended to take the Portal bungalows as these became available. The emergency huts had no bathrooms or WCs but were provided with services for a sink in a kitchen recess and a cooker and with a grate for burning solid fuel in the centre of the hut. Separate free-standing blocks were provided for a WC and fuel

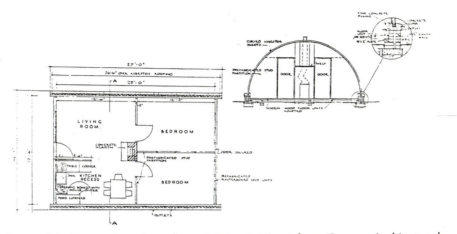

Figure 6.4. Plan and section of an emergency Nissen hut. (*Source: Architectural Design and Construction*, November, 1944)

store for each unit. Where possible all the sanitary fittings and cookers were supplied from salvage, but the local authorities were to be responsible for connecting the huts to the services and for the installation of suitable artificial lights and connecting the cookers.

The Uni-Seco hut was made of the standard Seco units already used in the hutting programme. These consisted of a light timber filled with wood wool and faced both sides with asbestos cement sheet. The Nissen hut was also constructed to the standard Nissen format of curved asbestos cement sheets anchored in a concrete kerb section sitting on a dwarf brick wall. Whereas the Seco panel system was in every way similar to the construction used for the Uni-Seco temporary bungalow as exhibited at the Tate Gallery, the Nissen system was never adapted for use in the Temporary Housing Programme despite its widespread use during the war and the durability of many Nissen huts since. In fact the dimensions of the Nissen hut (a gross external dimension of 19 ft 1 in × 27 ft 0 in) are not dissimilar to those of the revised Portal bungalow at 21 ft 3 in × 24 ft 4 in, and the Nissen format could have been stretched to meet these dimensions and provide a similar internal arrangement.

The most obvious reason that the Nissen hut was not used as the starting point for a prefabricated bungalow produced as part of the Temporary Housing Programme was its curved shape. The complexity of inserting windows into the curved roof/wall would place limitations on the internal arrangement, and in fact the Nissen emergency huts were only glazed within the brick gable ends. Another possible reason that the Nissen hut never became the Nissen bungalow may have been that its distinctive shape would have given it immediate associations with the war-time hutment programme, thereby looking back to the war rather than forward to the peace. Even though the temporary bungalows were an emergency response to housing shortage and the problem of finding a peace-time product for fully working factories, the bungalows had to embody a promise of the better future. They could not afford to look experimental and temporary even though both the public, parliament and those involved in their design and manufacture knew that they were. The earlier theories of Buckminster Fuller[20] might suggest that the curved or domed structure made efficient use of materials and manufacturing techniques to make it thereby a more appropriate form for the factory-made house, but the climate surrounding the temporary housing programme dictated that the detached house on its own plot, with a pitched roof and a traditional arrangement of rooms was essential, even in a factory-made building with a limited life-span.

The introduction of the Uni-Seco and Nissen huts as an answer to a real emergency housing need resulting from the V1 and V2 attacks could be seen as creating a further model for temporary emergency housing in this country. By this time, however, because the Temporary Housing Programme had been given form through the exhibition of the prototype and despite rising costs for the bungalow through the inclusion of suggested improvements, it was too late to question what the real emergency housing needs might be at the end of the war and how these might be met through a variety of solutions. To avoid confusion Mr. Lyttelton (Minister of Production) had to make it clear that the emergency huts were not temporary dwellings:

> He [Sir Malcolm Eve, executive controller of the agencies meeting the crisis] has a special appointment to deal with the problem created by the flying bomb. He is concerned with what really are huts. He is going to put up only 10,000 or 11,000 of them . . . They are to be erected at the Government's cost and are not to be regarded as any form of temporary houses. They are merely shelters particularly for this winter while we can get round to the matter of repairs . . . I expect that their utility will not extend beyond a year or 18 months.[21]

Nor could the programme be curtailed at a time when, in London, further damage to housing was so apparent. The factory-made temporary bungalow was what the nation was expecting and, despite continuing arguments in parliament as to the purpose and viability of the exercise, this was the house that was provided for the people. The arguments continued during the progress of the Bill through both the House of Commons and the House of Lords. Such arguments are probably best summarized by the following extracts from the criticism offered by Mr. Silkin during the Second Reading Debate in the Commons:

It [the Portal house] was sub-standard in a large number of respects . . . In the first place, both bedrooms lead out of either the living room or the kitchen. To get to one you have to go into the living room, then into the kitchen, and then into the bedroom. In order to go into the second, you go from the living room into the bedroom. All housing opinion will condemn leading into bedrooms out of kitchens. Moreover, the living room, of about 145 feet [ft^2], has three doors in it, one leading into the hall, one into the kitchen, and one into a bedroom. Obviously there must be draughts coming from these various doors. Then the house will suffer from condensation, from noise and from excessive heat in summer.

. . . the house will not stand up to rough weather. It may not outlast the ten years, especially if there are young healthy children in it. As to the height of the rooms, that is a defect, particularly in congested areas, and I imagine that the majority of the houses will be built in congested areas. A height of 7 feet 6 inches in the country is all right, but in towns it is bad. In London the minimum height is 8 feet 6 inches. Then there is a real danger of warping, and, where this happens, the cost of repair will be enormous. It will mean substituting the warped part by a new part. I take it that the vast majority of these houses will be of the two-bedroom type. No other types are at present available. The prospect of anything like 250,000 of these houses, all alike, scattered all over the country, fills me with horror . . . I am advised on high authority that these houses are particularly susceptible to vermin . . . Where are you going to put these houses? . . . Is he [Mr. Willink] going to recommend that these houses should be put on blitzed sites? If so these houses, by reason of their construction of one storey instead of the normal two, would take up twice as much space as the ordinary house. That is confirmed by the frontage of the house, which is 34 feet 6 inches against the normal frontage of 16 to 20 feet. As these houses cannot be put close together and do not lend themselves to terracing, but will have to be separated by some yards of air space and light, it follows that not more than half the number of houses can be put on a site as compared with permanent houses.

. . . it may well be 18 months to two years before we turn out these houses on any scale at all. Is it really worth while, for the sake of that amount of saving, to put up a temporary house which will last only a limited period and then have to be dismantled?[22]

Such criticism could not be answered. However, by then the Temporary Housing Programme had become an acknowledged part of post-war reconstruction thanks to the efforts of Lord Portal and the existence of the bungalow in a tangible form. As Mr. Hicks said, speaking in reply to the debate, 'Who had come forward with a house of comparable quality? If anyone had ideas let him come along with them.'[23] From this time on it was a question of what type of house and where and when, no longer whether such housing should be built at all.

PROGRESS OF THE TEMPORARY HOUSING PROGRAMME

Despite the fact that the original Housing (Temporary Accommodation) Bill was, 'designed to assist housing authorities in meeting the immediate shortage of housing accommodation by the speedy provision of temporary houses in large numbers,'[24] neither the numbers nor the speed were immediately apparent. The Act, when passed in October 1944, authorized the expenditure of £150 million on the programme. However, by 31 July 1945 only 1701 temporary houses appeared in the Housing Returns, a number that was to rise to 12,023 by 31 January 1946,[25] still well short of the 250,000 that were to be purchased by the £150 million set aside. Moreover, by this time the Portal bungalow had been abandoned and the problem of the cost of the units that had been built had become apparent.

At the time the Act was passed the steel bungalow was expected to cost £600. By 7 December 1944 the Minister of Works anticipated a problem with the steel bungalow as, 'actual production of the pressed-steel bungalow could not be proceeded with until the necessary labour and manufacturing capacity were released at the end of the war in Europe.'[26] By 23 February 1945, almost exactly a year after Churchill's private announcement to the Cabinet of the programme,[27] and 11 months after the public announcement, capacity could still not be released from munitions production and the government found that it had to proceed with the programme using 'less highly prefabricated types of houses,'[28] together with pushing on the construction of permanent houses. The programme rested on the Arcon, Uni-Seco and Tarran bungalows, but by this time it was apparent that there could be surplus capacity in the post-war aluminium industry and the Aircraft Industries Research Organisation for Housing had initiated work on the design of their factory-made aluminium bungalow.[29] A month later the costs were also acknowledged to have risen, with all types likely to exceed £800 per unit, apart from the proposed aluminium unit which was to cost about £900 'owing to the cost of fabrication in the factories.'[30] This was the first admission that complete houses from the factory might be more rather than less expensive. These cost estimates were to rise again almost immediately.

In another White Paper on housing in March 1945 the government's enthusiasm for the Temporary Housing Programme appeared to be waning. The programme was to continue with the rate of production dependent upon the supply of materials, labour and capacity, but after 1945 the production of temporary houses would depend upon the speed of construction of permanent homes. The target for numbers of temporary bungalows was, therefore, to be curtailed although it was recognized that temporary house production would fulfil the then current allocation of such accommodation to the local authorities, amounting to 145,000 units.[31]

Table 6.1. Costs to supply and erect the temporary bungalows, 1945.

	Earlier estimate £	Revised estimate £	Increase £
Arcon	816	1085	269
Uni-Seco	772	1020	248
Tarran	721	1000	279
Spooner	710	992	282
Universal	756	1135	379
Phoenix	935	1099	164
Aluminium	914	1365	Price still negotiable

When Labour took office in July 1945 a statement on the costs of the temporary bungalows was prepared. Table 6.1[32] represents the full costs including site preparation (but not the cost of the land, roads and sewers), supply and erection of the bungalows and the provision of the components and fittings. Additional bungalow types had been approved by this time (the Spooner, Universal and Phoenix[33]).

Some reasons for the increase in cost above the original estimates were analysed, Some 46 per cent was accounted for either by overlooked items or by over optimistic estimates, a situation that would not have received much sympathy in the conventional contracting building industry. Such items included increased costs per bungalow of £11 for abnormal site conditions, a figure that represented 1 per cent of the total bungalow cost. Such an increase did not pass without comment:

> Eleven pounds sterling for slightly more uneven ground! The facts of the matter, as known to everyone who has anything to do with these sites and by anyone who has watched progress being made, are that the procedure permitted is definitely slack and that men have worked in a way no ordinary builder on a private job would permit.[34]

A further £47 for site works was incurred both because higher standards of infrastructure were required[35] and because of the size of site used. Original estimates had been based on the assumption that the bungalows would be constructed in groups of 200 on the edges of towns to give an economical use of the infrastructure, whereas the actuality was that the average size of site, 'in the provinces is for 39 houses and in London 9'.[36] The need to clear the rubble left by bomb damage further boosted the site work costs. Such circumstances might well have been foreseen given the purpose of the temporary accommodation. The original estimate of the time required for the erection of the bungalows was also optimistic, and the cost of the actual time for erection added an extra £10 to the total. The type of labour required had also been wrongly represented in the original estimate of costs. Assumptions had been made that only local labour would be used with either a low expenditure on subsistence or none at all. In fact teams of mobile labour, such as had been used to repair bomb damaged houses, had to be used because local labour was not available. In consequence, contractors had to pay much higher subsistence rates, adding £21 to the costs. Since the temporary houses were to provide homes where there was a shortage of accommodation, labour in those localities might not be available having nowhere to live, and the use of a mobile labour force might have been anticipated. No allowance was originally added for breakages and losses, another item that might have been foreseen, though the addition of £15 per unit, or 1.5 per cent of the total cost, for breakages seems high. Finally, no allowance was ever made for the cost of administering the scheme and when the Ministry of Works Agency costs were added in the price rose by another £20, or 2 per cent of the total cost. Other cost increases might have been harder to predict because of the course of the war itself. When the working drawings were prepared modifications and improvements added to the cost, as did the need to change materials in response to shortages. Subcontracting of parts to smaller firms because the large firms were still engaged on war work added to the cost, these items together producing an increase of £96 for each type of bungalow. A further £25 increase was incurred because the fixtures and fittings had to be ordered from a large number of small firms so that the predicted cost reduction through economy of scale of production did not happen. In addition the contingency sum was raised to a figure that represented 5 per cent of the total, giving an additional cost of £23 per bungalow. Given that a contingency of 1.5 per cent already existed to cover breakages, it is hard to see exactly what the increased contingency sum was to cover. Perhaps the revised contingency was there to provide an excuse, however implausible, for the wide discrepancy between the estimates and the reality.

Although some cost increases might be attributable to the war, the rise in cost might also be attributed to the problems of putting any prefabricated house system into production. As a product for prefabrication a house is very complex and the record of unconventional housing has never suggested that such housing might be cheap. Following earlier experiments with non-conventional forms of house construction after World War I the following observation was made:

> In the issue of 26th April, 1920, in an article called *Hints to Inventors*, the writer said that many of the proposals put before the Ministry were more complex and costly than traditional methods using proved materials, although they claimed simplicity, economy and novelty. Such methods were generally approved if they were structurally acceptable, regardless of cost or

of the class of labour required. Inventors, said the writer, were proverbially optimistic and it was only when they came to prove the commercial advantages of a system that they found themselves unable to compete.[37]

Chief amongst the problems of the cost estimate of a factory produced system is the proportion of the cost represented by overheads. The building industry traditionally has existed and still does exist with low overheads. The builders of the Victorian cities that grew rapidly following industrialization, and even those of some of the mass house building of the inter-war period, had operated and made a profit with overheads that amounted to little more than a ladder, a bucket and a notebook. They built little at a time, selling as they built and using the money to finance the next house. With houses made totally or partially in the factory, the situation had to be different. In considering the cost of new methods of house construction after the war the Ministry of Works stated:

> The cost of site labour has been accurately established, and normal materials supplied to sites can be written in at their correct prices, but the difficulty arises with the special components and elements which characterise the new methods of construction . . . The main problem turns on the overhead charges; the factory labour, and the cost of the materials supplied to the factory can be estimated with some confidence. The overhead charges may vary enormously, depending on the rate of production and period of production over which they must be spread.[38]

The Temporary Housing Programme, representing a consistent and standardized house from the factory, incurred overheads very different from the conventionally constructed house against which it was measured. It may, therefore, not be surprising if the cost estimates varied widely from the actual practice at a time when war had just ended.

The Temporary Housing Programme had other problems with cost that emerged in 1945. The list of approved bungalow types had been further expanded to include a projected 30,000 units to be shipped in from the USA under the Lend-Lease agreement (see Chapter 3). The price of the American bungalow rose dramatically because of the cancellation of Lend-Lease in 1945. The bungalows were to have been supplied at a cost of £800 a unit, a price which included customs duty of £210 per bungalow. After the cancellation of Lend-Lease the full cost of £1330, including customs duty, was incurred, thereby making it more expensive than all prefab types except for the aluminium bungalow. The exchequer felt that this could not be afforded so only the 8150 houses already shipped or about to be shipped were accepted and the remaining order cancelled.[39] Since the full number of US bungalows had been included in the 165,000 units allocated to the local authorities, additional monies were needed for extra UK produced bungalows. The allocation was itself revised to 158,480 units at a cost 23 per cent above the original £150 million allocated to the programme,

Table 6.2. Temporary bungalow costs, 1945.

	Provisional number	Estimated cost/unit £	Total cost £
Arcon	40,000	1085	43,400,000
Uni-Seco	29,000	1020	29,580,000
Tarran	21,000	1000	21,000,000
Tarran	1,000	1074	1,074,000
Spooner	1,200	992	1,190,400
Universal	1,200	1135	1,362,000
Phoenix	2,430	1099	2,670,570
Aluminium	54,500	1365	74,392,500
USA	8,150	*	10,000,000*
			184,669,470

*The final cost depended on the results of discussion over the numbers supplied under Lend-Lease.

divided by house types as shown in table 6.2 (two Tarran types are included at differing costs).[40]

From this table it can be seen that the estimated cost of the temporary aluminium bungalow exceeded the cost limit of £1300 available for those building a two-storey house under licence (licences were required for private house building at this time and limits were given for both size of dwelling and costs).[40]

> A rather amusing side-light appears when it is remembered that the Minister of Health has announced no building of houses in the London area over £1,300; or in rural areas of over £1,200 – and yet the present price of the Temporary Aluminium House exceeds both these figures![41]

The slow progress made by the programme can be attributed to a number of reasons. The priority for the available building labour and materials was to provide as many homes for as many people as possible and even though the local authorities had been informed that, 'The use of temporary accommodation will . . make it possible approximately to double the number of dwellings which could otherwise be provided with the limited amount of skilled labour available in the first year after building can be resumed',[42] when the situation was reviewed afterwards it was found that during 1945 resources had been mainly concentrated upon the repair of war damaged buildings, thus limiting the amount of work that could be undertaken on the preparation of sites for permanent or temporary houses.[43] Set against the 12,023 temporary houses provided by 31 January 1946 are 99,123 additional units of accommodation supplied by the local authorities in the period between 31 March 1945 and 31 January 1946. Approximately 70 per cent of these latter units came from the repair of severely war damaged and unoccupied premises, a further 10 per cent from the conversion of existing premises, 16 per cent from the requisitioning of unoccupied houses for residential purposes and the remainder from the construction of temporary huts.[44] Thus, the resources of the depleted building industry were directed to the repair of existing units. This situation was to change over the next two years. During 1946 the provision of temporary accommodation more or less kept pace with the repair of war damaged dwellings, although by September 1947 the provision of permanent dwellings began to overtake both,[45] but by then the Temporary Housing Programme was drawing to its end.

The organization of the programme also worked against its speedy completion. As initially conceived the houses were meant to be produced in the factory using surplus capacity and labour and then sent from the factory to the site. Only the aluminium bungalow was constructed and organized in this fashion. The remainder of the bungalow types were less highly prefabricated and individual parts rather than sections of buildings were manufactured in the factory. This entailed a complex organization of demand, supply, allocation, storage, transport and erection to produce the finished house. Moreover, although the programme was run by the Ministry of Works, the Ministry of Supply was involved in a variety of roles from designating firms for production to providing vehicles for the transportation of the aluminium bungalow.[46] In addition the local authorities were responsible for the preparation of the sites and had to, 'Construct roads, sewers and electricity, gas and water services up to the point of junction with the house connections.'[47] They had also to furnish the Ministry of Works with all the information required about site levels, layout and finished floor level for each house, soil conditions, distance from local railway stations (to allow method of house delivery to be assessed) and a colour scheme for the external painting of doors and windows (the Ministry of Works supplied a restricted colour card). The site works were let to contractors on the basis of competitive tenders on a standard priced bill of quantities on which the contractors quoted percentage variations, either higher or lower depending on the site conditions, although a ceiling price existed for each type of house.[48]

The task of the Ministry of Works was complicated by the variety of contracts with manufacturers for the different types of house. Firms responsible for supplying few of the total number of bungalows, such as Orlit and Miller,[49] arranged the production of the basic structure of the house while the Ministry supplied separately fittings, including doors and windows, the kitchen and bathroom units (including refrigerator, wash-boiler, immersion heater and cooker and the cupboard units with their drawers and shelves).

For the Arcon bungalow the Ministry placed contracts for the component parts with a large number of firms, with the sponsoring firm, Arcon, being responsible for making sure that contracts were met, and thus acting as agents for the Ministry. The components were tendered for on a competitive basis except where it was not possible to obtain competitive tenders. Then the Ministry of Supply or the Board of Trade stepped in and designated a suitable firm. The order was then placed on the basis of a maximum price, but this was followed by a Ministry investigation of the actual cost of production on the basis of which a further price was negotiated. The manufacturers of the Uni-Seco, on the other hand, placed their own sub-contracts for component parts, initially at a negotiated fixed price for the first 6 months of manufacture. The future contract price was then set after a similar investigation of costs as for the Arcon. However, inducements to save were introduced: if the cost for the second or subsequent 6 month period of production was lower than that of the previous 6 months 40 per cent of the saving thus accrued was divided between the subcontractor and sponsoring firm in the ratio of 3 : 1, with the Ministry taking the remaining 60 per cent of the saving. This approach reduced the cost of the Uni-Seco structure minus fittings from £309 in 1945 to £284 by the end of the programme.[50] The Tarran bungalow was ordered through yet another system. Here the contracts were placed with two firms for the manufacture of the complete house structure with the windows. Payment was initially at prime cost plus profit for a fixed price of £330 after which a cost investigation lowered the price to £310 for each unit including the separate shed. Contracts for the other bungalow types tended to follow this model, the eventual price being agreed after investigation of the production process.

Although complex, the cost investigations tended to lower the price paid by the Ministry for the bungalow structures (in fact all the bungalows mentioned above dropped in price after investigation[51]). The complexity is also in some part due to the problems of the supply of materials as it was never possible to standardize exactly what was to be used in each house.[52] However, the aluminium bungalow did not follow a similar pattern of contracting. Although the roads and main services for all aluminium bungalows were still produced by the local authorities and the Ministry of Works produced the foundations, paths, fences and services from the roads to the houses, the Ministry of Supply contracted directly with ex-aircraft factories for the production of the bungalows:

> it was a question of making use of manufacturing capacity as it was released from aircraft work and the normal method of selection by competitive tender was not appropriate.[53]

This statement only serves to underline the fact that the Temporary Housing Programme was never seen as a way of providing a reasonable standard of housing for less cost, as so many advocates of prefabrication had claimed.[54] Instead it was to provide a diversion for the industries that had developed as a result of the war to ensure full employment through the difficult transition from war to peace. Of the five factories that produced the aluminium bungalow four were in fact owned by the government and one was mainly in private ownership.

Allocation of orders from the Ministry of Supply depended upon the capacity and location of the factory and the first batch of nearly three thousand bungalows was produced on a fixed cost plus profit basis. After this the prices for batches of bungalows were fixed in advance of manufacture although the costs rose, 'by the fact that aluminium has been employed in substitution for other materials on a larger scale than was originally contemplated.'[55,56] Overheads also rose because of the problems of maintaining factory production through the winter of 1946–47 and because sites could also not be prepared fast enough which slowed the production cycle down. The erection of the aluminium bungalows was also undertaken by designated contractors, three contractors for each of the five factories. The overall breakdown in costs of the aluminium bungalow, the most expensive and biggest contributor in numbers to the programme is shown in table 6.3.[57]

Table 6.3. Cost breakdown for the aluminium temporary bungalow.

Aluminium bungalow	Estimate 1945 £	Estimate 1947 £
1. Production		
(a) materials, fixtures and fittings	635	847
(b) factory fabrication and assembly	220	278
(c) other production costs	6	44
(d) factory plant and equipment	40	43
(e) contingency	89	24
2. Transport		
(a) vehicles, spares and repairs	18	25
(b) haulage	80	43
3. Erection	21	53
4. Maintenance	–	11
5. Contingency on 2, 3 and 4	12	4
6. Ministry of Supply expenses	20	25
Total	1141	1397
7. Ministry of Works expenditure	224	238
Total	1365	1635
8. Less residual value of assets	–	25
Total	1365	1610

The majority of the cost of the aluminium bungalow is contained in the materials and the work undertaken in the factory. As the bungalow was completely finished in four sections in the factory for delivery to site, this is not surprising. The higher costs for erection of the aluminium bungalows were attributed to a general reduction in numbers of bungalows on the sites, as mentioned earlier, and the consequent increase in the cost of the temporary roads required for the special haulage vehicles. However, for the other bungalow types the fact that components were not subcontracted and that the bungalows did not issue complete from the factory (the underlying tenet of the programme when originally announced) meant an increase in the complexity and cost of distribution.

To cope with the problem the Ministry of Works set up distribution centres where components were stored until required, made up into house sets and dispatched. The centres were run by managing contractors who also had responsibility for any necessary repairs to components. The original number of supply centres was based on two wrong assumptions, namely that the programme would be complete by the end of 1946 and that storage for 3 weeks supply of stocks was all that would be needed. Initially the local authorities were slow to complete site acquisition and development works so that sites were not handed over in any numbers until 1946. There were also problems with production of components:

> there was, up to the autumn of 1946, an unbalanced production of the many component parts, fixture and fitments that made up a complete house. Factories were changing over from war to peace-time production, labour was being redeployed, and there were continual production set-backs owing to shortage of materials and factory capacity.[58]

As a consequence storage of components under cover on airfields increased 'from 1,700,000 ft. to 2,700,000 ft.'[59] and since many of the airfields were far from railway stations, more expensive road haulage had to be used. Such an approach added to the complexity and costs of organization of the programme. The complexity can be seen in a map which shows the movement from factories supplying components for the Arcon Mark V hull to one of 33 distributions centres (figure 6.5). Moreover, breakages were more likely as, unlike the passage of the aluminium house from factory direct to site, the other temporary bungalows were shipped from factory to site in two phases. The Arcon Mark V required four lorries; one for the steel work; a second for the cladding; a third for internal partitions, floors and ceilings; and the fourth for the kitchen/bathroom unit, metal trim and other finishes.[60] Because the supply responsibilities were split between the Ministry of Works and the local authorities there was no impetus on the part of the local authorities to expedite site preparation. Eventually this was to lead to claims from contractors over 'delays by local authorities in making sites available,'[61]

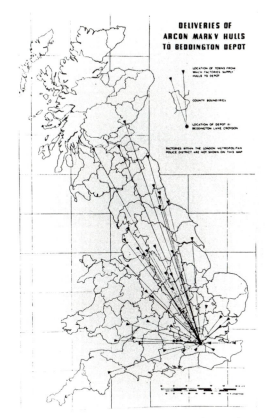

DELIVERIES OF
ARCON MARK V HULLS
TO BEDDINGTON DEPOT

Figure 6.5. Map showing location of factories outside London making hulls for the Arcon Mark V (*Source*: *Building*, May, 1948)

adding further to the overall cost of the programme. There is also evidence to suggest that the Ministry of Works took over some site preparation from the local authorities:

> Under arrangements agreed with the Treasury and the Health Departments in May 1945 the Ministry of Works, at the request of local authorities, may carry out the preparation of sites for both permanent and temporary houses and may also supply prisoner of war labour for the work.[62]

By the time the programme had been wound up, in place of the 250,000 for a price of £150 million some 156,623 bungalows were supplied at a cost of more than £200 million and at an average price per bungalow of £1324.

WINDING UP

The original date for the end of the scheme had been set at 1 October 1947, but because of the problems discussed above the scheme continued until,

Table 6.4. Breakdown of costs, 1948.

	Number	Estimated cost Oct 1945 £	Dec 1947 £	Total Cost £
Arcon	38,859	1085	1209	46,981,000
Uni-Seco	28,999	1020	1131	32,798,000
Tarran	1.015	1074	1022	1,037,000
Tarran	11,000	1000	1147	12,617,000
Tarran	6,999	1000	1126	7,881,000
Spooner	2,000	992	1079	2,158,000
Universal	2,000	1135	1218	2,436,000
Phoenix	2,428	1090	1200	2,914,000
Orlit	255	978	1202	307,000
Miller	100	976	1139	114,000
Isle of Lewis	50		2000	100,000
USA	8,462		663	5,610,000
Aluminium	54,500	1365	1610	87,745,000
Total	156,667			202,698,000

'The approved programme of 156,623 temporary houses was completed during the year of account and the last house was handed over in March 1949.'[63] An earlier White Paper had set the final figure at 156,667 bungalows with the proviso that 'subject to minor adjustments, this figure may be taken as final.'[64] The numbers, types and cost of the provisional figure were then broken down as shown in table 6.4.

When the costs of the programme were finally presented and the account closed on 31 March 1956 they, in fact, amounted to £207,309,000 for the 156,623 approved bungalows.[65] Additional money had been voted to the programme in two stages. The programme was first augmented by an additional £50 million in 1945 under the Building Materials and Housing Act[66] and then by a further £20 million under the Housing (Temporary Accommodation) Act in 1947.[67] The annual breakdown for the total expenditure is shown in table 6.5.

Of the cost of the total programme 69 per cent was for the manufacture and construction of the temporary bungalows and their fittings, including the cost of transport and storage, 25 per cent was accounted for in the erection of the temporary houses on sites provided by the local authorities, 3 per cent was for capital assistance to contractors and 3 per cent was for departmental expenses.[68] Thus, although the aim was to produce temporary houses from the factory and save labour, the costs of site erection were a relatively large part of the total programme. The overall average cost of the bungalows at over £1300 (though this average will be

Table 6.5. Annual expenditure for the Temporary Housing Programme.

Year	Expenditure £
1944/45	1,100,000
1945/46	46,000,000
1946/47	88,500,000
1947/48	57,000,000
1948/49	8,400,000
1949/50	3,100,000
1950/51	1,650,000
1951/52	650,000
1952/53	530,000
1953/54	365,000
1954/55	13,000
1955/56	1,000
Total	207,309,000

weighted by the higher costs, around £1600 for the aluminium bungalow which accounted for about a third of the total units supplied) does not compare favourably with the total cost of the permanent house in 1947.

The total cost of the average local authority three-bedroom house completed in the latter part of 1947, including site costs and professional fees, may therefore be computed as follows:

Building cost	£1,242
Cost of land and site development	£ 122
Quantity Surveyor's fee	£ 12
Subtotal	£1,376
Architect's fee, say	£ 24
Total	£1,400[69]

This cost was for a typical three bedroom house of 934 ft^2 and an out-building of 95 ft^2 and must be compared with the temporary bungalow of 643 ft^2 with a shed of 32 ft^2 (the Arcon Mark V).

What had begun as an exercise for employment in the steel industry had ended in the provision of factory prefabricated and standardized bungalows from a variety of available materials. The original steel bungalow, of which only four prototypes were ever produced, left an indelible trace upon the whole programme. Tooling up for the steel bungalow and for steel fitments, both the kitchen and bathroom unit and the cupboards, had been undertaken by the time it was realized that manufacturing capacity in the steel industry would not be available for the programme. This initial misplaced investment always remained as a cost to the programme. In fact only 28,500 kitchen and bathroom units and 27,000 cupboard units out of the total numbers supplied to the programme through the Ministry of Works were made of steel. The remainder were constructed more or less in timber with a subsequent saving to the programme despite the shortage of the material (the steel kitchen cost £129 and the timber one £114, while the relevant prices for the cupboard units were £77 and £51.5, respectively.[70] The aluminium bungalow, the type that most closely resembled the concept of the original Portal steel bungalow, was also the most costly provided under the programme. As an exercise in demonstrating the extra costs of producing complete houses in the factory the Temporary Housing Programme was a success.

Nevertheless, housing had been provided during a period of emergency and in a way that housing on some scale had never before been provided in Britain. The programme, in its uniqueness, could almost be viewed as a beacon of the changes that were to happen in the post-war world. At a time of rationing and privation, despite the fact that the war had been won,[71] the temporary houses appear as something fundamentally 'new' and representative of the better future:

> But we shall improve human beings. We shall improve them by teaching them, by legislation, by planning for them a better environment and a saner world. We are going to build a new Britain after the war.[72]

How far this attitude of an expectation of a new and better future may have affected other possible responses to the problem of housing provision after the war is debatable. At times any methods of providing shelter appeared to be worthy of publication. *Picture Post* ran an article in 1944 that showed the packing cases for the D-Day gliders converted by the GIs to housing in place of the standard issue tents.[73] By 1946, D-Day landing craft were shown for sale, converted and furnished, for any who could find the £875 cash and convince the Admiralty that they had a genuine housing need.[74] However, other but less esoteric methods of meeting the post-war housing shortage were discussed seriously, even if such discussion had little eventual effect on the course of the Temporary Housing Programme.

ALTERNATIVE APPROACHES

One obvious way of avoiding the shortage of materials and skilled labour after the war was to turn to materials that were plentiful and that did not require craft skills to work. This method had been tried after the Great War, when similar conditions prevailed. One of the strangest experiments of this type resulted, in the 1920s, in the construction of an estate of houses at Amesbury, Wilts, where a number of the houses were built using different methods of chalk mud walling. The economics of the experiment suggested that mud building was too expensive in terms of the necessary labour costs to warrant any large scale resurrection of the craft.

At first there was little apparent saving in the experimental methods as labour and materials, apart from those available on site, still had to be obtained from elsewhere and were expensive. However, towards the end of the programme a definite decline in the costs occurred as, with the experience gained earlier, it was possible to make greater economies in construction methods and in the planning of the houses.[75]

The Amesbury experiment did not lead to any revival of traditional materials for public housing although some architects, such as Clough Williams-Ellis, continued to experiment with the possibilities.[76] However, the idea of a return to the vernacular materials, which required considerable amounts of unskilled labour to manipulate them into an acceptable building, was also suggested after World War II, to meet the problem of housing people in rural areas:

> And yet I understand that the unimaginative councillors in many Wiltshire towns which actually stand on chalk are delaying their post-war building programmes until sufficient transport is released to carry clay bricks and concrete to them. Whilst there is the acute shortage of both houses and the skilled labour with which to construct new dwellings, surely the chalk daub house which can be built with unskilled labour has much to commend it? Better chalk houses built with unskilled labour to last two hundred years, than the prefabricated semi-detached closets.[77]

An example of such an approach was the suggestion that the traditional 'beehive' buildings of the outer Hebrides, the bothan (a name that meant temporary dwelling), might be reinterpreted and constructed using local materials and labour, since the 'normal type of house so much under discussion in Great Britain, whether rural or urban, is of no use in the Outer Hebrides'.[78] The walls were curved in the traditional manner and were to be constructed of a battered facing of local stone with an inner facing of peat blocks with layers of heather at intervals (figure 6.6). The stone was to be dry laid. The outer walls were to carry the roof of timber with a thatch of heather or bracken. A stone chimney was formed in the centre of the house in the traditional manner with the staircase built into it. Fittings, such as windows and doors, were to be supplied from the mainland. The house was intended to 'be entirely constructed with local labour and local materials.'[79]

Although the attraction of traditional materials like mud was that only unskilled labour was required for digging and the manipulation of the raw material, some skill was still necessary. The Amesbury experiment had shown that a period of familiarization with the method was essential and the later Amesbury experimental houses were cheaper and less difficult to build.[80] If such materials were to be used, what was required was a system of construction that would enable the users to put up houses with a limited quantity of professional and craft skilled input. Since, however, the nation possessed a skill base that was situated in the factory, following the

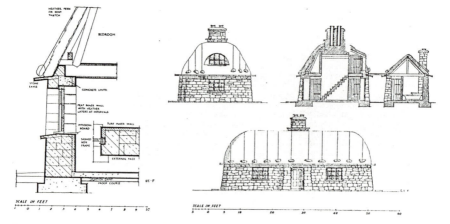

Figure 6.6. Proposal for traditional temporary dwellings for the Outer Hebrides, 1945. (*Source*: *Architectural Design and Construction*, January, 1945)

development of mass production techniques in response to the war, the natural place to look for housing skills was the factory and no such return to traditional materials was made.

The situation might well have been different if truly sub-standard emergency housing had been the response to the post-war shortage. Throughout this period, however, the aim was to provide the best possible house for those returning after the war. The situation in Germany provides an interesting contrast. Writing in *Building* in 1945 a refugee architect, 'who has now established contact with friends in Germany'[81] provides evidence of a totally different approach to the problem. To relieve the housing shortage, attributed to the allied bombing campaign, the first steps were the same as those taken after the Blitz in Britain – that is repair and requisition. Wherever possible existing accommodation was used for housing and lower space standards became the norm. The writer describes how river and canal barges were made habitable for sharing by several families. However, it became apparent that the replacements could not match the high numbers of dwellings that had been destroyed. In response, in 1944, Dr. Ley[82] ordered that a million 'emergency houses' should be built.

As skilled building workers were being needed for the armament industry these emergency houses were to be built as far as possible by unskilled labour and preferably by the persons who were going to live in them. These houses had to be built from clay, rough timber, and bricks and rubble from bomb-damaged houses. Other materials were controlled and not allowed to be used for dwellings. Steel was prohibited, except for an R.S.J. for the construction of air-raid shelters.

Transportable machines, designed to sort in one operation bricks, pieces of brick, and rubble from bombed sites were being used. The salvaged rubble was treated in various ways, moulded into solid bricks, hollow bricks, and flagstones or used as crushed concrete. As there was not sufficient cement, substitutes made from rubble were used.[83]

The plan and size of the emergency dwelling was controlled with an overall floor area of approximately 21 m^2 and a ceiling height of 2.5 m. The services that were permitted within the dwellings were very basic.

For all types of emergency houses the electric lighting installations were kept to a minimum, that is, if there was electrical installation at all. Furnishing provided was: 1 range with 4 kg. fluepipes and 2 elbows (if possible salvaged from bombed houses); 1 bucket; 1 wooden hygienic closet with lid; 1 paraffin lamp; 1 hand water pump (which had to serve for 4 houses), and the assurance from Dr. Ley that 'our grandfathers did not think it a sacrifice to live under similar conditions'.[84]

Although the German approach had been to underline the emergency of the situation and to accept that sub-standard accommodation, which might also be poorly constructed by the unskilled users of the dwellings, was necessary, in Britain it appeared that those who had been victorious in the war were thought to want something better than mere emergency shelter. Indeed, another of Dr. Ley's measures for providing emergency housing, the donation of grants of money to the owners of sheds on allotments in the towns to make them habitable, was presented to the British people as, 'the Herrenvolk are reaping the bitter fruits of the Hitler harvest.'[85]

Whether the economic cost of war is greater for those who lose or for those who win is, perhaps, a speculation of marginal value, since the cost of war to any nation is great. What is of more relevance is the housing expectations of the winners compared to those of the losers in these particular circumstances. The British people had been led to expect better homes after the war and the temporary accommodation provided to meet the emergency needs was of a far higher standard than that of Germany. The fact that many of the temporary bungalows have remained in use long after their initial design life is a testament to the expectations that the victors in war had of their 'emergency' accommodation. Moreover, it is possible to speculate that if the newly formed families from the years during and immediately after the war were not given such a home, they might put off starting a family and the women would possibly have wished to continue in work. Since the much publicized Beveridge Report had promised full employment some means had to be found to bring women out of the factories where they had enjoyed money and independence. To do this proper 'homes' had to be provided so that the woman's 'job' of raising the family within the home could be continued in the post-war world.

THE EXTENDIBLE HOUSE

In pursuit of this goal of decent homes, the architectural profession toyed with another idea for the provision of much needed short-term accommodation after the war – that of the extendable rather than the temporary house. The idea of building housing in wartime that could house families in lowered space standards but that could be extended to acceptable standards in peacetime can be traced to a competition that the RIBA ran early in the war, the results of which were published late in 1940 (figure 6.7). The competition concerned the design of new housing for industrial workers that could withstand air-raid damage and that would be suitable for use in peacetime.

> The workers moving to new factories are mostly single men and women, for whom hostel accommodation would prove to be the most satisfactory form of housing. Several hostels are being built to meet the need, but it has generally been the policy of the authorities to encourage the building of houses, rather than hostels, as the latter are not likely to be required after the war. Houses, on the other hand, will be required. In this way a wartime need can be made to serve a future peacetime requirement.[86]

The competition was centred around four approaches to the problem. The first involved the design of a two-storey house that was suitable for peacetime use but which was constructed to be totally protected from blast and splinter damage. The second looked at the design of a normally

Figure 6.7. Winning submission in the RIBA competition showing the dwelling in both wartime and peace time use. (*Source*: RIBA, 1940)

constructed two-storey house that contained an air-raid shelter within its volume (in one of the submissions of this version the shelter under the stairs in the centre of the house became a fuel store and larder in peacetime[87]). The third approach was the design of a single-storey dwelling that was protected from air-raids either completely or in part, and to which extra ground floor rooms could be added in peacetime to provide full family accommodation. The last solution, which was considered by those who reported on the competition to be the most practical, involved the provision of the ground floor of a standard two-storey house plan with the intention to build the second storey after the war. The ground floor plan was designed for use as hostel or family accommodation and protection from air-raids was provided in the bedroom area. A design of this last type won the competition. The protected dormitory area became the living room in the peacetime arrangement with a staircase inserted against the front wall of the house; the wartime unprotected lounge area became a peacetime kitchen and the washing area became a downstairs bathroom. Three good bedrooms were to be added on the first floor to give a wide frontage semi-detached family house. Between the running of the competition and the publication of the report nightly bombing raids had commenced on London. The behaviour of the people affected by the bombing suggested to those reporting that this approach to wartime housing, that is providing a minimum of well protected accommodation that could later be extended, had relevance.

> In the more heavily bombed areas . . . many families assemble in the ground-floor rooms of their home, to sleep there or in the shelters, leaving the bedrooms unused at night. In such cases, it would be waste of labour and materials to complete the bedroom floors of new houses while night bombing is prevalent, especially in the most vulnerable areas, and the single-storey unit appears to give accommodation which seems suitable for vulnerable area wartime housing programmes.[88]

The architectural press persisted with the idea of the design of accommodation for war-time use that could be extended and altered after the war, as shown in *The Builder* of 1941.[89] Such an approach would delight designers as it required skilled planning for the dwelling to work equally well in both circumstances without any need for costly structural alterations.

Similar ideas were also carried forward into the period of post-war reconstruction. Rather than investing in prefabricated temporary structures that would be sub-standard, it was recognized that permanent housing could be provided that would initially contain two families and later, once the immediate urgency was over, be converted to contain only one. In this way, fewer resources would be wasted on sub-standard accommodation. The *Housing Manual 1944* suggests the following:

While the housing programme generally will be mainly concerned with the family of five to six persons, during the first transitional period, when many newly married couples will be setting up a house, the small family will, in most places, require special consideration. Accommodation may be provided for such families without unbalancing the housing programme as a whole by the erection of a three-bedroom house of normal size so planned that it may be temporarily occupied by two small families, usually in separate flats. This is a solution which may commend itself to some local authorities as a useful alternative to the emergency factory-made house of temporary construction.[90]

The proposed plans (figure 6.8) show what is ultimately a standard semi-detached house with three bedrooms and a bathroom upstairs and, downstairs, a living room, dining kitchen, utility room,[91] hall and WC. When first built it was to be arranged as two flats, the ground floor flat for two persons (although a pram space is indicated under the stairs and the bedroom could easily contain a cot, so that a family with a child up to about two years in age could be accommodated), and an upper flat for three persons.

Similar ideas are found in other official publications. In their 1944 report, the Department of Health for Scotland suggested four possible strategies for relieving the housing shortage in the post-war period:

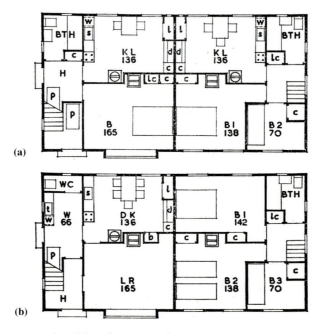

Figure 6.8. Ground and first floor plans for a pair of semi-detached houses arranged (*a*) as four flats to provide emergency dwellings and (*b*) for peace time. (*Source*: Ministry of Health/Ministry of Works, 1944*b*)

(*a*) Transitional accommodation, whereby structures which had been put up for use during the war were converted into temporary accommodation.
(*b*) Accommodation capable of being converted or upgraded, whereby permanent homes were erected which could house more than one family during a transitional period.
(*c*) Accommodation provided by alternative building methods, whereby homes would be built using non-traditional materials and alternative (presumably factory) labour.
(*d*) Accommodation provided by normal methods, whereby houses were to be built to model plans based on improved pre-war designs rather than an ideal post-war design.

Of these four approaches most information was provided on the second.[92] The suggestions were similar to those discussed earlier:

> We suggest that the most careful consideration should be given to the possibility of providing accommodation on what we describe for convenience as the 'duplex' principle. By this we mean that a proportion of the houses to be built in permanent construction on their final sites should be so designed that in the immediate post-war period they can accommmodate two families and can subsequently be converted into single family houses which will conform to the higher standards of planning and conveniences recommended in this report.[93]

Although this particular 'emergency' form of the permanent house received publicity at this time it does not appear to have become a serious rival to the prefab. By the time the 1949 *Housing Manual* appeared it was no longer necessary to refer to an emergency situation. The Manual discusses optimum layouts for a variety of house types and for blocks of flats, the only concession to the stringency of those times being a discussion of 'New methods of construction' but with the rider that:

> The future of any non-traditional systems of house construction will depend, however, on their success in competing in price and on equal terms with traditional houses. Theoretically, the increase in speed of erection which all approved methods are designed in varying degrees to effect should produce a price below that of the traditional house, and the opposing factor, the initial outlay on plant and equipment which has been responsible for the higher price, should gradually cease to operate.[94]

Clearly, with the passing of the immediate apparent emergency in housing, prefabrication, which had been hailed as a necessity and which found an outlet in the Temporary Housing Programme, now had to compete on equal terms with traditional building.

Although the emergency 'sub-standard' accommodation which could be later upgraded was no longer recognized as necessary by the Ministry of Health, this architecturally elegant solution to post-war housing problems was to find some expression in the private sector, although in a different form. Those building private houses after the war were restricted in both the size and cost of any new home so as to avoid unnecessary use of scarce materials. Costs were first fixed at £1200 for a house in the country and £1300 for an urban house, this price to be inclusive of the land cost. The maximum area that could be built was 1000 ft^2 for a two-storey house and 930 ft^2 for a bungalow. The answer for those who wished for something larger was to design a house which met immediate requirements but which was capable of extension once restrictions had been lifted, 'Those who are planning the building of a home should bear in mind such possibilities.

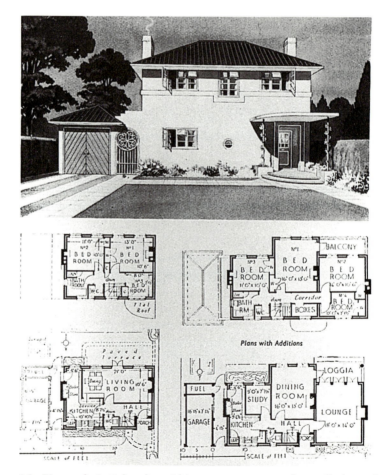

Figure 6.9. House designed to be within post-war cost and area limits and which could be extended later – front view of the original house with plans showing house as first built and house as extended. (*Source*: Church and Drysdale Smith, 1947, reproduced by permission of Barrie and Jenkins Ltd)

Choose a frontage which will allow extensions. Restrictions will not always be with us.'[95]

An example of such a house has the basic three-bedroom plan which can be extended by the addition of a lounge with two bedrooms over to one side and a garage and fuel store to the other (figure 6.9). However, the house is apparently of traditional construction and the main extension as illustrated would have involved considerable disruption with the alteration and extension of the hipped roof (figure 6.10). It would appear that, with one or two exceptions, the link between an extendable house and prefabrication of components was not made in the private sector after the war. This idea is discussed by Whittick:

> If it is proposed to extend a house when required, it should be designed complete at each stage, and the construction should be such that the extensions can be made as simply and efficiently as possible. It is much simpler, for example, to make extensions to a house with a flat roof than to a house with a pitched roof. This applies both to horizontal and vertical extensions. Further, where the walls, floors and roof are made of large factory-made sections, and the house is designed on a grid of, say, three feet for each of its completed stages, the extension will be simpler than if the house is of traditional brick construction.[96]

The idea emerged again in 1953 as the result of a *News Chronicle* competition for the design of a house. Presented as an accompaniment to the competition results, the 'house that can grow' showed a two-bedroom house for a young family which could later be extended by additions at either side to provide a five-bedroom house with a double height void over dining and living rooms (figure 6.11). Even the increased size of car that would come with increasing affluence is allowed for, the house growing from 1050 ft^2 to 2100 ft^2 exclusive of the garage space. Although the

Figure 6.10. Front view of extended house. (*Source*: Church and Drysdale Smith, 1947, reproduced by permission of Barrie and Jenkins Ltd)

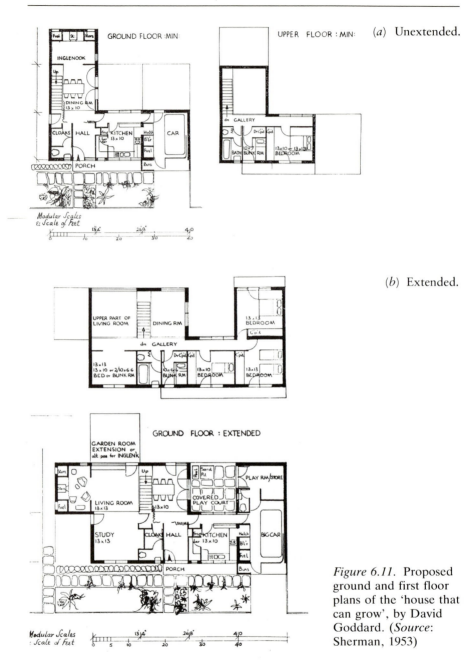

(a) Unextended.

(b) Extended.

Figure 6.11. Proposed ground and first floor plans of the 'house that can grow', by David Goddard. (*Source*: Sherman, 1953)

architect, Goddard, admits that the house could be built of traditional load bearing materials, the design was conceived on a 3 ft 4 in module with the view that the components could be prefabricated in the factory:

When a house like this is geared to full factory production it will be less costly and a far better proposition than its predecessor the traditional house – like the motor car of today compared with the relatively costly models of the twenties . . . But it will put a well-designed and well-equipped house within the reach of everyone. The house might be ordered from a catalogue, and all the bits and pieces put together just as the purchaser wished to suit his own personal and family needs.[97]

By 1953, however, this cry seemed no more than an echo of what a factory produced housing system might have been. The progress of prefabrication and system building reliant on site organization in public sector housing that was to emerge later in the post-war period has been chronicled elsewhere[98] but in the private sector the house from the factory was supplanted by traditional building, even if the organization of large firms engaged in speculative house building using the traditional methods of construction resulted in an increase in productivity. Only firms such as Colt,[99] with a system of prefabrication and factory production in timber, appear to have made any impact on the UK private housing sector and then only for the relatively well off.

The extendable house, it would appear, was proposed first as alternative emergency accommodation and then as a solution to government restrictions on house building in the private sector. What does not appear to have been addressed in any very serious way was the relationship between extendability and the house from the factory. Providing that the case was made for a factory made house be to both standardized and modularized, the development of a building form and a technology that would allow the house to be easily extended would seem a logical progression. In this light, the temporary bungalow belongs to the 'Utility' era, a standard well-made and well-designed product available in one size for all. In their turn industrialized building systems, as were applied to flats and houses post-war, appear equally inflexible and designed only to increase productivity or decrease costs. The dream of the factory made house arranged like the original Edison Phonograph so that it could be constantly updated as technology improved[100] remained exactly that; a dream:

Factory-made houses, well designed and using to the best advantage all powers of mass-production and modern materials, are in less danger of social obsolescence than traditional buildings . . .

The initial design of the house could also enable extensions to be made, to accommodate additions to the occupying family. It should be just as possible for the small householder to add a new wing, containing a couple of extra rooms, to his factory made house as it was for the eighteenth century nobleman to add a new wing to his mansion, containing ten or twenty bedrooms. Adding to a traditionally built house is a costly business: adding to a factory-made house could be relatively simple: the unit construction of such houses making it a matter of the greatest mechanical ease, and the additional units necessary for the extension could be erected in a few hours after they had been ordered from the factory.[101]

NOTES

1. Ministry of Health (1949), p. 104.

2. Official Report House of Lords, 1943–44, Vol. 131, col. 564.

3. Official Report House of Lords, 1943–44, Vol. 130, col. 699.

4. Official Report House of Commons, 19 July 1944, Vol. 402, col. 187.

5. *Ibid.*, col. 204.

6. Official Report House of Commons, 1 August 1944, Vol. 402, col. 1251.

7. Official Report House of Commons, 26 September 1944, Vol. 403, col. 171.

8. Official Report House of Commons, 10 October 1944, Vol. 403, col. 1686.

9. Finnemore (1985*b*), p. 47. Quoting PRO CAB 66/55: Minister of Reconstruction, 'Production of Prefabricated Houses', September 22, 1944.

10. Parliamentary Papers (1943–44), Vol. 1, pp. 588–687.

11. Official Report House of Commons, 1 August 1944, Vol. 402, col. 1260.

12. *Ibid.*, col. 1374.

13. *Ibid.*, col. 1255.

14. *Ibid.*, col. 1266.

15. *Ibid.*, col. 1310: Mr. Hicks in reply to Mr. Hopkinson.

16. V1 = *Vergeltungswaffe* or 'reprisal weapon', being in response to the obliteration bombing of Germany.

17. Lewis (1986), pp. 217–218.

18. *Ibid.*, p. 219.

19. 'Emergency Accommodation', *Architectural Design and Construction*, 1944, **XIV**, p. 271.

20. For Buckminster Fuller's steel house design for USA defence needs, see *The Architect and Building News*, 24 December, 1943.

21. Official Report House of Commons, 26 September 1944, Vol. 403, col. 168.

22. Official Report House of Commons, 1 August 1944, Vol. 402, cols. 1290–1295.

23. *Ibid.*, col. 1299.

24. Parliamentary Papers (1943–44), Vol. 1, pp. 588–687.

25. Minister of Health (1946), p. 4.

26. Minister of Works (1945), p. 2.

27. See Finnimore (1989), p. 31. Finnimore states that 'In the Cabinet meeting of 24 February 1944, Winston Churchill announced his intention to manufacture half a million temporary homes from steel.'

28. Minister of Works (1945), p. 2.

29. Finnemore (1985*a*), p. 60 also, Madge (1946), p. 207, and 'Production of prefabricated aluminium houses' *Journal of the RIBA*, July, 1946, p. 402.

30. Minister of Works (1945), p. 2.

31. Ministry of Reconstruction (1945), p. 4.

32. *Ibid.*, p. 3.

33. The Spooner bungalow was timber frame and clad externally with steel sheet. A version was exhibited at the Tate Gallery at the start of 1945. The Universal bungalow was a steel frame with asbestos cement cladding. The Phoenix bungalow was timber frame with asbestos cement cladding.

34. Bossom (1945), p. 309.

35. It had been assumed that the surface water would drain to soakaways. In addition more paths and fences were required than first estimated. There was always uncertainty over the true temporary nature of the programme as local authorities were encouraged to think in terms of reusing sites and infrastructure at a later date. In these terms additional infrastructure costs might have been warranted. However, extra monies spent on the provision of fencing and paths would seem to suggest a more 'permanent' approach to the temporary houses.

36. Minister of Works (1945), p. 3.

37. White (1965), p. 91.

38. Ministry of Works (1948), p. 9.

39. Minister of Works (1945), pp. 2–3.

40. *Ibid.*, p. 5.

41. Bossom (1945), p. 310.

42. Ministry of Health/Ministry of Works (1944), p. 3.

43. Minister of Health (1946), p. 2.

44. *Ibid.*, p. 5.

45. Ministry of Health (1948*b*), p. 37

46. Ministry of Health/Ministry of Works (1944), p. 6.

47. Minister of Works (1948), p. 3.

48. *Ibid.*, p. 5.

49. The Orlit hutting system was precast concrete frame and cladding and the company's bungalow appears to use the same technology. The Miller bungalow was no-fines concrete and all were erected in Scotland. A number of special bungalows, of concrete, had to be designed for the Isle of Lewis as it was felt that the standard types would not withstand the severe weathering.

50. Minister of Works (1948), p. 5.

51. *Ibid.*, p. 4–5.

52. At one time £10 was added to the average cost for two separate reasons. The supply of plasterboard diminished and fibreboard had to be used for ceiling linings. The hard winter of 1946 and the problem of the fuel supply meant that the tenants were forced to burn soft coal rather than the smokeless fuel for which the stove had been designed. This produced a real fire risk and for further units the flues were lagged to a greater extent and a detail devised to set the fibreboard back around the flue. *Ibid.*, p. 4.

53. *Ibid.*, p. 8.

54. The final sentence of Bruce and Sandbank (1944) perpetuates this myth: 'And probably the biggest lesson, for all of us, will be when we learn that Prefabrication is simply another term for better, more economical building under modern conditions – a goal we are all striving to reach'.

55. Minister of Works (1948), p. 9.

56. West (1945, p. 322) states: 'The application of the aluminium alloys to building, though not so far-reaching or intensive as in the United States and continental Europe, was making steady progress in this country until the outbreak of war diverted all supplies of the alloys to war purposes, particularly to aircraft production.'

This would suggest that far from looking for a market in the building industry after the war the pre-war market existed to be exploited. In this light the aluminium bungalow was not to be an idealistic realization of the house from the factory but rather a means of tiding over production until the conventional building industry had picked up.

57. Minister of Works (1948), p. 8.

58. *Ibid.*, p. 6.

59. *Ibid.*

60. Arcon, Chartered Architects (1948*c*), p. 118.

61. Parliamentary Papers (1948–49), Vol. 22, p. 416.

62. Parliamentary Papers (1946–47), Vol. 15, p. 75.

63. Parliamentary Papers (1948–49), Vol. 22, p. 420.

64. Minister of Works (1948), p. 2.

65. Parliamentary Papers (1956–57), Vol. 20, p. 441.

66. Parliamentary Papers (1945–46), Vol. 1, p. 217–229.

67. Parliamentary Papers (1947–48), Vol. 3, pp. 390–489.

68. The information is extracted from Parliamentary Papers (1956–57), Vol. 20.

69. Minister of Health (1948), p. 12.

70. Minister of Works (1948), p. 100.

71. Bread rationing ended in July 1948 and other forms of rationing were gradually withdrawn, for instance clothes rationing ended in November 1949.

72. Joad (1943), p. 94. The soldier is speaking and it is his assumption that the world will be better after the war.

73. *Picture Post*, 11 March, 1944, pp. 10–11.

74. *Picture Post*, 18 May, 1946, p. 16. The original cost of the D-Day landing craft was £1500–£1600.

75. Vale (1973), p. 5.

76. Williams-Ellis (1919).

77. Duncan (1947), p. 102.

78. 'Houses for the Outer Hebrides', *Architectural Design and Construction*, January, 1945, p. 23.

79. *Ibid.*

80. Vale (1973), p. 37.

81. 'Wartime Housing in Germany', *Building*, **20**, June, 1945, p. 161.

82. Dr. Robert Ley was Reichsleiter and head of the German Labour Front. He was the author of the famous 'Kraft durch Freude' slogan. See Speer (1970).

83. 'Wartime Housing in Germany', *Building*, **20**, June, 1945, p. 161.

84. *Ibid.*

85. *Illustrated London News*, Part 2, 13 December, 1947, p. 657.

86. RIBA (1940), p. 6.

87. *Ibid.*, p. 10.

88. *Ibid.*, p. 23.

89. *The Builder*, 5 September, 1941, pp. 214–215.

90. Ministry of Health (1944*b*), p. 22.

91. The utility room appears as part of the standard features of the postwar home. Two out of the three alternative ground floor plans of the modern three bedroom house in the Dudley Report include a utility room for laundry (see: Ministry of Health (1944*a*), p. 14.) In 'Plans and elevations of the house women have chosen' the kitchen and utility room are shown as separate areas with the comment, 'The separate washhouse-utility room for laundry work and storage is considered essential in a family house' (see Pleydell-Bouverie, 1944, pp. 56–57). Whether the conversion of the old term washhouse to the new term utility room has more to do with contact with the USA or with the associated use of 'Utility' in connection with the austerity production of clothes, furniture and other necessities of life is open to speculation.

92. Department of Health for Scotland (1944), pp. 67–68.

93. *Ibid.*

94. Ministry of Health (1949), p. 104.

95. Church and Drysdale Smith (1947), p. 51.

96. Whittick with Schreiner (1947), pp. 137–139.

97. Sherman (1953), p. 63.

98. See White (1965) and Finnimore (1989).

99. Diamant (1964), pp. 161–162.

100. When Edison first marketed the phonograph all improvements that were incorporated into new models, such as the diamond stylus and the 4 minute as opposed to the 2 minute cylinder record, were available as conversion kits for the basic model. No such retrospective upgrading was developed for Emil Berliner's disc playing Gramophone and yet the gramophone was to become ultimately the more successful development of recording technology.

101. Gloag and Wornum (1946), pp. 89–90.

7

BUILDING HOMES

'I shan't feel really happy about the temporaries unless one of the fixtures in each of them is a fifteen-year-time-bomb guaranteed not to be a dud!'[1]

Any historical phenomenon can be interpreted in a variety of ways. It is possible through analysis of the available material to arrive at more than one series of related events that could be said to give rise to a particular phenomenon. The stance taken here was to look at the public face of the Temporary Housing Programme and to attempt to examine a variety of reasons given within the public domain for its establishment. Hence, it was considered worthwhile to look at people's ideas of the type of house that they expected to see built after the war; reactions to the prototypes exhibited in 1944; public discussion in parliament; and the reactions of architects, in order to establish the background against which the Temporary Housing Programme emerged.

The problem with this approach to history is that it tends to suggest that a certain chain of events gives rise to a certain outcome. It might be far more convincing, however, to view the Temporary Housing Programme rather more in the light of the Burgess Shales controversy[2] and see it as one possible, but perhaps unlikely, outcome of the factors of that time. Just as the Burgess Shales suggest that of a diversity of flora and fauna fossilized in the mud only some survive to evolve into creatures that are recognizable as antecedents of modern life, so of the diversity of ideas and opportunities that existed immediately after the war to provide housing for people, the Temporary Housing Programme was only one possible outcome. It also proved an outcome that, like some creatures in the evolutionary scheme, appeared to come to a dead end, never to develop further.

Surrounding the emergence of the Temporary Housing Programme has to be set a strange group of circumstances. The nation was still at war when the programme was first announced to the public in 1944. Although the tide of the war had turned by the battle of El Alamein in October–November 1942 and the Anglo-American landings in North Africa afterwards, in the midst of rationing and general shortages of food and fuel the exhibition of a type of house, new both in form and concept, just over a year after these victories, seems unlikely. Nor was the house the only 'new' phenomenon to appear during the war. The whole development of the mechanism of the welfare state was to emerge and be published during the war[3] as a herald of the changes that were to come in a peacetime, which was then viewed as more or less certain if not actual.

Nor was the house ever to be produced in such numbers as to make it a true change in the nature and composition of the housing stock. At the end of the war 4 million homes were required because of destruction, lack of new building and the deterioration of the housing stock. The majority of this short fall was made up by the permanent housing programme and the 156,623 temporary bungalows produced by 1949 could only make a small contribution. Immediately before the war more than 300,000 houses were being constructed and the government set a similar target for the production of permanent houses in the second year after the end of the war in Europe.[4] In the light of this target and of the later Conservative promise to build 300,000 houses a year, a promise which aided their re-election in 1951, and which was broadly achieved in the period 1953–58, the temporary bungalows seem unimportant.

As a demonstration of the applications of factory production to housing the programme had obvious drawbacks. Although the aluminium bungalow was produced in the factory and formed the largest number of a single type in the programme it was significantly more expensive than the other types. The less expensive bungalows were less highly prefabricated and the methods of storage and distribution are, perhaps, more reminiscent of a war time campaign to ensure as wide a spread of component stores and manufacture as possible to avoid total annihilation of the programme through bombing. The design and prefabrication of the bungalows was obviously linked to the availability of materials and skilled labour after the war but, overall, the majority of different bungalow types had frames of that most traditional building material, timber. The exceptions of the aluminium bungalow and the light steel frame of the Arcon, representing almost 60 per cent of the total bungalows constructed do, perhaps, suggest ways in which alternative materials can be used for small houses but neither produced any very radical change in the long term. Even today the steel industry is still considering ways in which the material might be effectively used for low-rise houses.[5] The efforts to use prefabrication for housing in the post-war period were soon to be transferred from low-rise individual units to high-rise system built blocks, a phenomenon which was also relatively short lived but which did have a numerical effect on the numbers of dwellings produced, particularly in cities.[6,7] However, as Esher suggests, the antecedents for the high-rise system built flat are not the same as those of the prefabricated bungalow:

It was easy enough to roll off complete dwellings; indeed the emergency housing programme had done just that at the end of the war. But for obvious environmental reasons this was unacceptable to architects, who were looking for a kit from which a humane variety of low-rise types could be assembled faster and cheaper than bricks and mortar could do it. They never succeeded. But what were available, mainly from France and Sweden, were patented systems for the rapid building of multi-storey flats, which met the demand in continental countries. For Ministers and for housing committees seeking to beat all productivity records for new dwellings, this had to be the answer.[8]

If the accidental nature of history is accepted it is not hard to picture the consequences that might have resulted had the Swedish prefabricated 'Magic House' been used as a prototype in place of the continental flat; the former would allow the occupants some measure of control over the construction of their houses, the latter did not. Although housing expert Elizabeth Denby in her pre-war survey discussed both Swedish low-rise houses and Swedish flats she did not fail to comment that the cottages of the self-build communities, 'are at present the cheapest accommodation in Stockholm'[9] (figure 7.1). In the light of the rising costs of post-war high-rise flats in the UK, this statement becomes a prophetic warning. However, it was, perhaps, from the 'Magic House' that the author Ethel Mannin developed her images of a post-war Utopia:

> The modern houses and flats in Utopia have deep windows and sun-balconies, and a great many of them have been not merely designed but built

Figure 7.1. Swedish family at work on the foundations for a factory-made timber house. (*Source*: *Architects' Journal*, 31 May, 1945)

by the people who are to live in them, since the Utopians consider that there are few activities in life more satisfying than building one's own house – few things, the cultivation of the soil apart, more truly creative.[10]

The other side of the experiment with post-war prefabrication highlighted by the Swedish self-build experience, was the need to cope with the reductions in both numbers and skills of those working in the building industry. Such shortages touched not just those involved in new housing but those who had need to employ craftsmen in existing houses: as a contemporary author noted, 'The difficulty of obtaining skilled labour for simple household repairs makes it more than ever desirable for the householder to equip himself with the little knowledge necessary to keep his household apparatus in good working order.'[11] Nevertheless, for the aluminium bungalow, the most highly prefabricated of the types, 21 per cent of the cost was labour costs of which 16 per cent was for erection of the four-section bungalow on site.[12] In the factory some labour costs were also of necessity skilled.[13] For the less highly prefabricated types proportionately more labour was required on site and there is some circumstantial evidence to suggest that this was not unskilled labour,[14] since any prefabricated system, unless like the TVA Trailer House it arrives completed on site, inevitably needs adjustments in the move from the ideal world of the factory to the irregularities of the real site. Most systems of prefabrication rely on 'simple' joints to fix together prefabricated sections of floor, roof and walls. If the joints do not exactly correspond, on site alterations are far more complex than with a traditional system of building with brick and timber, where the 'prefabricated' brick forms a very small and infinitely adjustable unit of the whole. For this reason complex tolerances are built into any system of prefabrication[15] but even these have very limited possibility for adjustment when compared with traditional building. For this reason more skilled labour may be required on some sites rather than less and even the Ministry of Works found that they had originally underestimated the cost of erecting the temporary bungalows.[16]

The only material from which prefabricated building sections can be made and which is capable of relatively unskilled adjustment is timber, such as used for the Swedish self-build house, but this was not available on any scale for the emergency bungalows.[17] A difficult paradox can, therefore, arise whereby adopting unfamiliar systems of prefabrication to save labour can increase the skilled labour required when the system breaks down. Moreover, at the time it was pointed out that prefabrication was not synonomous with unskilled labour:

the current tendency to stress the amount of 'unskilled' labour that can be used in the process of prefabricating is indefensible from the national point of view. Prefabrication is essentially a movement towards precision in building and in the long run only the highest skill is good enough.[18]

Traditional systems of building are traditional just because they invariably represent the best use of available labour and materials to achieve a particular goal. In the case of the temporary bungalows the reasons given for turning to prefabrication were to provide a new peace-time product for factory production, and to make up for a lack of trained building labour and the run down of the traditional building industries. In the light of what occurred in the post-war period these latter assumptions are questionable.

In terms of the numbers of houses produced in the post-war period the temporary bungalows represent just over 6 per cent of the total of 2,488,110 new permanent and temporary houses and flats built in the UK under the post-war housing programme in the decade after the war.[19] Even in England and Wales, by January 1946, ten months after the end of the war only 10.6 per cent of the 113,057 families rehoused in new and temporary dwellings and destroyed houses rebuilt were housed in the temporary bungalows, making the repair teams using traditional building techniques the more successful providers of houses.[20] In total, of the half million emergency bungalows originally promised by Churchill, the programme delivered just over 150,000. Therefore, in terms of numbers of dwellings only, the traditional skills of the building industry produced more than the programme established to make the prefabricated units. More-over, proposals existed to use permanent traditional houses in an 'emergency' way through the use of the same house for initially two families and then one. As a use of resources this would seem more expedient than investing in temporary units with a fifteen year life.

As a means of giving a new product to industry the temporary bungalows also had limited success. The original all steel Portal bungalow never became more than a prototype because capacity could not be released from industry. The war in Japan originally occupied the industry and this was to be followed later by the war in Korea, and the build up of defence needs in response to the Cold War. Perhaps more importantly, society itself was to demand alternative products from industry – the consumer products of the car and the washing machine – once all war time controls were finally released in the early 1950s. As a measure of such changes in society after the war Hopkins states:

> In 1956 after a long inquiry into actual household expenditures, the basis of the official cost-of-living (retail prices) index was changed. The weighting given to food was reduced; candles, lump sugar, rabbits, turnips and similar items were thrown out of the basket, and into it was poured the brimming cornucopia of the mid-twentieth-century industrial civilisation – soda water and dog food, nylons and washing machines, apples and pears and camera films, telephone rentals and school ties, dance-hall tickets and second-hand cars.[21]

Although the aluminium industry produced more temporary bungalows than any other type in the programme, in the event it appeared that it was looking for a diversity of post-war products rather than a straight substitution of houses for aircraft. The 1945 'Aluminium from War to Peace' exhibition had shown not only the bungalow but also a Rolls Royce Merlin engine, electrically driven hand power tools of aluminium, aluminium windows and curtain tracks, furniture, heating appliances, saucepans etc.[22]. The failure of the aluminium industry to develop a prefabricated house as a long-term product, given that the Temporary Housing Programme offered a guaranteed market during the difficult developmental stage, would suggest that although the bungalows gave a useful cushion for the industry at a difficult time, prefabricated houses of aluminium were never going to be viable.

The temporary bungalows also failed to achieve the image possessed by designers of what the mass-produced house should be like. The later system built flats probably came much closer to this image than did the bungalows:

> Working in the twentieth storey of an office building . . . and watching the astonishing growth of a similar office building . . . I began to understand to what extent building could be organised to use the machine as its chief tool.

> . . . The point is that the bulk of house-building is for the poorer classes of the community for whom the price margin is a very important item. Every saving of superfluous labour . . . if reflected in the dwelling in terms of better equipment and lower rent, raises their standard of living. For them old-time building method is a luxury.[23]

Nor did the form of the temporary house, the dwelling on its own plot, receive much support from those interested in the cities of the post war future:

> endless rows of individual or semi-detached houses, however well designed, are both irritating and monotonous . . . The solution is surely terraces around open quadrangles of lawns and trees, punctuated with high blocks of flats.[24]

At the same time, other educated commentators did not see the prefab as an artistically appealing product:

> When this book first appeared I was accused by certain left-wing reviewers of waxing sentimental and nostalgic over a vanished and largely mythical past, and of ignoring that bright 'progressive' future which, according to their philosophy, lies always just round the next corner. But the portents of this future which I saw in the course of my 1947 voyage were fungus-like outcroppings of those tin huts called 'pre-fabs'.[25]

The materials from which the prefab was constructed, particularly the asbestos cement sheet, linked it far more closely to the war-time hut or hostel than any vision of a 'new' prefabricated product for the post-war world. Earlier this has been suggested as a reason for the temporary nature of the programme, since the public, the designers and the building industry may, therefore, have more readily accepted the product. Paradoxically, this very disbelief in the viability of the bungalow as a permanent prefabricated house may have undermined the future of the latter. Through linking the words prefabricated and temporary in the public mind the future for the production of the low-rise house in the factory may have been limited. As Sheppard commented at the time, 'There is a tendency to assume that prefabrication has been developed only to supplement orthodox methods of construction during a period of emergency.'[26]

If, therefore, the temporary bungalow apparently failed in terms of what the government gave as its *raison d'être*, that is the transfer of labour to the factory, the production of a large quantity of houses during the emergency period post-war, and the development of a new peace time product for the expanded war time industries, why has the product survived long beyond its design life and why did the people lucky enough to be allocated a prefab welcome the dwelling and praise its qualities? It seems unlikely that houses with a 15-year life could have survived for nearly five decades without some quality that could make them homes.

> The pre-fabs up Cow Lane showed what could be done if the government thought seriously about better housing. By today's standards maybe they look small, but they were no smaller than the average flat in a tower block.[27]

The prefabs may have had problems with condensation and corrosion but many have been repaired. In contrast, schemes of prefabricated flats from the 1960s in Sheffield and Manchester have been demolished because of poor performance resulting from corrosion and condensation problems while only half way through their projected design lives. Some quality about the bungalows must suggest that they are worthy of repair and an extended life. At the time the temporary bungalows appeared they represented a housing form that had been associated in the UK with holidays and a healthy life and with the chance to build and own a house for those near or at the bottom of the housing pyramid. At a time when the war had of necessity forced people into much closer proximity with each other, whether in the crowded shelters or the dormitories of service camps, the prefab offered immediate privacy without any divisive hierarchy since every bungalow was the same with the same fittings. By being placed detached in its own plot, with its own front door, the bungalow offered a chance for personalized display in the garden but also for immediate withdrawal into the private realm. In this it parodied the model of the inter-war semi-detached house which had, through the cottage estates, formed the backbone of housing provided by the state through the local authorities up to this time. At the same time this model for housing had emerged through war-time surveys and discussion as the house type the people wanted after the war. Internally, the levels of fittings, both in terms of the kitchen and general storage provision, were higher than had been hitherto provided in houses from the state.

All these factors combined to give the prefabs a unique quality which may indicate a specific reason for their success. At a time of upheaval and change each temporary bungalow managed to combine both traditional and futuristic qualities without compromising either. It was a cottage on its own plot but a cottage that contained the latest labour saving kitchen and a central heating system. This wish to combine both the traditional and the modern can be found in statements such as that by Godfrey:

> And if some should say: 'These things must be; change must come and with it loss and disappointment; have faith in the future which will bring greater triumphs than in the past', I would answer that all this may well be, but it is poor advice to cut away the lower part of the ladder before we have reached the top. The more completely we jettison the achievement so far reached, the more difficult and the more distant will be the desired progress and development.[28]

Or as Tubbs was to comment in relation to the concept that modern architecture ignores tradition:

> The English tradition is one of good workmanship and of the honest expression of materials and structure. It is also one of change. It is only by evolving our own forms, based on our own outlook and methods of construction, not by copying, that we can follow tradition.[29]

If the prefabs, therefore, formed housing that the people valued, the extent to which they were to survive many years beyond their design life is influenced not just by their technology and their form but by the way in which they were used to provide homes in the widest sense of the word, through the creation of communities. However, because of the temporary nature of the programme, it was recognized that the land on which the bungalows were placed might not even be land ultimately set aside for future permanent housing developments. This produced two potential reactions to the layout of the bungalows. The first viewed the houses as temporary settlements only, with the layout being of minor significance, so that images emerge of row upon row of identical bungalows. Alternatively, other authorities viewed the temporary bungalows as precursors to permanent housing schemes, so that the infrastructure of roads and the layout of the bungalows became more important. This fact was recognized in the Memorandum for local authorities:

> The bungalows may be erected on either temporary sites or permanent housing sites. On the temporary sites the land will revert to its present use or

will be used later for other than housing purposes. The development works may then have no permanent value and will in most cases have to be demolished. Where the site is to be used for permanent housing in the future, the development works will have been designed or should now be designed to have permanent value.[30]

Such temporary sites as might be thought appropriate included cleared bomb sites, recreation land and vacant infill sites which were not set aside for housing. The problem with this approach was that the numbers of sites in the programme as a whole rose as the numbers of bungalows on each site could be relatively small. This was later to be a recognized factor in the increasing costs of the programme.[31] However, it may also have been significant in the creation of community; the private prefab, with ownership identified through its garden, within a recognizable cluster of like prefabs, the later forming an identifiable unit within the wider urban or suburban development.

Not all bungalows appeared in small numbers, however. The Shrublands Estate, at Great Yarmouth, consisted of 711 Arcon bungalows laid out by the Borough Engineer with a mixture of road frontage and footpath access, with the intention to use the road layout for a later permanent housing scheme (figure 7.2). The layout of the estate with its emphasis on formal geometry resembles a small scale version of the estates of public housing produced in the 1920s. The Shrublands estate, because it was planned for

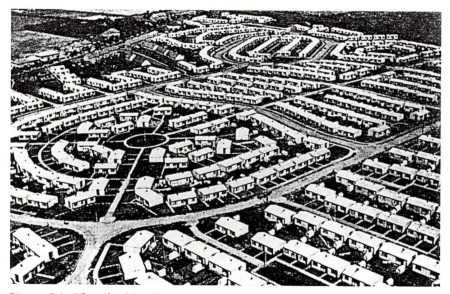

Figure 7.2. The Shrublands Estate of Arcon prefabs, Great Yarmouth, 1947. (*Source: Building*, October, 1947)

permanent housing, also made provision for 'Permanent shops in blocks of four, with three self-contained flats above, and two public houses.'[32]. Some attempt, however, was made to establish a sense of community for the tenants who came from bombed out areas of Yarmouth with a high proportion of ex-service men: the contractors made over one of their huts for a club house for the tenants and 'cultivation of gardens is encouraged by means of competitions.'[33] Shrublands is also interesting as the 711 bungalows housed some fourteen hundred children, emphasizing the fact that however sub-standard the bungalows may have been for families with children, these were exactly the people who were to inhabit them.

> We heard the prefabs were going to be available, so when Bill came home from the Forces, we went to the Housing, taking Brian, our boy, with us. 'We won't even consider you with just one child,' they said. 'You'll have to have another,' they said.
>
> 'Anyway,' says Mrs Dowding, 'from 1945 to 1947 we had to wait until Alan, our second, came along. Then we were all right.'[34]

For a few bungalows on an infill site the question of the individual identity of each house did not become a problem. With an estate as large as Shrublands or that which still exists, at least in part, at Kirkconnel in Dumfries, the problem of identity within the repeated units became, perhaps, more severe than on an estate of more traditional houses. Because of the way in which the temporary bungalows were constructed they were seen at the time as more difficult to personalize:

> Perhaps the extreme case of a home that deters home-making is the temporary 'prefab', which in almost every way – its layout, its equipment and the construction of its inside walls – makes it either unnecessary or impossible for the tenant to express his personality.[35]

This lack of opportunity for personal expression did not go unnoticed in the press. An article in *Crusader* (the Eighth Army Weekly) provided a record of the support and criticism for the Portal bungalow as exhibited in the spring of 1944, and followed this with comments on the potential for the personalization of the mass-produced house:

> Whole communities will live in prefabricated houses, yet monotonous outward uniformity will be avoided. Additions of various designs of porches and garages need not interfere with the standardisation of panel sections.[36]

Although the variety of prefabricated additions (apart from differing types of garden shed) never formed part of the programme, the garden itself provided a way in which the bungalows could be personalized. Such personalization is still in evidence today, for the temporary bungalow was a suburban prototype and the layout on the ground allowed the psychological characteristics of suburbia to be established. As Oscar Newman states:

The single-family house set on its own piece of land, isolated from its neighbour by as little as six feet, has been the traditional expression of arrival in most every Western culture. It is the symbolic token of having a stake in the social system; it is deeply rooted in notions of proprietorship and belonging to the establishment. To many it represents the reaching of maturity and the achievement of success and potency.[37]

The temporary bungalow gave the occupier this important token in a way that the later prefabricated architect-designed flats failed to do. Moreover, the very presence of the garden as part of the layout allowed individual expression to flourish. However much designers felt that suburban taste was ill-informed and unarchitectural it did allow the occupiers to be creative on their own terms:

One moral . . . is that creative activity can only be encouraged among the mass of people by building on a foundation of their own existing modes of expression. For this purpose – especially when looking at the suburbs – sophisticated standards of taste and criticism can conveniently be forgotten.[38]

What the prefabs offered was sophistication of housing in the correct place. The design and technology of the method of production broke new ground in British housing but the final single-storey form and detached layout produced a type of housing that allowed the occupier control. For once the designer was to be servant rather than master.

There is also evidence to support the idea that the war itself had emphasized the importance of tradition, even amongst former supporters of the Modern Movement. When abroad during the war Richards, the author of *Modern Architecture*, wrote a nostalgic and supportive description and analysis of suburbia, commenting that, 'when the public is given a choice, the kind of architecture it chooses is very like that which it is already being given.'[39] Bertram's pre- and post-war editions of *The House: A Machine for Living In* also indicate a change in attitude to houses and tradition. As he states in the comments added to the later edition:

I prefer, in this dark interim, to be less cocksure than I was in 1935. One sees but dimly. I have no longer the confidence even to guess what the little man will want, or myself to face with equanimity the nomadic or mechanised futures I so glibly and cold-bloodedly prophesied.[40]

Bertram may have been unsure but at least part of the nation appeared to hold the traditions of the country in esteem. *Picture Post* noted the success of Gibbings' book *Sweet Thames Run Softly*, illustrated with wood engravings of a pre-war English countryside stating that it, 'was published in the second grim winter of the war. It was unquestionably the book of the year'.[41] Such nostalgia appeared to run through all levels of society. The very fact that *Recording Britain* was commissioned during the war to show the nation the vanishing traditions of the countryside is further support for this idea. Within the four volumes very few pictures show a view of field or city under the influence of war,[42] the majority looking towards a timeless way of living.

Even the 1951 Festival of Britain, a showcase for all that was modern and new in the post-war world, was not immune to the attractions of tradition. The catalogue to accompany the Festival Ship Campania begins the section on 'Homes and Gardens' with the words, 'In any display . . . it is well to be reminded that most of the inhabitants of Britain live in towns,'[43] but illustrates the same with the image of the thatched cottage in its garden with roses round the door. Moreover, the appearance of the prefab with the smoke curling from its chimney as the homeless family cooked lunch where, the day before, there had been only a concrete slab, parallels the rights of the independent cottager who could claim his strip of land if he could build a shelter and have smoke rising from the chimney between daybreak and sunset. The prefab did no more than fulfil the myth.

To those who lived in the prefabs what mattered was not the technology used to construct them but the chance offered to make some kind of home. All that can be said of the technology is that it did not appear to impede the latter aim:

> It was never my intention to live in a pre-fab. Many people, myself included, said that they looked like flat-topped hen houses . . .
>
> One day a terrific gale hit a row of them and number 22 lost its roof. The bedroom walls were also damaged. At the time my husband, two year old son and myself lived in a condemned house. A housing officer came round and offered us number 22. My immediate reaction was, I didn't want to live there, but he explained that a new roof had been put on, and the bedroom wall was rebuilt and emulsioned. After a short while I was persuaded to at least go and view it . . .
>
> We saw a square box with grubby-looking walls. I said, 'I'm not going to live there.' However, going through the gate, down two steps, into a small garden, we entered a different world . . .
>
> To us the pre-fabs were the ideal accommodation; the only thing they needed to be perfect was a brick casing on the outer walls. I wish even now to be back in our 'hen hut', for it housed us during the happiest years of our lives.[44]

What emerges as important about the temporary bungalows is not what interested the architectural press at the time, that is the technology used to make them, but rather the simple and acceptable housing model that emerged. In Nottingham, in 1990, under the aegis of 'The Tarran Bungalow Replacement Programme' single-storey brick bungalows were being constructed in the same spaces occupied by the former prefabs leaving the hedges and gardens around them intact (figure 7.3). Finally the post-war permanent house has arrived on the foundations of the temporary bungalow.

Figure 7.3. New bungalow built as a Tarran replacement, Nottingham, 1990.

The programme also impresses as a planned, nationally accepted, drive to produce housing to meet a particular need. Such planning ensured an equitable share of resources at a time when resources were scarce. Looking at the prefab it may appear superficially that, 'austerity reduced house design to the simplicity of a child's drawing',[45] but this simplicity belies the detailed design effort that went into the prefab, giving levels of fittings in excess of anything that had gone before and of single details such as hollow steel architraves which formed the trunking for the electric wiring.[46] Such simplicity could alternatively be viewed as the natural outcome of attempting to derive maximum shelter from the minimum available resources given the methods of production. As such, the Temporary Housing Programme may provide a parallel to the current quest for sustainable development, which in turn depends upon equity within limited resources. Unlike the Temporary Housing Programme, which at least presented proposals and elicited criticisms, and where the physical planning of where houses were to be produced, distributed and erected formed an essential part of the delivery, the current approach to sustainability is to leave the issue to market forces. In neither the United States not Britain did market forces produce the house from the factory. The market for this type of house was stimulated by war conditions and supported by the respective governments through the orders they placed for the product. The lessons that might be carried forward from the Temporary Housing Programme are that producing for people the houses that they want may well aid the success of the venture; that new technologies depend upon the stimulation of artificial markets;[47] and that planning is an essential tool of government if equal access to resources is regarded as essential.

Nevertheless, during the evolution of the prefab the chance was missed to use the techniques of prefabrication and demountability to involve the occupants in the construction of their own houses, but the same people have been quick to use the opportunities offered by the technology of the prefabs to recycle them into other uses. Unseen by those who commissioned the programme this, too, must be judged as one of its strengths.

The mass-produced factory-made house appeared in the UK as a result of a series of disconnected incidents, not least the public utterance by Churchill that the government was to order the production of houses from the factory. Those involved in their design and manufacture were only too aware of the complexities of such a project, complexities that only emerged as the programme continued. For their part, the homeless were thankful to be housed in a modern bungalow where they could enjoy some privacy after the enforced communality of war. Those who watched, however, usually only offered criticism:

> Faced with two evils – families without homes or unsightly dwellings – we have chosen the lesser. Nevertheless, a sub-standard dwelling is an evil. The 4,625 factory-made bungalows known as 'prefabs' erected in Birmingham were originally given a life of ten years; twenty-five is a more likely period, but it is to be hoped that all these ill-conceived and unsightly temporary dwellings will have ceased to disfigure the landscape by 2002.[48]

Perhaps only time will tell.

NOTES

1. BBC (1944), p. 17.

2. The Burgess Shales controversy concerns the unpredictable nature of evolution. Rather than the view that evolution is a rational process where change happens in an ordered manner, the fossil evidence of the shales suggests that a vast 'soup' of potential animal and plant forms existed, only some of which, by chance, survived to evolve further. This suggests that history can only be observed rather than predicted; see Gould (1990).

3. Beveridge (1942).

4. Ministry of Reconstruction (1945), pp. 2–3.

5. In 1989 the Steel Construction Institute commissioned a study of the development of a steel framed two-storey house. The study was undertaken but no further developments have yet ensued, or seem likely to (private communication).

6. For a study of post-war prefabricated and system built housing see Finnemore (1989).

7. Darke and Darke (1979, p. 114) offer the following statistics to demonstrate the influence of system building on public sector housing:

Year	Houses	Flats			% System built
		<4 storeys	5–9 storeys	>10 storeys	
1955	71.0	23.1	5.2	0.7	n.a.
1958	57.4	31.5	5.0	6.1	n.a.
1961	51.0	32.0	5.6	11.3	n.a.
1964	44.8	31.0	5.4	18.7	21.0
1967	50.0	27.0	9.4	13.6	42.6
1970	51.5	38.6	7.2	2.7	19.4
1973	54.9	41.7	2.7	0.7	24.4
1976	57.3	40.9	1.3	0.5	12.1

Figures refer to tenders approved for the dwellings in the selected years: n.a. means no information available.

The collapse of Ronan Point occurred in 1968.

8. Esher (1981), 1983 Pelican edition, p. 57.

9. Denby (1938), 1944 second edition, p. 74.

10. Mannin (1944), p. 148.

11. Wiseman (1945), p. 6.

12. The rule of thumb for traditional brick and timber low-rise construction is that one-third of the total cost is for the site, one-third for labour and one-third for materials. An examination of the costs of the aluminium bungalow without site costs gives 21 per cent for labour and 53 per cent for materials, the remaining being absorbed in overheads and the cost of the programme.

13. The floorboards for the prefabricated sections of the aluminium bungalow were nailed and punched by hand. See *The RIBA Journal*, July, 1946, p. 403.

14. In an estimate for the cost of erecting a Nissen hut in 1942, 40 hours work were required for a joiner and 24 hours for a labourer. In this prefabricated structure, therefore, the proportion of skilled labour required for erection was greater. Information taken from a hand written insert found in Nissen Buildings Ltd. (1939).

15. Edric Neel (1945, pp. 298–303) explained the approach taken to the design of tolerances in the Arcon bungalow: 'In England, where only a limited number of building materials are available, the difference between one prefabrication system and another will lie chiefly in detail. It is hoped that the above record of a development has served to emphasise the enormous detail involved. This point is stressed not to deter new entrants to the field, but to equip them with fore-knowledge so that they may be properly prepared to withstand the long seige.'

16. Minister of Works (1948), p. 3. A 40 per cent increase was incurred for the costs of site work and erection between 1945 and 1947.

17. Architecturally, the most elegant proposal for a temporary bungalow was probably the Jicwood stressed skin plywood bungalow by Sheppard and Chitty, which was widely publicized at the time but could not be used because of the problem of obtaining plywood. See Sheppard R. (1946), pp. 118–122.

18. Madge (1946), p. 142.

19. Minister of Health and Local Government and Secretary of State for Scotland (1955), p. 2.

20. Minister of Health (1946), pp. 4–5.

21. Hopkins (1964), p. 310.

22. 'Aluminium from War to Peace Exhibition' (1945) *The Architect and Building News*, 8 June, 1945, pp. 151–152.

23. Fry (1944), pp. 56–57.

24. Tubbs (1942), p. 37.

25. Rolt (1948), Preface.

26. Sheppard (1946), p. 9.

27. Rooney, Lewis and Schule (1989), p. 42.

28. Godfrey (1946), pp. 81–82.

29. Tubbs (1942), p. 49.

30. Ministry of Health/Ministry of Works (1944*a*), p. 41.

31. Ministry of Works (1948), p. 10.

32. 'Prefab. Estate', *Building*, October, 1947, Vol. 22, p. 336.

33. *Ibid*.

34. Marks (1987), pp. 53–54.

35. Madge (1948), p. 10.

36. *Crusader* (1944), No 108, Vol. 11, 25 June, quoted in *Union Jack* (1989), p. 191.

37. Newman (1972), p. 51.

38. Richards (1946), pp. 79-80.

39. *Ibid*., p. 53.

40. Bertram (1945), p. 111 (the title was changed for the second edition).

41. *Picture Post*, 14 October, 1944, p. 20.

42. Phyllis Ginger produced a series of water colours of Cheltenham and Bath for the Recording Britain project. The former include people in uniform and one of the latter shows the consequences of a Baedecker Raid. Of all the pictures these contain some of the few visual references to the war situation. See Anon (1946).

43. Cox (1951), p. 26.

44. Rooney, Lewis and Schule (1989), pp. 42–43.

45. Keith (1991), p. 32.

46. For the Arcon Mark V steel was used as cold rolled sections for skirtings, architraves, picture rails and vertical corner cover strips. These sections had a dual purpose as they acted as cover strips for the inevitable tolerance gaps between floor, wall and ceiling panels and, 'since they are hollow, also form a path for electrical wiring'. See Arcon, Chartered Architects (1948*c*), p. 118.

47. The costs of the development of a nuclear power programme could not have been generated if left to market forces.

48. Cadbury (1952), p. 29.

BIBLIOGRAPHY

Abrams, C. (1946) *The Future of Housing*. New York: Harper and Brothers.

Addison, P. (1985) *Now the War is Over*. London: BBC/Cape.

Anon (1946) *Recording Britain*, Vols. III and IV. Oxford: Oxford University Press.

Anthony, H. (1945) *Houses: Permanence and Prefabrication*. London: Pleiades.

Architectural Forum (1942) Prefabrication gets its chance. **76**, February.

Arcon, Chartered Architects (1948*a*) The design, organisation and production of a prefabricated house. *Building*, **23**, March.

Arcon, Chartered Architects (1948*b*) The design, organisation and production of a prefabricated house. *Building*, **23**, May.

Arcon, Chartered Architects (1948*c*) The design, organisation and production of a prefabricated house. *Building*, **23**, April.

Army Bureau of Current Affairs (1943) *Building the Post-War Home*. No. 56, 20 November.

Army Bureau of Current Affairs (1944*a*) *What Has Happened At Home?* No. 82, 18 November.

Army Bureau of Current Affairs (1944*b*) *The Yank in Britain*. No. 64, 11 March.

Army Bureau of Current Affairs (1945) *Housing Brief*. 15 December.

Association of Building Technicians (1946) *Homes for People*. London: Paul Elek.

Banham, R. (1960) *Theory and Design in the First Machine Age*. London Architectural Press.

Bateson, R.G. (1948) *The Economy of Timber in Building*. London: Crosby Lockwood.

BBC (1944) *Homes for All*. Worcester: Littlebury.

Bertram, A. (1935) *The House: A Machine for Living In*. London: Black, republished in 1945 as *The House*.

Bertram, A. (1945) *The House*. London: Black.

Beveridge, W. (1942) *Social Insurance and the Allied Services*, Cmd. 6404. London: HMSO.

Block, A. (1946) *Estimated Housing Needs*. London: Architectural Press.

Boesiger, W. and Girsberger, H. (1967) *Le Corbusier, 1910–1965*. London: Thames and Hudson.

Bossom, A.C. (1945) Excelsior! *Building*, November.

Boudon, P. (1972) *Lived-In Architecture* (translated by Onn, G.). London: Lund Humphries.

Bournville Village Trust (1941) *When We Build Again*. London: Allen and Unwin.

Bowley, M. (1960) *Innovations in Building Materials*. London: Duckworth.

Bowley, M. (1966) *The British Building Industry*. Cambridge: Cambridge University Press.

Briggs, R.A. (1901) *Bungalows and Country Residences*. London: Batsford.

Bruce, A. and Sandbank, H. (1944) reprinted 1972 as *A History of Prefabrication*. New York: Arno Press.

Bruce Milne, M. (ed.) (1946) *Future Books*, Vol. II, The Stage is Set.

Brunskill, R.W. (1978) *Illustrated Handbook of Vernacular Architecture*. London: Faber.

Burnett, J. (1980) *A Social History of Housing, 1815–1970*. London: Methuen.

Cadbury, P.S. (1952) *Birmingham – Fifty Years On*. Birmingham: Bournville Village Trust.

Casson, H. (1946) *Homes by the Million*. Harmondsworth: Penguin.

Central Statistical Office (1982) *Social Trends*. London: HMSO.

Chadwick, E. (1842) *Report on the Sanitary Condition of the Labouring Population of Great Britain* (1965 edition). Edinburgh: Edinburgh University Press.

Church, G. and Drysdale Smith, R. (1947) *What About A House Again?* London: Rockcliff.

Churchill, W. (1944) The hour is approaching. *The Listener*, **XXXI** (794), 30 March.

Cinematograph Film Council (for the Board of Trade) (1944) *Tendencies to Monopoly in the Cinematographic Industry*. London: HMSO.

Cooney, E.W. (1974) High flats in local authority housing in England and Wales since 1945, in Sutcliffe, A. (ed.) *Multi-Storey Living, the British Working-Class Experience*. London: Croom Helm.

Council for Research on Housing Construction (1934) *Slum Clearance and Rehousing*. London: P.S. King & Son.

Cox, B.H. (1945) *Prefabricated Homes*. London: Paul Elek.

Cox, I. (1951) *Festival Ship Campania*. London: HMSO.

Cullingworth, J.B. (1966) *Housing and Local Government*. London: Allen and Unwin.

Cullingworth, J.B. (1975) *Environmental Planning 1939–1969*. Vol. 1: *Reconstruction and Land Use Planning 1939–1947*. London: HMSO.

Darke, J. and Darke, R. (1979) *Who Needs Housing?* London: Macmillan.

Darley, G. (1978) *Villages of Vision*. London: Granada.

Daunton, M.J. (ed.) (1984) *Councillors and Tenants: Local Authority Housing in English Cities, 1919–1939*. Leicester: Leicester University Press.

Denby, E. (1938) *Europe Re-housed*. London: George Allen and Unwin.

Department of Health for Scotland (1944) *Planning Our New Homes*. Edinburgh: HMSO.

Diamant, R.M.E. (1964) *Industrialised Building*. London: Iliffe Books.

Duncan, R. (1947) *Home-Made Home*. London: Faber and Faber.

Eccles, S. *et al.* (1945) *Women and the Peace*. London: Signpost Press.

Elsas, M.J. (1946) *Housing and the Family*. London: Meridian.

Esher, Lord (1981) *A Broken Wave*. Harmondsworth: Allen Lane.

Finnemore, B. (1985*a*) The A.I.R.O.H. house: industrial diversification and state building policy. *Construction History*, **1**.

Finnemore, B. (1985*b*) The Use of New Technology in Post World War II Social Housing. PhD Thesis, University of London, p. 47.

Finnemore, B. (1989) *Houses from the Factory*. London: Rivers Oram Press.

FitzGerald, M. (1944) The house that Martha wants. *Weldons Ladies' Journal*, January.

Fletcher, B. (1967) *History of Architecture on the Comparative Method*, 17th ed. (revised by Cordingly, R.A.). London: Athlone Press.

Ford, H. (1926) *Today and Tomorrow*. London: Heinemann.

Freeman Allen, G. (1982) *Railways: Past, Present and Future*. London: Orbis.

Fruges, H. (1967) Speech given in 1967 and quoted in Boudon (1972).

Fry, M. (1944) *Fine Building*. London: Faber & Faber.

Gaskell, M. (1987) *Model Housing*. London: Mansell.

Gloag, J. and Wornum, G. (1946) *House out of Factory*. London: Allen and Unwin.

Godfrey, W. (1946) *Our Building Inheritance*. London: Readers Union.

Gould, J. (1977) *Modern Houses in Britain, 1919–1939*. London: Society of Architectural Historians of Great Britain.

Gould, S.J. (1990) *Wonderful Life*. London: Hutchinson Radius.

Gray, G.H. (1946) *Housing and Citizenship*. New York: Reinhold.

Greenhalgh, R. (1944) The post-war house. *Building*, **19**, March.

Gropius, W. (1935) *The New Architecture and the Bauhaus* (translated by Morton Shand, P.) London: Faber and Faber.

Gropius, W. (1956) *Scope of Total Architecture*. London: George Allen and Unwin.

Hall, D.C. (1940) The case for prefabrication. *The Builder*, **158**, 3 May.

Hardy, D. and Ward, C. (1984) *Arcadia for All*. London: Mansell.

Harper, R.H. (1987) *The First Hundred Years of the Sheffield Society of Architects*. Sheffield: Sheffield Society of Architects.

Heath Robinson, W. and Browne, K.R.G. (*c* 1930) *How to Live in a Flat*. London: Hutchinson.

Herbert, G. (1978) *Pioneers of Prefabrication*. Baltimore: Johns Hopkins University Press.

Herbert, G. (1984) *The Dream of the Factory-Made House*. Cambridge, Mass: MIT Press.

Hesketh, J. (1980) *Industrial Design*. London: Thames and Hudson.

Hodson, J.L. (1944) *Home Front*. London: Gollancz.

Hopkins, H. (1964) *The New Look*. London: Readers Union/Secker and Warburg.

Hubbard, J. (ed.) (1985) *We Thought It was Heaven Tomorrow, 1945–1955*, People's History of Yorkshire, Volume XIV. Pontefract: Yorkshire Art Circus.

Huber, B. and Steinegger, J.-C. (eds.) (1971) *Jean Prouve*. London: Pall Mall Press.

Huxley, J. (1943) *TVA: Adventure in Planning*. London: Architectural Press.

Joad, C.E.M. (1943) *The Adventures of the Young Soldier in Search of the Better World*. London: Faber and Faber.

Keith, H. (1991) *A Lovely Day Tomorrow*. Aukland: Random Century.

Kerr, R. (1972) *The Gentleman's House* (first published 1864). New York: Johnson Reprint.

King, A.D. (1984) *The Bungalow*. London: Routledge and Kegan Paul.

Kohan, C.M. (1952) *Works and Buildings* London: HMSO.

Le Corbusier (1927) *Towards a New Architecture* (translated by Etchells). London: Architectural Press.

Le Corbusier (1929) *The City Tomorrow* (translated by Etchells) 1946 edition. London: John Rodker.

Leathart, J. (1944) Architectural opinion. *Building*, **19**, March.

Lethaby, W. (1911) *Architecture: An Introduction to the History and Theory of the Art of Building*. London: Williams and Norgate.

Lewis, P. (1986) *A People's War*. London: Thames/Methuen.

Local Government Boards for England and Wales and Scotland (1918) *Report of Committee to Consider Questions of Building Construction with the Provision of Dwellings for the Working Classes in England and Wales and Scotland, and Report upon Methods of Securing Economy and Despatch in the Provision of Such Dwellings*. Cd. 9191. London: HMSO.

Lock, M. (1939) The administrative aspect of housing in Sweden. *Journal of the RIBA*, 14 August.

Madge, J. (ed.) (1946) *Tomorrow's Houses*. London: Pilot Press.

Madge, J. (1948) Human factors in housing. *Current Affairs*, No. 50, 20th March. London: The Bureau of Current Affairs.

Mannin, E. (1944) *Bread and Roses*. London: Macdonald.

Marks, C. (1987) Prefabulous. *Telegraph Sunday Magazine*, 15 February.

Mass Observation (1943) *An Enquiry into People's Homes*. London: John Murray.

Minister of Health (1946) *Housing Returns for England and Wales*, Cmd. 6744. London: HMSO.

Minister of Health (1948) *The Cost of House Building*. London: HMSO.

Minister of Health and Local Government and Secretary of State for Scotland (1955) *Housing Summary 30th April 1955*, Cmd. 9478. London: HMSO.

Minister of Works (1945) *Temporary Housing Programme*, Cmd. 6686. London: HMSO.

Minister of Works (1948) *Temporary Housing Programme*, Cmd. 7304. London: HMSO.

Ministry of Health (1942) *The Care of the Homeless*. London: HMSO.

Ministry of Health (1944) *Design of Dwellings*. London: HMSO.

Ministry of Health (1948*a*) *The Cost of House-Building* (Girdwood Report). London: HMSO.

Ministry of Health (1948*b*) *Housing Summary 31st July 1948*. London: HMSO.

Ministry of Health (1949) *Housing Manual*. London: HMSO.

Ministry of Health and Local Government (1964) *Housing Returns for England and Wales*, Cmd. 2432. London: HMSO.

Ministry of Health/Ministry of Works (1944*a*) *Temporary Accommodation: Memorandum for the Guidance of Local Authorities*. London: HMSO.

Ministry of Health/Ministry of Works (1944*b*) *Housing Manual*. London: HMSO.

Ministry of Information (1944) *Manpower*. London: HMSO.

Ministry of Reconstruction (1945) *Housing*, Cmd. 6609. London: HMSO.

Ministry of Works (1944*a*) *Methods of Building in the USA*. London: HMSO.

Ministry of Works (1944*b*) *House Construction*, Post-war Building Studies, No. 1. London: HMSO.

Ministry of Works (1944*c*) *Demonstration Houses*. London: HMSO.

Ministry of Works (1948) *New Methods of House Construction*, National Building Studies Special Report No. 4. London: HMSO.

Muthesius, S. (1982) *The English Terraced House*. New Haven: Yale University Press.

Myerscough-Walker, R. (n.d. [*c.* 1939]) *Choosing a Modern House*. London: The Studio.

Myles Wright, H. (ed.) (1937) *Small Houses*. London: Architectural Press.

Neel, E. (1943) Tarran system of construction. *Architectural Design and Construction*. October.

Neel, E. (1945) Prefabricated panels. *Building*. November.

Newman, O. (1972) *Defensible Space*. London: Architectural Press.

Nissen Buildings Ltd. (1939) *Memorandum containing information concerning Nissen Huts*. Hoddesdon, Herts: Nissen Buildings Ltd.

Orbach, L.F. (1977) *Homes for Heroes*. London: Seeley Service.

Osborn, F.J. (1942) *New Towns After the War*. London: J.M. Dent.

Osborn, F.J. (ed.) (1946) *Planning and Reconstruction 1946*. London: Todd.

Peak District Advisory Panel (1934) *Housing in the Peak District*. London: Council for the Preservation of Rural England.

Pleydell-Bouverie, M. (1944) *The Daily Mail Book of Post-War Homes*. London: Associated Newspapers.

Randal Phillips, R. (1920) *The Book of Bungalows*. London: Country Life.

Rankine, A. (1942) A war-time hospital at Hull. *The Builder*, 6th March.

Ravetz, A. (1974) *Model Estate*. London: Croom Helm.

RIBA (1940) *Industrial Housing in Wartime*. London: RIBA.

Rice, A. (1973) The heyday of bungalow town. *Country Life*, **153** (2), 19 April.

Richards, J.M. (1946) *The Castles on the Ground*. London: Architectural Press.

Robertson, H. (1944) *Architecture Arising*. London: Faber and Faber.

Robertson, H. (1947) *Reconstruction and the Home*. London: The Studio.

Rolt, L.T.C. (1948) *Narrow Boat*, 2nd ed. Reprinted 1990. London: Mandarin.

Rooney, R., Lewis, B. and Schule, R. (1989) *Home is where the Heart is*. Castleford: Yorkshire Art Circus.

Rose, F. (1947) *Your Home*. London: Nicholson and Watson.

Rowntree, B.S. (1945) *Portrait of a City's Housing*, Rebuilding Britain Series No. 13. London: Faber.

Roy, R. and Cross, N. (1975) *Technology and Society*, T262 Units 2–3. Milton Keynes: Open University.

Russell, B. (1977) Mending the modern movement. *The Architects' Journal,* 30 March.

Sant'Elia (1914) *Messagio*, quoted in Banham, R. (1960).

Scottish Development Department (1970) *Housing Return for Scotland*. Edinburgh: HMSO.

Scottish Development Department (1971) *Housing Return for Scotland*. Edinburgh: HMSO.

Scottish Office Building Directorate (1987) *A Guide to Non-Traditional Housing in Scotland*. Edinburgh: HMSO.

Setright, L.J.K. (1989) Revolutions. *Car*, December.

Sharp, T. (1932) *Town and Country*. Oxford: Oxford University Press.

Sheppard, R. (1945) *Cast Iron in Building*. London: George Allen and Unwin.

Sheppard, R. (1946) *Prefabrication in Building*. London: Architectural Press.

Sherman, M. (ed.) (1953) *New Elizabethan Homes*. London: News Chronicle.

Short, J.R. (1982) *The Post-War Experience: Housing in Britain*. London: Methuen.

Simon, E.D. (1945) *Rebuilding Britain – A Twenty Year Plan*. London: Gollancz.

Smithells, R. (ed.) (1939) *Country Life Book of Small Houses*. London: Country Life.

Speer, A. (1970) *Inside the Third Reich*. London: Macmillan.

Squire, R. (1984) *Portrait of an Architect*. Gerrards Cross: Colin Smythe.

Summerfield, P. (1984) *Women Workers in the Second World War*. London: Croom Helm.

Swenarton, M. (1981) *Homes Fit for Heroes*. London: Heinemann.

Thorpe, M.F. (1946) *America at the Movies*. London: Faber.

Towne, C.A. (1942) Portable housing. *New Pencil Points*, July.

Towne, C.A. and Purnell, W.H. (1946) An appraisal of the Tennessee Valley Authority's research in prefabrication, in Osborn (ed.).

Tubbs, R. (1942) *Living in Cities*. London: Penguin.

Union Jack (1989) London: HMSO.

Vale, B. (1973) A Review of the Ministry of Agriculture's Earth Houses.

University of Cambridge, Department of Architecture, Technical Research Division.

Weaver, L. (1926) *Cottages: Their Planning, Design and Materials*. London: Country Life.

Weidenfeld, A.G. (ed.) (1947) *The Changing Nation*. London: Contact Publications.

Weller, J. (1982) *The History of the Farmstead*. London: Faber.

West, E.G. (1945) Aluminium alloys and the architect, in Drew, J. (ed.) *Architects' Yearbook*. London: Elek.

West, T. (1971) *The Timber-Frame House in England*. Newton Abbot: David and Charles.

White, R.B. (1965) *Prefabrication. A History of Its Development in Great Britain*. London: HMSO.

Whittick, A. and Schreiner, J. (1947) *The Small House: Today and Tomorrow*. London: Crosby Lockwood.

Williams-Ellis, C. (1919) *Building in Cob, Pise and Stabilised Earth*. London: Country Life (revised and enlarged 3rd ed, 1947).

Williams-Ellis, C. (1928) *England and the Octopus*. London: Geoffrey Bles.

Williams-Ellis, C. (ed.) (1938) *Britain and the Beast*. London: Readers' Union.

Wiseman, F. (1945) *The Penguin Handyman*. London: Penguin.

Women's Group on Public Welfare (1951) The effect of the design of the temporary prefabricated bungalow on household routine. *Sociological Review*.

Woodforde, J. (1976) *Bricks to Build a House*. London: Routledge and Kegan Paul.

Yorke, F.R.S. (1943) *The Modern House*, 4th ed. Cheam: Architectural Press.

Your Inheritance: The Land: An Uncomic Strip. (1942). London: Architectural Press.

INDEX